The Silver Canvas

The Silver Canvas: Daguerreotype Masterpieces

from The J. Paul Getty Museum

Bates Lowry

Isabel Barrett Lowry

Thames and Hudson

The sizes of the daguerreotypes reproduced here are given using the traditional terminology from the daguerreian era. Within each category, the actual sizes of the plates vary slightly from image to image.

Whole plate	8½ × 6½ inches
Three-quarter plate	7⅛ × 5½ inches
Half plate	5½ × 4½ inches
Quarter plate	4¼ × 3¼ inches
Sixth plate	3¼ × 2¾ inches
Ninth plate	2½ × 2 inches

Front cover:
CHARLES H. FONTAYNE and WILLIAM SOUTHGATE PORTER
A Family Seated in Its Garden, 1848–1852
Plate 71

Frontispiece:
JOHN JABEZ EDWIN MAYALL
The Crystal Palace at Hyde Park, London, 1851
Plate 6

Page vi:
JOHN PLUMBE, JR.
Portrait of a Man Reading a Newspaper, about 1842
Detail, Plate 25

Page viii:
UNKNOWN AMERICAN PHOTOGRAPHER
Portrait of a Girl with Her Deer, about 1854
Detail, Plate 33

Page xii:
PLATT D. BABBITT
Niagara Falls, about 1855
Detail, Plate 62

First published in Great Britain in 1998 by
Thames and Hudson Ltd, London

Copyright © 1998 The J. Paul Getty Museum

British Library Cataloguing-in-Publication Data
A catalogue record for this book is available from the British Library

ISBN 0-500-23762-X

Printed in the United States of America

Contents

FOREWORD

WHEN THE GETTY MUSEUM began to collect photographs in 1984, among the most notable were nearly two thousand daguerreotypes, many of which were made in the first dozen years after January 1839, when the invention of this new art form by Jacques Louis Mandé Daguerre was announced to the world.

Daguerre's success at producing images on silver-coated copper plates by the action of light took the world by surprise. So miraculous were these pictures in the eyes of the first witnesses that the caricaturist Théodore Maurisset drew artists committing suicide out of fear that the new medium would make their work obsolete. In reality, the daguerreotype and subsequent developments in photographic techniques prompted a dialogue between traditional graphic art and photography that continues to this day, illuminating and enriching both forms.

Photography now occupies an important place in the Getty Museum. Over more than a decade, the Museum has held forty-five exhibitions and published approximately twenty books and catalogues drawn mostly from the collection's sixty-five thousand paper photographs. Despite this, our daguerreotypes remain too little known by the public. This book presents for the first time a generous and expertly chosen sample of the Getty's holdings. Its publication has required treating, rehousing, and rephotographing all the works included in it—work that has been ably performed by the curators, conservators, and other staff members.

Bates Lowry and Isabel Barrett Lowry have written an engrossing essay on the relationship of the daguerreotype to the artistic traditions of Europe and America during the first half of the nineteenth century. They have selected nearly eighty examples from our collection and written texts that provide each picture a context and a sharper definition. In so doing, they have managed the difficult job of weaving together cultural and art history with the development of photography. I am very grateful to them.

This book owes its existence to the wisdom and persistence of Weston Naef, curator of photographs, who five years ago proposed the idea of publishing and exhibiting the best of the Museum's daguerreotypes during the opening year of the new Getty Museum at the Getty Center. I want to thank him and the other members of the Museum staff whose efforts brought this book into being.

Deborah Gribbon
Associate Director and Chief Curator

PREFACE

THE GETTY MUSEUM is one of the few locations in the world where the several threads constituting the early history of photography can be studied. Although the Museum's holding of early photographs on paper is much better known through exhibition and publication than its daguerreotypes, with the advent of this book the imbalance is remedied.

The majority of the daguerreotypes in the collection were acquired as a block in 1984, and acknowledgment is due to the efforts of a handful of serious collectors who believed in the importance of this art form and persevered to obtain the very best examples they could find.

Of the major collections acquired in 1984, seven were the source of the daguerreotypes chosen for this book: those of Arnold Crane, Bruno Bischofberger, André and Marie-Thérèse Jammes, Samuel Wagstaff, Daniel Wolf, Michel Auer, and Werner Bokelberg. The Crane collection, built with considerable advice from the dealer George Rinhart, contributed fully one-third of the total (twenty-seven items), most of American origin. The Bischofberger collection, which concentrated on pieces of European origin, contributed sixteen. The Jammes collection contributed eleven items, all but two of French origin. The Wagstaff collection contributed seven items to the total, and the Wolf collection six. Four

items each are included from the Auer and the Bokelberg collections. In addition to the works acquired in 1984 from these seven collections, four daguerreotypes included in this book were acquired later: *Portrait of Louis Jacques Mandé Daguerre,* by Charles Meade (opposite page 1); *Portrait of Edward Carrington, Jr. ("Uncle Ed"),* by Jeremiah Gurney (Plate 8, page 48); *The Arch of Hadrian, Athens,* by Philippos Margaritis and Philibert Perraud (Plate 40, page 104); and *The United States Capitol,* by John Plumbe, Jr. (Plate 69, page 189).

The Museum holds an example of almost every subject that came before the cameras of the daguerreian artists: images made for experimental scientific and educational purposes; records of historic events; now-vanished objects from the built environment; and, not least, portraits of people famous for their accomplishments in the arts, literature, science, or politics of the preceding century. The Museum also contains a number of experimental plates that chronicle the evolution of the special technology involved with the daguerreotype process. However, the largest number of daguerreotypes in the collection comprises people whose names have been lost to us and whose makers are often unknown. Some of these are among the most successful from the purely visual perspective.

The selection of nearly eighty items for this book was guided by the twin criteria of aesthetic quality and condition. This book is neither a catalogue of the collection nor a history of the daguerreotype in all of its manifestations. Its purpose is to provide both an overview of the very best of the Museum's holding and an introduction to the art of the daguerreotype. The choices were made chiefly on the basis of the visual properties of the daguerreotypes, a yardstick for gauging importance established by centuries of practice evaluating traditional art.

In determining quality, physical condition played a large role, since the polished surface of a daguerreotype is extremely fragile and subject to abrasion, fingerprints, oxidation, and other forms of deterioration. Nevertheless, some images with damage or deterioration are so beautiful or unusual in composition that their inclusion was mandatory. The most important element of quality is the visual acuity of the maker—the choice of light, viewpoint, posing, setting, and gesture all contribute to the artistic success of a daguerreotype.

In 1972 Bates Lowry and Isabel Barrett Lowry started down a path that eventually led to this book, first as collectors of daguerreotypes and then as scholars. This book represents considerable new research attained in the authors' pursuit of original sources—letters, periodicals, and other documents of the period—as well as the study of other public and private collections of daguerreotypes. Each daguerreotype plate took the authors on a search for new information concerning the historical background, the social context, and the aesthetic factors guiding its makers style. For their dedication and skill at this work I am deeply grateful.

While the authors have shaped the content of this book in every possible way, its undertaking incorporates some form of contribution from the entire Department of Photographs. On behalf of the authors I would like to acknowledge and thank a number of these individuals. The several visits by the authors to the Museum for study and research were coordinated by Peggy Hanssen and Marcia Lowry, with the help of Jean Smeader. Assistance in the Study Room was cheerfully provided by Gordon Baldwin, Katherine Ware, Joan Gallant Dooley, and Julian Cox, who also coordinated the several rounds of new photography that were required to faithfully copy the originals. Judith Keller read and commented insightfully on the manuscript during its preparation. I am particularly grateful to Michael Hargraves, who catalogued the objects, compiled the Roster of Daguerreian Makers, prepared a preliminary draft of the index, and pursued elusive items in the literature of photography.

The high quality of the reproductions is due to a combination of efforts. Marc Harnly, conservator, and Ernest Mack, assistant conservator, with the occasional assistance of conservation consultant Valerie Baas, have cleaned or replaced the cover glass, as well as providing other mitigating treatments to the plates and the restoration of their cases.

The conserved daguerreotypes were skillfully photographed before and after treatment by Ellen Rosenbery, who benefited from the advice of Charles Passela, head of Photographic Services, and his consultant, Dennis Waters. It has been our good fortune to benefit from an excellent editorial and design team. The editing of the manuscript was handled by David Featherstone, with contributions in house from Shelly Kale, working under the guidance of Mark Greenberg, managing editor, and Chris Hudson, head of Museum Publications. The design and layout of the book by Vickie Sawyer Karten preserves the integrity of the daguerreotypes and is sensitive to the authors' text. In addition, I wish to acknowledge Cecily Gardner, for successfully procuring illustrative materials from other institutions, and Stacy Miyagawa, for overseeing the production of the book. To the staff of the Getty Trust Publications Department—Richard Kinney, director of publications; Karen Schmidt, production manager; and Deenie Yudell, design manager—we entrusted the challenge of translating these images on fragile, mirror-like surfaces into ink on paper.

Special thanks are due to Deborah Gribbon, associate director and chief curator, who in 1985 first heard of my desire to eventually publish and exhibit our daguerreotypes, and to Barbara Whitney, associate director of administration, for their administrative support of this project over its several years of gestation and completion.

Weston Naef
Curator of Photographs

INTRODUCTION

WHEN FRANÇOIS ARAGO, French scientist and champion of Daguerre, formally announced the invention of the daguerreotype to the world in 1839, he described the new creation as a "canvas." We have adopted his term for the title of our book because we believe it reveals how Daguerre's contemporaries first thought of his invention. The traditional woven canvas on which the painter created illusionistic scenes was now extended to include the metallic silvered plates on which the miracle of photography would produce its imagery.

Choosing a word used at the time also underscores our approach to the history of the daguerreotype's discovery: to reconstruct events through first-hand reports, not later interpretations. Doing so, we believe, has resulted in a more accurate and unbiased account of developments leading up to the daguerreotype's introduction and its immediate widespread use.

The historical narrative of the Prologue serves as a foundation for six essays discussing key qualities we have identified as inherent in the daguerreian form. In each instance our perceptions were guided by the original works, which are illustrated and discussed at the close of the individual chapter. Presenting the works in this way will, we hope, allow the reader both to appreciate the incredible importance of Daguerre's invention for all branches of human thought and, above all, to enjoy the amazing beauty of the daguerreian image—the first silver canvas.

The quality of the daguerreotype is unlike that of any other form of photography. Even the act of perceiving the image contained within the confines of the small silver-coated copper plate is unique, for before the smooth, mirror-like surface will reveal its contents to the viewer, it must be held at a certain angle to allow the surrounding light to pick up the microscopic grains—scattered across its surface—that make up its image. Handling the daguerreotype in this way creates a personal relationship between the viewer and the work of art. The intimacy of this act enhances the viewer's visual experience by making it become one of discovery and surprise, intensifying the detection of the incredible details the daguerreotype contains within a display of textural richness unique to its art. Because it produces a visual image of such a special nature, the daguerreotype stands alone as a work of art whose manner of being produced caused it to be considered a miraculous creation. The controlling hand of the artist, always evident when viewing a drawing or painting, no longer dominates the experience of seeing the visual image produced by the daguerreotype. With Daguerre's invention, a new form of artistic expression was born.

This book is our response to the generous invitation by Weston Naef, curator of photographs at the J. Paul Getty Museum, to explore the treasure trove of nearly two thousand daguerreotypes assembled by the Museum as part of its comprehensive photographic collection. Our challenge was to select roughly eighty outstanding works to represent the excellence of the collection and demonstrate the nature and importance of this art form. Undertaking the search afforded us the pleasure of holding in our hands daguerreotypes already famous for their quality and historic significance, but it also provided us with daily surprises as we uncovered daguerreotypes of equal caliber that had escaped previous attention. The number of such works proved time and time again what a truly rich and uniquely valuable collection had been created by the Museum, but at the same time made our task of selection infinitely more difficult.

We discussed our preliminary choices with Weston Naef, as well as with others whose extensive knowledge of daguerreotypes in private and public collections proved indispensable. Particularly helpful in this regard were Denise Bethel, Arnold Crane, Nicholas Graver, Joan Murray, George Rinhart, Grant Romer, and John Wood, each of whom provided comments and information that led us to see our selections in a new light.

During the following three years of research and writing we were fortunate to be able to share ideas and problems with many others who have wide experience and knowledge in the daguerreian field. We profited on many occasions from talking with Floyd and Marion Rinhart, who always were willing to answer our questions and to suggest new directions based on their many years of studying and collecting daguerreotypes. We also are grateful to them for introducing us to W. Robert Nix of the University of Georgia, whose extensive knowledge of the daguerreotype process and experience as a practicing photographer gave us valuable insights into the source of the quality of particular works.

Our work was greatly rewarded by many long sessions with Matthew R. Isenburg. His generous sharing of both his knowledge and his outstanding collection and library benefited our work on innumerable instances, especially when he used original equipment to teach us how daguerreotypes were created.

Discussions—and sometimes heated debates—with Dennis Waters over how various light effects had been achieved contributed to our understanding of the problems faced by the daguerreotypists. As a professional photographer he is particularly sympathetic to the intent of the maker.

In all stages of this book we have benefited from the correcting and guiding pen of Randall Holton, whose disciplined mind and sensitive ear for language were invaluable. It also has been a privilege to have been able to profit from Eugenia Robbins's long experience as an editor of art books and journals. Her sense of style and her critical judgment were important contributions to the book. We are pleased our publisher chose David Featherstone to edit our manuscript, as his queries and suggestions pushed us into clarifying certain sections of the text with great profit. Finally, the book has benefited from Shelly Kale, whose keen attention to editorial detail was crucial in the final stages of the galleys.

To answer questions raised by the subject matter of the daguerreotypes included here involved a wide range of expertise, and it was our good fortune to discover many people who generously shared with us information not otherwise available. Their specific contributions are acknowledged in the relevant endnotes.

The Research Library of the Getty Research Institute for the History of Art and the Humanities was fundamental for all phases of our work, and we wish to thank the staff for its expert help.

The rich collections and generous people at many other libraries and museums were vital to our research. We especially want to thank: The Boston Athenaeum (Sally Pierce); Boston Public Library; Boston University Library; Fogg Art Museum (Deborah Martin Kao); George Eastman House (Rachel Stulhman, Joseph Struble); Harvard University Libraries; Library of Congress (Carol Johnson); Massachusetts Historical Society (Chris Steele); Massachusetts Institute of Technology Library; Musée des Arts et Métiers, Paris (Christiane Delpy, Nathalie Naudi); Musée Hyacinthe Rigaud, Perpignan, France (Marie-Claud Valaison); National Museum of American History (Debbie Griggs Carter, Michelle Delaney); National Portrait Gallery (Alan Fern, Ann Shumard); New England Historic Genealogical Society (Jerome Anderson); Société française de photographie, Paris (Katie Busch); University of Massachusetts/Boston Library.

We have been fortunate to have had the constant support of Weston Naef and the generous assistance of the entire staff of the Getty Museum's Department of Photographs. Special thanks are due to Michael Hargraves, who has played a critical role as our liaison with all parts of the Getty Museum as well as answering our many requests eagerly and enthusiastically. He also proved invaluable in tracking down obscure books and articles for us.

In addition to all the members of the Department of Photographs, we have been generously assisted by many others within different parts of the Getty Trust. Throughout the entire period we have relied upon the staff of the Museum's Publications Department, which has patiently and successfully pursued our requests for photographs and efficiently and graciously assisted us with the many details involved in the editing process. In the latter part of our work, the design and production of the book benefited greatly from the care exercised by the staff of the Getty Trust Publications Department.

In making these acknowledgments we have been very conscious of one whose wisdom, counsel, and enthusiasm we were able to benefit from only at the very beginning of our work—Daniel Robbins. We dedicate this book to him in memory of all the other many times when we worked so closely together on our shared interests.

Bates Lowry
Isabel Barrett Lowry

Overleaf:
CHARLES RICHARD MEADE
American (1827–1858)
Louis Jacques Mandé Daguerre
1848
Half plate
84.XT.953

Prologue

THE ORIGINS OF THE DAGUERREOTYPE

———

The Magician of Light

IN 1835, WORD began to spread around Parisian ateliers and salons that the city's favorite master of illusionistic displays had discovered a new way to enchant the eye. Expectation, not surprise, greeted this news because by this time Louis Jacques Mandé Daguerre (1787–1851) was widely recognized and admired for having provided the capital city over the past quarter century with events of visual excitement and delight. In the beginning, his stunning stage designs had thrilled theatergoers by transporting them far from their theater seats into an unfamiliar world of sights and sounds where the moon rose and set before their eyes at the will of the designer. Even more miraculous to the viewers were his productions staged in a theater of his own design called the Diorama. There, through a mysterious mix of colored lights and special pigments spread on an enormous canvas, Daguerre had been able to convince his enchanted visitors that they had actually been in faraway places or at the scene of historic events. Such visceral effects had never before been experienced by the Parisian public, and it became entranced by these innovations. Again and again, critics and the public alike professed their inability to know what was real and what was fantasy. Through his own talents with paint and light, Daguerre had transported his audiences into a world beyond their own, and they came to think of him as a master of illusion, or, more poetically, as the magician of light.

Daguerre's genius flowered at a particularly fortunate moment within the theatergoing world of Paris, which itself had been formed by a centuries-old tradition of public spectacles of great pomp and fantasy staged by the church and heads of state to dramatize and support their special points of view. More recently, the Parisians' love of fictional or historical tales in dramatic form had been given free expression when, during the revolution of the 1790s, censorship had disappeared and an amazing sixty-nine theaters came into being. Gradually, as a centralized government regained control, the number was reduced by decree until by 1816 only eleven theaters were still operating in Paris, including the Odéon, the Opèra, and the Academy of Music.

Consequently, the introduction at the beginning of the nineteenth century of a new form of entertainment that required no actors but provided spectators with a comparable sense of theatrical experience by viewing vast illusionistic paintings was enthusiastically received. These new presentations, called panoramas, were exhibited in large interior spaces where, upon entering, the visitors truly believed they had been transported to a faraway city. The appeal of this new theatrical form was

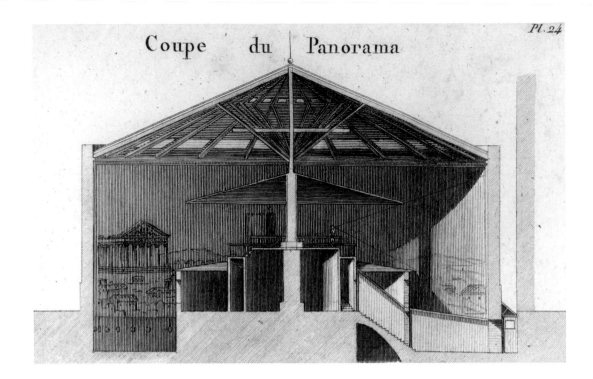

FIGURE I
Cross Section of the Panorama
Published in Alexis Donnet, *Architectonographie des théâtres*
(Paris 1840), pl. 24 (detail)
Courtesy of The Trustees of the Boston Public Library

instantaneous, and its success helped form the audience Daguerre would inherit—one whose long tradition of taking delight in observing elaborate visual spectacles was now embellished with a more recent fascination in being deceived.

By his later successes and his singular concern with the art of illusion, Daguerre's course as an artist almost appears to have been preordained.[1] From his early training as an architect's apprentice in his hometown of Orléans, southwest of Paris, where his ability was apparently directed toward making impressive renderings of architectural monuments, to his apprenticeship in 1804 with Eugène Marie Degotti (d. 1824), one of France's most celebrated stage designers, Daguerre set out on a path unlike that followed by others wanting to be artists. Their traditional instruction began by copying classical casts at the École des Beaux Arts. Daguerre's training concentrated on learning how illusionistic effects were created in the greatest theatrical space in France, the Paris Opèra. As the theater most renowned for the decorative brilliance of its presentations—which critics often said was superior to the musical quality of its performances—the Opèra was a training ground perfectly suited to Daguerre's interests and to the development of what would prove to be his principal talents. From then on, his concern was how the corporeality of the natural world could be defined simply by the differences between light and shadow as conveyed by light and paint.

Daguerre's first opportunity to display his talents for this type of work occurred in 1807, when he was chosen by the celebrated illusionistic painter, Pierre Prévost (1764–1823), to join his team of talented artists in executing panoramas, or as they were called, "paintings without bounds."[2] Daguerre joined Prévost's workshop just as the painter/entrepreneur opened a new and larger panorama building in which the painted view was about 350 feet in circumference and fifty feet in height.[3] It completely filled the surrounding circular wall, located some thirty-five feet away from the spectators, who stood on a platform beneath a tent-like canopy, isolated in the building's center (Figure 1). Since access to the platform was by way of a dark, tunnel-like passage from the street, the

FIGURE 2
UNKNOWN ARTIST
View from Spectators' Platform of "The Panorama of Rome"
About 1804
Drawing
Musée du Louvre, Cabinet des Dessins; Photo © R.M.N.

spectators arrived on the platform—itself in semi-darkness—to find themselves completely engulfed by a brilliantly lit panoramic scene.

Natural light entering from above was controlled so that it fell only on the painting, creating a realistic appearance of light and shadows and depriving the viewers of any sense of distance between themselves and the painted scene (Figure 2). They were free to stroll about the platform to study the scene from different points of view as if they

were moving about the city portrayed. Spellbound by their visits to such realistically depicted cities as Rome, Athens, and Jerusalem, the spectators, according to the press of the time, were completely overwhelmed by the impact of these illusionistic scenes of reality. One report even quoted the revered painter Jacques Louis David (1748–1825) as telling his students that rather than going to the countryside to study nature, they should go to the panorama.[4]

One reporter's description of his experience reveals the powerful effect of a visit to the panorama. Attempting to startle his readers, he began by saying that although he had been in Rome yesterday, he already was back in Paris today. Such a trip, unimaginable then, had been made possible, he said, by an act of magic—an hour-long visit at the panorama to

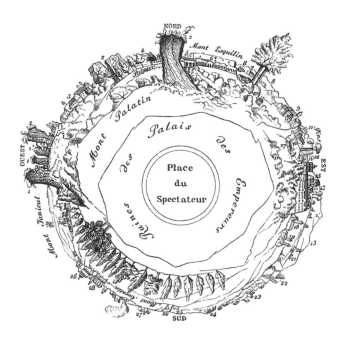

FIGURE 3
Ground Plan of "The Panorama of Rome"
From brochure provided to panorama visitors
Reproduced in Germain Bapst, *Essai sur l'histoire
des panoramas et des Dioramas* (Paris 1891), p. 10
Courtesy of The Research Library,
Getty Research Institute

see an entire vista of the Eternal City (Figure 3). He vividly described the different sites he had seen and even expressed his dismay about the ruined condition of monuments once so significant in the history of Rome. In ending his account, he said he would not even mention the actual *painting* of the panorama because, after five minutes, a viewer was no longer conscious of the painting, but only of "nature itself." [5]

Daguerre's work with Prévost led to his being asked to become the principal stage designer for one of the popular Parisian theaters, the Théâtre de l'Ambigu-Comique. When his first stage creation was unveiled there, in 1817, it was immediately hailed by the critics, who claimed the superb decorations by Daguerre the sole merit of the play. Each of his subsequent productions received still more extravagant praise, particularly those in which oil lamps were used to create dramatic lighting effects. In 1818, a moonlit scene caused such an enthusiastic response

that only Daguerre's name, not that of the author, was mentioned in the critical reviews. The following year, he went even further by showing the moon seeming to rise against a darkened sky, an effect applauded by critics as the most elegant presentation ever produced in the art of stage design. [6]

This concern for the visual presentation of plays was a new element in dramatic appraisal. A decade earlier, the visual aspect of a production would not have commanded the same attention, nor have been considered significant. Now, however, the illusionistic effects of the drama became as highly valued as the contributions of the playwright or actors. The work of Daguerre helped formulate the aesthetic arguments then being voiced over the role illusion, realism, and idealism should play in the arts. [7]

Daguerre's much-acclaimed success at the Ambigu led to his being invited, in 1820, to also become a designer of productions staged at the Paris Opèra. His return to where, fifteen years before, he had worked as a student apprentice no doubt gave Daguerre enormous confidence, as well as enhanced celebrity. He was responsible for designing, with the other principal Opèra designer, Pierre Cicéri (1782–1868), the sets for *Aladdin or the Marvelous Lamp* (Figure 4). [8] The entire artistic presentation was greeted with enthusiastic acclaim on its premiere on February 2, 1822, but the final scene, "The Palace of Light," was singled out as the most captivating one by critics and audiences alike. The palace was an architectural fantasy of brilliantly painted columns with arches and walls covered with glass jewels, all transformed into a glittering image bathed in the rays of a sun that moved across the sky before their eyes. The audience was bewitched by what seemed to be nothing more than a transitory apparition, an effect enhanced by an ingenious use of gaslight—the first time it had been used in a theater. From then on, gaslight would become a regular feature of theater design, but viewers of "The Palace of Light" always

FIGURE 4
LOUIS JACQUES MANDÉ DAGUERRE (attributed)
French (1787–1851)
Set for a Scene from the Opera "Aladdin"
About 1820–22
Drawing
Cliché Bibliothéque Nationale de France / Bibliothéque-
Musée de l'Opéra de Paris

would remember it as the first moment when they were transported into a fairy world far removed from reality.

Only six months after this grand success, with the public still clamoring to see the magical setting for "The Palace of Light," Daguerre left his work in the theater to offer the public, in July 1822, a totally new form of optical pleasure—the Diorama. In making this change he shifted from using illu-

sion to create images of fantasy to using illusion to suggest scenes of reality. Combining what he had learned from painting panoramas with his experience in manipulating sources of light for his stage designs, Daguerre unveiled in the Diorama a new creation that gave the Parisian public even more amazing spectacles.

Since Daguerre was able to open his new attraction so soon after his work at the Ambigu and the Opèra, he must have been working on the invention for some months, if not years. It had required, first of all, organizing a group of investors to underwrite the construction of a completely new type of building of large dimensions (Figure 5). In addition, at least two enormous illusionistic paintings, each one nearly forty-five feet high and seventy-two feet wide,

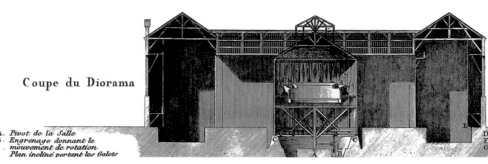

Coupe du Diorama   sur la ligne C.A.D.

A. *Pivot de la Salle*
B. *Engrenage donnant le*
   mouvement de rotation
C. *Plan incliné portant les Galets*

D.E. *Tableaux*
F. *Galleries de service*
G. *Emplacement des Chassis modificateurs*
   de la lumière

Vue intérieure de la Salle du Diorama

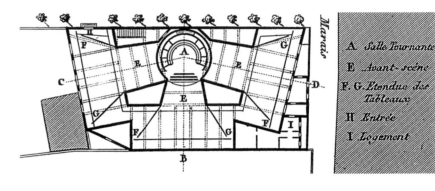

A. *Salle Tournante*
E. *Avant-scène*
F. G. *Etendue des*
   Tableaux
H. *Entrée*
I. *Logement*

FIGURE 5
Cross Section, Plan, and Interior View of the Diorama
Published in Alexis Donnet, *Architectonographie des théâtres*
(Paris 1840), pl. 23 (details)
Courtesy of The Trustees of the Boston Public Library

had to be created. Later remarks by Daguerre suggest that six to eight months were required to paint such scenes. Daguerre invited a scenic painter and former colleague at the panorama, Charles-Marie Bouton (1781–1853), to join him in creating the two scenes that would inaugurate the opening of the Diorama.

Unlike the panorama, which plunged the viewer into the midst of a completely encircling scene, the Diorama displayed two independent illusionistic scenes that were viewed successively. In both theaters, the spectators passed from the street through a dim corridor to mount stairs leading to a central viewing area, but unlike the panorama, where they could move about to obtain different views of the static painting, visitors to the Diorama were seated inside a small theater (Figure 5). They

were surrounded by an elegant white and gold drapery bearing the names of illustrious painters, a subtle suggestion of the quality of the work they were about to see. The viewers faced an opening like a proscenium arch, set forty-two feet away, through which they saw an enormous painted tableau. The audience was immediately caught up in the spell cast by the mountains, chalets, and streams of a Swiss valley, so like a natural scene that one critic of the time described himself as never having been so vividly impressed by any other representation of nature.[9] So rapt was the audience with this first scene that it found itself facing a second scene oblivious to the fact that the entire seating platform had been rotated from below.[10] Now, even though presented with a completely different subject, the spectators once again became total believers in a painted scene.

What made the audience's experience even more thrilling and deeply impressive was an innovation by Daguerre which persuaded audiences that, as they watched, a series of rapid changes occurred in the painted scene. Whether day became night or fair weather became foul, the viewers were convinced they were actually witnessing such transformations. Daguerre's secret in producing these effects lay in his ability to introduce multiple sources of natural light, not only from the front, but from above and behind the transparent linen hangings on which the scenes were painted. By regulating, through a complex arrangement of shutters and blinds, the source and amount of natural light, Daguerre was able to produce a variety of lighting effects that transformed a static view into an ever-shifting scene.

The audience's experience at the Diorama led to a fundamental change in the public's expectations of what an illusionistic presentation should achieve. No longer was it adequate simply to trick the audience into believing it was a visitor to a distant city, as at the panorama; now they also expected to experience a transformation in time. In this way, the Diorama amazed and delighted audiences for over a decade. Gradually, however, some critics began to remark that although the scenes produced at the Diorama were amazing, they nevertheless possessed a stillness or immobility that made them appear abandoned by the living.

No sooner was this slight murmur of discontent expressed than Daguerre skillfully overcame it by inventing a new and even more dramatic type of spectacle. In 1834, Daguerre, working with a pupil, Hippolyte Victor Sébron, met the criticism of immobility by adding the illusion of action to the painted scene. It was the result, Daguerre claimed, of his use of light. In fact, he boasted, light was the only source for the appearance of action within his new presentation.[11] It was, he said, a system of painting that he had invented that could transform the appearance of an object by switching between reflected and refracted light, as well as by changing the color of the light that fell upon it. He could even make an object appear or disappear by this use of light. The result of this new effect once again caused critics to hail Daguerre and the Diorama as magical.

Enthralled Parisians and foreign visitors crowded the Diorama to see the first of such new stagecraft marvels: the enactment of a midnight mass at the familiar Parisian church of Saint Étienne-du-Mont. The audience was first presented with a daylight view of the empty nave of the church, which gradually darkened as they watched. Candles were then seen being lit at the altar, ultimately filling the now-dark space of the nave with their glow. Miraculously, the previously empty chairs slowly filled with worshipers—an effect Daguerre specifically described as caused by the manipulation of light. Organ music filled the church, completing the illusion of the midnight service; and as the music diminished, the candles were extinguished one by one. Dawn's light crept in and the chairs were once again empty.[12] A rapt audience could only compare the spell cast by this performance to a mystical experience.

This new production at the Diorama played continuously for three years, and another equally popular and even more dramatic presentation joined it a year later—one that appealed to another side of human nature, the fascination with natural disasters. Again relying upon Daguerre's novel manipulation of light and pigment, the new production was one of both painted beauty and simulated action. It retold the story of a catastrophic 1806 avalanche that had destroyed a village in Switzerland. Opening with a foreground scene of a beautiful sunlit valley, the view deepened to expose a series of snowcapped mountain peaks whose slopes were dotted with chalets. No sooner had the audience enjoyed this delightful pastoral display, complete with tinkling cow bells, than an Alpine storm suddenly arose. Rain fell across the now-darkened valley, illuminated only by flashes of lightning and threatened by deep rolls of thunder. Villagers were seen leaving their houses to gather in the valley to implore God's grace, but a deafening sound of falling rock foretold that their pleas were in vain against this natural fury. As the clouds diminished, the moon emerged to light the valley, now seen covered with the vast debris and enormous rocks of an avalanche—and no sign of human life.[13]

The audience was struck dumb by its experience of an illusion created solely by Daguerre's ability to combine the effects of light and transparent painted surfaces. No greater depiction of reality was possible, according to one critic, who correctly attributed these amazing effects to Daguerre's great knowledge of optics. In creating these startling appearances of reality, Daguerre had indeed made light his servant. It was during this peak of acclaim as a magician of light that news began to spread that a new Daguerre invention promised even greater reality in the world of illusion.[14]

Fortified Vision

WHAT DAGUERRE HAD achieved so successfully during his years of work at the panorama, the theater, and the Diorama was to make people believe that what they saw before them was real, whether it was a moonrise or an avalanche. To inspire such belief, Daguerre used all the visual tricks of the artist, making whatever changes were necessary in his depiction of the natural world to give it the illusion of reality. His newest invention would also give the viewer an illusion of the real world, but without using any of the artist's deceptive practices. His aim was to put in the viewer's hands—literally—a small illusionistic scene, untouched by the hands of an artist but duplicating exactly, in every detail, a view of the real world.

How Daguerre intended to accomplish this feat was by transforming the drawing tool called a "camera obscura," or dark chamber, into a machine that could produce its own *permanent* images of nature. If he could succeed, a new tool for enhancing natural vision would be added to those already existing instruments—spectacles, microscopes, telescopes, and the camera obscura itself—that formed what the seventeenth-century German philosopher Gottfried Wilhelm Leibniz (1646–1716) called mankind's "fortified vision."

In appearance, the camera obscura Daguerre had been using was simply a wooden, lightproof box, one end of which was fitted with a lens that transmitted rays of light into it. Once the light from whatever object the camera was aimed at passed into the box, it would strike a surface, interrupting its passage. This surface, usually a mirror, was set at an angle to reflect the image it had received up onto a flat sheet of ground glass. Over this glass an artist could place a piece of paper on which to trace the transmitted image (Figure 6).

Amateurs who possessed no natural skill in drawing hoped that using the camera obscura would make up for their lack of talent, but their results rarely disguised their inadequacy. This tool was essentially a professional apparatus that was enormously useful to artists and topographical draftsmen who wanted to secure an accurate rendering of a three-dimensional scene on a flat surface.

Daguerre first became familiar with this draftsman's aid as a youthful architectural apprentice, and it had been a constant and important tool for all of his theatrical work. During these years, he had ample opportunity to become increasingly adept at its use; and like other users of the camera obscura over the centuries, he, too, must have become frustrated by

FIGURE 6
Artist Using Camera Obscura
Published in Dionysis Lardner, *The Museum of Science
& Art* (London 1855) vol. 8, p. 203
Courtesy of The Trustees of the Boston Public Library

the transitory nature of the beautiful images that appeared on the tracing glass, pictures that changed with every floating cloud and every passing moment. Struck by their perfection, artists yearned for the ability to transfer such images from the tracing glass to a permanent surface so they could refer to them again and again. Daguerre apparently became determined to find a way to accomplish this feat, a goal he was on the point of reaching at the time Parisians began to hear about his new invention.

When Daguerre began to pursue his dream is not known, but the idea for it probably first entered his thinking when he was wrestling with the problems of the Diorama presentations in the early 1820s. The conception and execution of the giant Dioramas involved complicated interactions of different kinds of light that played on diverse types of pigments covering both sides of a transparent screen. It was a complete break with all previous painting methods, and Daguerre had to perceive his ultimate image as coming into existence through a series of disparate steps. This perception would be important for guiding his later research in perfecting what came to be called the daguerreotype.

During the many years of experimentation that preceded the perfection of the daguerreotype process, its inventor could only work on it occa-

sionally, as his principal involvement was with his moneymaking projects at the theater and Diorama. What time he could devote to research was spent pursuing two main goals: the optical goal of increasing the sharpness of the lenses used in the camera obscura and the chemical goal of discovering the reaction of various light-sensitive materials when applied to different types of surfaces. Even though others were experimenting with light-sensitive chemicals at the time, the latter question was the most difficult for Daguerre both because of the innumerable variations possible and because his own knowledge in this area was limited. Nevertheless, he plunged into the search, picking up ideas from anyone he could question as well as attending scientific lectures.

Daguerre apparently had made little progress by 1826 when, by coincidence, he learned that a gentleman, an amateur scientist living near Dijon, Joseph Nicéphore Niépce (1765–1833), also was engaged in work similar to his own.[15] Niépce had begun to work with light-sensitive materials at least a decade earlier, hoping to find a way to produce a printing plate—of stone, copper, glass, or pewter— that, without the aid of an artist, could be used to make multiple copies. In part, Niépce's interest in finding such a medium came from his lack of talent as a draftsman, but he particularly foresaw the procedure as a lucrative means for reproducing multiple copies of existing prints or drawings. Niépce achieved some success in this pursuit and, without knowing it, provided the first step toward what would become the important technique of photoengraving. He also was experimenting, without success, in trying to secure an image through the camera obscura.

Niépce was both surprised and wary when Daguerre first wrote to him in 1826 inquiring about his work with the camera obscura, for Niépce had thought his research had been done in absolute secrecy. When writing about his experiments, he always used a secret code for key words, a practice he

FIGURE 7
JOSEPH-NICÉPHORE NIÉPCE
French (1765–1833)
View from the Window at Gras
1826
Heliograph (copy photograph enhanced by
Helmut Gernsheim in 1952)
Gernsheim Collection, Harry Ransom Humanities
Research Center, The University of Texas at Austin

and his older brother in London had followed earlier
when corresponding about their experiments to create a perpetual motion machine. Despite his reser-
vations, a tentative relationship grew between the
two men through a limited exchange of letters and
examples of their work. Niépce, writing on June 4,
1827, emphasized the fact that because they shared a
common goal they should reciprocate their efforts.[16]
Later that summer, when passing through Paris on

his way to London, Niépce met Daguerre for several
long discussions and was tremendously impressed
by the Diorama.

On his return from London in February 1828,
after a disappointing attempt to interest English scientists in his work, Niépce again visited Daguerre
in Paris, where they discussed the possibility of
working together.[17] Nearly eighteen months passed,
however, before the two men resumed contact. In
October 1829, Niépce took the initiative and sent
Daguerre an example of one of his recent pictures
taken in the camera obscura.[18] Although this piece
no longer exists, we can gain an idea of its subject
because of the descriptions of it by both Daguerre
and Augustin François Lemaître, a Parisian engraver
whom Niépce had also asked to criticize it.[19] Their
replies reveal that the piece resembled the only exist-

ing example of Niépce's work—now at the University of Texas, Austin—which he had left in London in February 1828 (Figure 7).[20] In fact, both of these images fit the description of other examples taken from nature that Niépce described in earlier letters to his brother.[21]

"Criticize my work severely," Niépce told Daguerre, and this he did, writing bluntly about its faults.[22] Daguerre objected to the lack of gradations in the light and dark areas of the plate, which he believed severely limited the truthfulness of the image. More importantly, he concluded from his inspection of the plate that, since shadows were cast on both sides of the objects in the scene, it must have taken an entire day's passage of the sun to make the image. Such a length of time, he said, made the objects so indistinct that the entire view appeared incomprehensible.

Lemaître went into even greater detail about this problem.[23] He noted that whereas, in nature, buildings opposite one another should appear parallel and equally lit, they did not do so in Niépce's work, and he concluded that the sun must have changed direction during the exposure. If Daguerre and Lemaître had known that the plate actually needed an exposure of several days, as recent scientific experiments have shown, they might have lost interest in Niépce's process altogether.[24]

As it was, however, Daguerre wrote that, despite his criticism of the image's faults, Niépce's actual "discovery could not be more extraordinary." For Daguerre, the importance lay in the fact that, for the first time, he was holding in his hands what he himself had so long sought, an image secured in the camera obscura on a light-sensitive surface that could be removed intact from the camera. For this reason, Daguerre always credited Niépce with this initial discovery.

He pressed Niépce, however, to continue working to improve the image that he harshly, but correctly, compared with what the least capable pupil could do simply by making a tracing with the aid of a camera obscura. He tried to impress Niépce with the importance of his discovery, pleading with him not to alter the plate in any way to produce multiple impressions. He also urged Niépce to continue his research, even though it might take several years to achieve perfection, and encouraged him to acquire an improved lens to get sharper images.

Above all, Daguerre said, the exposure time had to be reduced. He offered to help Niépce develop his process, but only if the impressions Niépce made in his camera obscura were superior to the one he had just sent to Daguerre. In reply to this criticism, Niépce proposed again that he and Daguerre work together to achieve perfection.[25]

Niépce's desire to have Daguerre join with him resulted in a formal partnership agreement that was signed December 14, 1829, during Daguerre's first visit to Niépce's home. Over the next four years, the two men worked together both through an encoded correspondence and side-by-side during visits by Daguerre to Niépce's laboratory in Chalôn-sur-Saône, several miles south of Dijon.[26]

Despite their close association over this period, they did not truly share the same priorities about perfecting the process. Niépce stated in August 1828 that he had foregone his search for a way of making printing plates in favor of producing images of nature in the camera obscura, but his initial purpose still continued to influence his research. Where this difference became most critical was in Niépce's lack of interest in what Daguerre believed was the crucial element for their discovery: the ability to produce an image with an exposure time short enough that each part of the natural scene would be distinguished clearly.

Again and again, Daguerre's letters encouraged Niépce to use different kinds of lenses to reduce exposure time. He even sent his colleague a camera obscura of his own design that he believed would cut the exposure to a third of the time. By Niépce's death in 1833, however, their joint endeavors had made almost no advance over the example Niépce had sent to Daguerre in 1829, which symbolized Niépce's first success but still represented only an ideal yet to be accomplished.

During the next two years, Daguerre worked not only on creating new, complicated scenes at the Diorama, each of which took over eight months to execute, but simultaneously experimented with ways to capture permanently the elusive images of the camera obscura. Although Isidore Niépce succeeded his father in the joint project, he apparently was not sufficiently knowledgeable to improve his father's process nor to contribute to the new direction Daguerre was taking in his research. This situation was formally recognized when, in May 1835, Daguerre called for the original contract with Nicéphore Niépce to be altered by replacing the section binding the two original participants to work together to perfect Niépce's process with a substitute clause that acknowledged the fact that two separate systems existed.[27] From then on, references about the process would refer to the new method invented by Daguerre and the older one conceived by Niépce.

How quickly and successfully Daguerre developed this new process we do not know, but in December 1834 he wrote Isidore to say he had found an important new way to make the plate light sensitive, although he still spoke of it requiring three to four hours to produce an image.[28] Writing on August 4, 1835, Daguerre pointed out that he had begun research on his new process as early as 1833, which had resulted in an exposure time sixty times faster than the old Niépce method.[29] We have few details of these steps, for although Daguerre mentioned these and other accomplishments in letters to Isidore, he did not give any details about how these breakthroughs were realized.

From the evidence of other commentators, however, it is clear that by 1835 Daguerre had, indeed, produced images similar to those that would be hailed in 1839. When, for example, the Paris correspondent of the London periodical *The Athenaeum* reported in January 1839 about the invention, he commented that Daguerre's current images were better than those he had seen "four years earlier." As Daguerre apparently also shared his work with a few friends, news of this amazing discovery began to circulate in the ateliers and salons around Paris, resulting in a notice in the September 27, 1835, issue of the *Journal des Artistes* alerting its readers to this incredible development.[30]

The following year, in September 1836, the father of Eugène Emmanuel Viollet-le-Duc wrote his son that a friend told him of seeing a work by Daguerre taken from atop the Diorama showing the hills of Montmarte one and one-half miles away. With only a weak magnifying glass, he wrote, it was possible to distinguish among the windmills on the hill the one serving as the telegraph tower, despite the fact that it measured only about three-quarters of an inch on the plate. It was even possible, he added, to distinguish all its working parts and sails, including the glittering iron wires used to operate arms of the semaphore telegraph. The letter concluded the description by adding that Daguerre's new device contained such minuscule details it could not possibly have been produced by an artist.[31]

During the period from 1835 to 1837, while still painting enormous scenes for the Diorama, Daguerre continued to perfect his discovery. He was particularly concerned with finding a way to ensure the stability of the finished image as well as with further reducing its exposure time. At last, he was satisfied both that his work could no longer be improved upon and that his process was a completely separate invention from the original work of Nicéphore Niépce. Accordingly, Daguerre called for a second change in the 1829 contract. On June 13, 1837, Isidore signed a "definitive agreement" affirming that Daguerre was the inventor of the "new process" and that it should carry only the name of Daguerre, but that the elder Niépce's name must be

FIGURE 8
LOUIS JACQUES MANDÉ DAGUERRE
French (1787–1851)
Still Life with Casts
1837
Whole-plate daguerreotype
Collection of the Société Française de Photographie

included in any announcement of the discovery. All other parts of the original contract were unchanged, thereby assuring that Isidore would continue to share in whatever gain might be made by exploiting the process.[32]

It was also in 1837 that Daguerre felt sufficiently confident of his work to present to the chief curator at the Louvre a still-life composition bearing an inscription on the back identifying it as proof of his discovery (Figure 8).[33] By April 1838, Daguerre became even more convinced of his success, for in a postscript to a letter to Isidore he casually announced that he had baptized his procedure "Daguerréotipe."[34]

The principal problem remaining for both Daguerre and Niépce was how to exploit the discovery. Over the next eighteen months, they sought a way to market the invention while protecting it from being freely used by others; for once revealed, even though patented, the process could easily be copied.[35] Daguerre was less concerned with reaping a montary reward from the invention than was Isidore, who was in severe financial trouble and was con-

stantly proposing ways to profit from the ten-year-old enterprise.[36] Daguerre frequently had to point out to him that it was difficult to sell shares to investors in a process when the value of their investment would plummet after the nature of the process was revealed. Daguerre also was against selling the invention abroad, to England or Germany, as Isidore had proposed. This dilemma continued until Daguerre reluctantly agreed to attempt to find subscribers for the invention, although he still hoped that some organization or individual could be found that would actually undertake making the invention available to the public.

Daguerre's hope became a reality when, near the end of 1838, he met François Arago (1786–1853), the respected astronomer and permanent Secretary of the Academy of Sciences. Arago was immediately struck by the importance of the discovery and, rejecting the viability of an open subscription, suggested instead that the government itself should purchase the discovery. Daguerre related this remarkable development to Isidore in a letter on January 2, 1839, saying that Arago intended to announce the discovery at the next meeting of the Academy of Sciences.[37] There Arago would take the first steps to convince the government that, by such an action, France would add to its reputation as the home of genius as well as demonstrate, once again, its role as the world's foremost contributor to the advancement of mankind.

The Dream Has Come to Pass

ARAGO WASTED NO TIME promoting Daguerre's discovery, taking advantage of the next meeting of the Academy of Sciences on January 7, 1839, to begin his campaign. He astonished his colleagues with his announcement that a way had been discovered to retain permanently the wonderous views previously seen only fleetingly in the camera obscura.[38] This long-sought goal had finally been reached, or, as Arago later would describe it, "the dream has come to pass." The artist who, over the previous twenty years, had brought so much excitement to the Parisian public with his illusionistic spectacles, J. L. M. Daguerre, had now succeeded in bringing about this new miracle. Although the natural colors of objects were not captured by Daguerre's system, his images on metal plates were otherwise perfect reproductions of what the camera obscura saw before it. Arago testified that he and two other scientists, Jean Baptiste Biot (1774–1862) and Alexander von Humboldt (1769–1859), had inspected the results—marvelous views of Parisian monuments—and were convinced that Daguerre had achieved an amazing breakthrough. The scientists agreed that a patent to protect the invention was not feasible and therefore accepted Arago's idea that a government subvention should reward the inventors. Arago proposed to pursue this goal with the government as soon as Daguerre had revealed to him exactly how the images were created. The pathway for Daguerre's public and financial success was thus laid out, and over the next eight months the steps along it were directed by Arago.

While the legislative process was proceeding, the press immediately hailed this magical discovery. To describe the invention was not an easy task, however, for they had to do so without fully understanding how or why it worked. Daguerre took every precaution to keep his process secret. Although willing to show his work to visitors—particularly the press—he made sure that the metal plates bearing the images were either framed behind glass or had their edges concealed by paper so the type of metal used could not be identified.[39] Seeing the results, however, was enough to send prose flying high. Typical of how the press reacted are phrases such as "marvels from a fairy tale"; "fabulous but true"; "nature drew herself"; "each picture produced an exclamation of admiration"; "the invention borders on the fantastic."[40]

After making such general observations, all of the early reports agreed that the most amazing feature of the daguerreotype was that it contained every detail of whatever scene it captured. Minute parts of the view, ones not even visible to the naked eye, proved to be present when the plate was examined through the powerful magnifying glass Daguerre provided to visitors. Reporters eagerly told how letters on a distant, barely perceptible shop sign became completely legible; how a scarcely visible window on a distant roof not only came into view but was found to have a broken pane patched with paper; how a leaf could be spied on the ledge of a distant monument whose masonry was revealed to be filled with chips and cracks. No commentator failed to report the awe brought about by looking at the daguerreotype through the magnifying glass. Such demonstrations turned doubters into believers, and the daguerreotype began to be thought of as a mirror that permanently retained every detail it reflected.

Accompanying this fascination with its accuracy was an amazement that this perfect mirror could be taken away from the presence of the object it depicted. When holding the image in one's hand, it seemed impossible to believe that this small piece of metal brought with it a detailed view of a distant street or landscape. One commentator attempted to describe this new phenomenon by saying it was as if Daguerre could order an immovable monument to come to him. He could, for example, order the towers of Notre Dame to appear before him, and they would obey.[41]

What the daguerreotype depicted was more easily described than was the object itself. Commentators took different approaches in characterizing the physical appearance of the daguerreotype, but most began by commenting that, because it lacked color, it was not a painting. Often it was compared with certain kinds of prints: engravings, etchings, mezzotints. However, as these processes depend on using lines both to outline objects and to create areas of darkness through crosshatching, such prints were not truly comparable to the daguerreian images, which took form through the subtle gradations of light. It was the more recent form of etching, the aquatint, that became the most accepted comparison. Like the daguerreotype, its images were not defined by line, but by contrast of areas of light and dark. It also possessed a wide range of tonal gradations that closely resembled the effects that

were produced by the action of the sun in the daguerreotype.[42]

Drawing also was frequently suggested as an object of comparison, but it, too, was not deemed totally similar since drawings, like prints, were mostly the product of lines. Although the term "pencil of nature" became a poetic way of referring to the process,[43] it did not accurately reflect the daguerreotype's appearance. Among drawings, only those made with fine black chalk or India ink–tipped brushes were thought to possess qualities similar to the daguerreotype, presenting the same exquisite tones, extraordinary softness of surface, satin-like shadows and gradations of luminosity.[44]

In England, the mid-January reports of Daguerre's discovery[45] came as a distinct shock to William Henry Fox Talbot (1800–1877), an English scientist respected for his experiments in many branches of science. Talbot believed he already had discovered such a process in experiments made four years earlier that he had not pursued. Therefore, to preempt Daguerre's being accepted as the discoverer of the process that Talbot felt was his own, he immediately took steps to make his work public. On January 25, without waiting to learn more about what the French discovery looked like, Talbot placed on display at the Royal Institution numerous works he had made in 1835, believing they were similar to what Daguerre had invented.[46] They included records of lace and botanical specimens laid upon chemically treated paper and exposed to the sun (Figure 9). In addition, he presented a view made on light-sensitive paper in a camera obscura showing a silhouetted roofline and chimneys (Figure 10), an image in no way comparable to the impressively detailed views of Parisian buildings produced by Daguerre.

Talbot's work was actually aided by the announcement of Daguerre's discovery, for it challenged him to continue the experiments he had abandoned earlier that would ultimately lead to the discovery of the positive / negative photographic

FIGURE 9
WILLIAM HENRY FOX TALBOT
British (1800–1877)
Linen Textile Fragment
About 1835
Photogenic drawing negative
85.XM.150.14

belief was surely what encouraged Daguerre to apply for an English patent for his process a month before the secret was given free to the rest of the world. Daguerre would not have dared to undertake such an act without Arago's blessing.

While this nationalistic jousting was taking place, reports of the wonders of the daguerreotype continued to pour forth. Arago continually encouraged Daguerre to show his work to visiting dignitaries, and an ever-increasing number of interested scientists from Italy, Russia, and Germany came to see him, as did the American, Samuel F. B. Morse (1791–1872), who had come from New York to Paris to demonstrate his invention of the electric telegraph. On March 7, 1839, Morse visited Daguerre's studio and was vastly impressed by what he saw. He wrote about his visit a few days later, calling Daguerre's invention one of the most beautiful discoveries of the age.[49] The day after Morse's visit, Daguerre's studio at the Diorama went up in flames, and most of his papers and daguerreotypes were destroyed. A few plates appear to have been saved, but an example Arago had made under Daguerre's tutelage was lost, a specimen Arago surely had planned to exhibit when announcing the specifics of the then-secret process to the world.[50]

To make up for the loss he suffered, Daguerre must have had to work feverishly to create additional images to display in support of the claims Arago was making. In particular, Arago wanted examples for the English scientists to examine so they could see for themselves the weakness of Talbot's claims. Sir John Herschel (1792–1871), the astronomer and physicist (and close friend of Talbot, with whom he often discussed photogenic drawing) led a group of British scientists to Paris in May 1839 to see examples of Daguerre's work for the first time. Talbot had refused an invitation to accompany them and remained in London, anxious to hear of their reaction.[51]

Although Herschel is quoted as saying that, in contrast to what Daguerre had produced, the English

process. As his sister expressed in a letter to him at the time, "I am glad M. Daguer [sic] roused you to life."[47] His claim for precedence riled the scientific scene, particularly when he asserted it before the Academy of Sciences in Paris, where Arago testily rejected it, pointing out (somewhat erroneously) that the Frenchmen Niépce and Daguerre had been working on this problem for the past twenty years.[48] Talbot's attempts to place his work ahead of Daguerre's had two consequences. First, a comparison of actual examples of each man's work established the superiority of Daguerre's process. The second result was a belief on Arago's part that the English were trying to steal France's glory. This

FIGURE 10
WILLIAM HENRY FOX TALBOT
British (1800–1877)
Rooftop and Chimneys, Lacock Abbey
About 1835
Salt-fixed photogenic drawing negative
84.XM.478.9

efforts were only "childish amusements," he was more tactful in his personal report to Talbot. He did, however, confess his amazement to Talbot at the quality of the daguerreotypes and called them miraculous.[52] Saying they surpassed anything he had thought possible, Herschel praised their incredible detail, their gradation of light and shade, and especially the beautiful effects of river scenes taken in the rain. Talbot could only have been dismayed to receive such positive comments about the daguerreotype from his friend.

Talbot's desire for recognition as the inventor of a miraculous new system of making images would continue, for the time being, to be thwarted. Even London newspapers came out decisively on the side of Daguerre, one asserting bluntly that

any comparison between Talbot's photogenic drawing on paper and the works of Daguerre was quite ridiculous.[53] Talbot was spared, however, from learning of one colleague's stinging comments. After viewing Daguerre's works in May 1839, the Scottish scientist James Forbes wrote his sister that "the daguerreotype baffles belief," and concluded with the dour remark that "As to Messrs Talbot & Company, they had better shut shop at once."[54]

The Secret Is Disclosed

FOR MANY LONG MONTHS, the mystery of how a daguerreotype was actually made was not revealed. All those who had seen one of the miraculous images or had read about them were kept in the dark by the absolute secrecy imposed by Daguerre and his supporters. Not until the late summer of 1839 was it finally announced that details of the process would be divulged on August 19. The heretofore strictly guarded procedure would be made public by Arago at the regular Monday meeting of the Academy of Sciences, to which members of the Academy of Fine Arts would also be invited. Held in the seventeenth-century home of the Institute of France, located on the Seine directly across from the Louvre, the prestige of the setting alone stressed the significance of the occasion.

Word of the impending event spread throughout Paris, and an enormous crowd began assembling several hours before the announced time of the meeting. By the time Arago started to speak, the auditorium was filled with distinguished scientists and artists, while hundreds of other curious Parisians packed the plaza outside and even spilled out onto the Quai de Conti.

Arago took full advantage of this epochal occasion by endowing it with an air of historic solemnity.[55] He first portrayed the moment as the culmination of a series of important chemical and optical discoveries begun in the Renaissance. He depicted how the insights of Daguerre's predecessors had led to the invention of the camera obscura and how its beautiful miniature scenes had inflamed a desire to preserve these fleeting impressions so they could be carried away to be enjoyed forever. Now, as if by enchantment, Daguerre had made that possible.

Arago related Nicéphore Niépce's role in the invention of the daguerreotype and affirmed that his son, Isidore, and Daguerre would be equally rewarded by the state for their work, but that Daguerre would receive additional compensation for disclosing the secret of his Diorama. Arago then went on to extol at length the benefits this new invention would bring to both the sciences and arts.

At last he turned to the disclosure everyone had come to hear—how the daguerreotype was actually produced. Although present at Arago's side, Daguerre requested that his sponsor speak on his behalf, pleading that a sore throat prevented him from doing so himself.

Despite the complexity and innovative character of this new process, no step-by-step demonstration was presented. Instead, Arago gave only an oral description of how the process worked. Under these circumstances, it is amazing that anyone present was able to understand the description sufficiently to realize the revolutionary implications of the process. Not even those with scientific training or laboratory experience could have anticipated the extraordinary chain of chemical effects required to produce the daguerreotype. How the image finally appeared on what Arago called the "canvas" of the daguerreotype thus seemed even more mysterious than they had expected.

At least one scientist in the audience predicted that thousands of daguerreotypes would have to be made before it could be known exactly how such effects were achieved. He was modest in his appraisal. Today, after millions of examples have been made, questions still remain about how the daguerreian image is formed. "The dream has come to pass," was the way Arago characterized the result of finally securing the elusive image seen in the camera obscura, but the *how* remained a mystery.[56]

Only a few who heard Arago's discourse learned enough about the process to actually make a daguerreotype. The next day, one newspaper printed a lengthy account written by the scientist Alfred Donné (1801–1878), who had been present at Arago's address. He included a careful summary of the steps to make a daguerreotype, but vital details, such as the time needed for each step, were still lacking.

Even Donné, with his scientific training, was led, after describing the first three steps of making a daguerreotype, to resort to a metaphor to explain the mystery of the process by saying it was as miraculous as the incubation of an egg which produces a live chick. He also poetically described the washing of the plate as a baptism of this new being resulting from human creation.[57]

Those eager to make a daguerreotype did not have to depend solely upon oral reports or newspaper accounts, because the next day a detailed instruction manual, prepared by Daguerre himself, was available for purchase. He also had made sure that complete outfits of the necessary equipment had been manufactured and were available for immediate sale. Obviously Daguerre had spent the prior months organizing his resources for this moment. Both the instruction manual and the official equipment quickly sold out and constantly had to be restocked.[58]

In Daguerre's manual, a novice could find a concise description of the successive steps necessary to make a daguerreotype using the custommade equipment. Following these instructions, as a fledgling daguerreotypist you would first need to polish a silver-coated copper plate scrupulously, until it shone like a mirror. Then, to make it sensitive to light, you would place the coated side over the vapors of iodine until it turned the "correct" shade of yellow. Now, in its sensitized state, your "silver canvas" was ready to be placed in a lightproof metal container (a version of today's plate holder), which slid into your new daguerreian camera, replacing the piece of ground glass on which you had composed your image visually. Now, rather than tracing the scene yourself, as you would have done in the past with your traditional camera obscura, you would remove the lens cap and allow light to fall on the plate, putting nature to work to "portray herself." Surprisingly, in spite of the fifteen to twenty minutes nature was left to work its magic, no visible image would have appeared on the plate when it was removed from the camera obscura. Only after putting it over the fumes of heated mercury—keeping the plate at a mysteriously mandated forty-five-degree angle—could you watch the image emerge. Nature had now described itself on your plate.[59]

After a bath in a chemical solution and a final rinse in distilled water, the image was fixed forever. Because, as Arago had said, the daguerreotype surface was as delicate as the wings of a butterfly, you had to protect it by covering it with a piece of glass. Finally, you held in your hand a permanent painting made by nature itself—but with more than a little help from you.[60]

Regardless of the detailed instructions in Daguerre's manual, the complicated and inexact procedure dismayed potential enthusiasts, who found it was not an easy task to turn the sun into an obedient painter. The ultimate purchasers of Daguerre's process—the citizens of France—started to wonder whether they had been misled.

Their unease about the process was aggravated by the scathing criticism of the entire discovery that appeared a week after Arago's presentation in an article by Jules Janin, an influential and previously enthusiastic supporter of the daguerreotype.[61] In the weekly publication *L'Artiste*, Janin gave vent to his anger at the lack of information Arago had provided at the Academy of Sciences. He was biting in his description of that event, particularly incensed that no actual demonstration had been given. He even accused Daguerre of hiding in the shadow of Arago, not daring to risk personally demonstrating the invention France had presented to the world. Janin was not alone in his outspoken views, and the opticians, chemists, artists, and curious amateurs who had taken up the challenge of this new wonder right away also began to lose faith in the process when their results proved worthless, or at best mediocre.

Daguerre, clearly dismayed by the discouraging response to his prized invention and perhaps concerned about the government's reaction to this attitude, acted immediately to turn the disgruntled and angry critics into supporters. He sought out Janin directly, berating him for failing to understand the process and telling him to come with him to his studio that very moment to watch him make a daguerreotype. Janin agreed and became completely convinced that it was indeed possible for others to learn the technique. As a result, in the next issue of *L'Artiste*, Janin totally reversed his negative opinion about the ease and practicality of carrying out the process.[62] He softened his previous approach by saying that, as he watched Daguerre place the exposed plate over the mercury fumes, it was as if Mab, the queen of fairies, had used her magic to make the image appear. More importantly, he went on to say that what Daguerre must do was to personally demonstrate his process to others. If he did, Janin said, there soon would be hundreds who would become experts in the art.

Daguerre began doing just that, giving weekly public consultations and demonstrations. At his first session, held early in September, he demonstrated each step of the process slowly and deliberately. He even asked three people in the audience to examine the plate after it had been exposed in the camera obscura so they could testify that at that point nothing could be seen traced upon the iodized surface. Then, as they watched, the fumes of mercury made the image appear. The finished picture, painted by the sun—much like the one reproduced here (Figure 11)—was handed about the group and proclaimed a complete success.[63] Such demonstrations turned pupils into disciples who began to spread the news of the unbelievable process into the far reaches of the world.

Chapter One

The World Poses for the Sun

———

W HEN, IN 1839, word first began to make its way from the scientific and literary gazettes into the popular press that a French artist had found a way to make the sun itself create a work of art that exactly copied a scene from nature without any aid from an artist's brush, the general public was suspicious. After all, only four years earlier these same newspapers had startled the world by reporting that people actually lived on the moon, even showing illustrations of winged moon-creatures lolling on the beach of a lunar lake.[1]

Such images had been described as coming from sightings made by the eminent scientist Sir John Herschel through his gigantic telescope in South Africa. For months, detailed articles traveled around the globe and were taken so seriously that a group of clergy began planning how missionaries could be sent to the moon to spread the word of the gospel. Although finally revealed as a hoax perpetrated by an ingenious *New York Sun* reporter and denounced as false by Herschel, the moon story had made such an impact that the world greeted other startling scientific news with skepticism.

Now, only a few years later, should the public believe these astonishing reports of "sun pictures," especially when the same scientist, Herschel,

endorsed them as being genuine? What was one to believe from such reports? If people had unscrupulously been led to believe winged creatures occupied the moon, why should they now believe the sun would be willing to be shut up in a box to produce works of art on a metal plate with the curious name *daguerreotype*?

During the months before any accurate details emerged about what appeared to be more a concoction of fiction than a scientific invention, newspapers compounded, rather than explained, the mystery of the daguerreotype because the editors themselves were not actually confident of their own understanding. One of the earliest examples of such reports appeared in the *Cincinnati Republican* of March 1839, where it was intriguingly entitled "Farewell to Ink, Types, Clocks!"[2] This headline represented what the editors understood from early London reports about this new invention—that the daguerreotype could do everything previously accomplished by painting and printing and could show the passage of time because plates made early in the morning looked different from those made at noon or in the evening.

Fantasies about this new use of the sun blossomed during this early period of little precise information, and one American wrote a lengthy poem about what the new solar device would allow him to

Detail, Plate 5

see. He dreamed of being able to look through all the "picture pages" the sun had been daguerreotyping since the beginning of time! He longed to see the first pictures of the world when only dark and chaos prevailed, as well as ones of Adam "when he stroll'd about his charming garden." He listed all the great Biblical events he hoped to witness as they had happened—like the parting of the Red Sea—as well as scenes from the ancient histories of Athens, Rome, and Egypt. "Give back the lost," he implored, and restore them "in one vast gallery of pictures of the Sun."[3] Imaginative ideas like these give an insight into the expectations the concept of the sun as an image maker inspired during the period when the secret of the new process remained hidden.

In Paris, however, the availability of Daguerre's manual, equipment, and demonstrations, as well as the existence of a group of critics and artists who were constantly exchanging ideas about this new process, led not to fantasies about the daguerreotype but to the desire to make one. A frantic struggle took place to succeed in producing an actual example of this new art form. The energy of those anxious to experiment with the camera swept through Paris as they tried to photograph the same monuments and urban views Daguerre had translated so successfully into miniature, but exact, representations of Parisian scenes. One bystander described the autumnal days of 1839 as a time when "the opticians' shops were [so] besieged" they could not "rake together enough instruments to satisfy the onrushing army of would-be daguerreotypists."[4] In the following days, he observed, this army was dispersed so thoroughly throughout the city that there was not a square in Paris that was without a "three-legged dark box planted in front of churches and palaces." Like their master, Daguerre, these neophytes attempted to capture, through the magic of the lens, the majestic forms and rich ornamentation present in the architectural masterpieces of the capital city.

They could immediately judge their results by comparing the appearance of the actual monuments with the images that nature, and they, had painted on their plates. It was a painful learning process, for unlike Daguerre, who had worked with the camera obscura for years, few of these devotees had any experience in composing a scene through a ground-glass viewer. Another critical problem the early enthusiasts were distressed to discover was that, in their carefully composed views of the monuments along the Seine, the Louvre had surprisingly been transferred to the other side of the Seine, or that, in their views down the narrow shop-lined streets, all the signs were reversed. They had ignored the fact that the daguerreotype—this mirror image of a scene—would be reversed left-to-right unless their lens was fitted with a reversing prism such as Daguerre had described in his manual and used in his demonstrations. Adding the reversing prism, however, lengthened the exposure time, so many daguerreotypists omitted using it. Seeing images with their familiar surroundings displaced caused the public both discomfort and amusement, which satirists of the day took great sport in exaggerating.

Only by trial and error were the results with this new instrument gradually perfected. Happily, the "mistakes" and the "less-than-acceptable compositions" could be wiped off the silver plates and their surfaces repolished, producing new silver canvases ready to be sensitized for another try.[5]

During what must have been a series of frustrating attempts, these pioneers had in front of them the superior works created by Daguerre himself; when they visited their local opticians they faced window displays of the very daguerreotypes they were striving to emulate. They got little sympathy if they complained that it was the system that was at fault, for as Jules Janin had already cautioned them, they would only sound like those who, having bought a Stradivarius violin, complained of not being able to play like Paganini.[6]

Seeing these models of perfection could only make the novices question where they had gone wrong. The potential for error or lack of success was so broad that today it seems amazing that so many triumphed over the obstacles. They had to be concerned with chemical, physical, and artistic failure simultaneously when they sought to find out why their results were less than perfect. Was it because the plate had been inadequately sensitized? Had it been exposed in the camera too long, or not long enough? Had the fumes of mercury been heated to precisely the right temperature? Or was it their choice of viewpoint that had prevented the image from appearing as they had hoped? What was it that kept them from being able to capture the tonality, the subtleties of light and dark, of highlights and shadows, they had perceived in the astonishing prototypes? Only when we realize the multitude of variations possible in this complex process can we begin to comprehend the revolutionary zeal and dogged determination of these pioneers. They were motivated by the stunning possibilities Daguerre had presented to them of a completely new art form. In addition, after several decades of viewing the spectacles Daguerre had presented to the Parisian public in the panorama, the theater, and the Diorama, this new art form enabled individuals, for the first time, to create their own illusionistic representations of the world.

Despite the difficulties and vagaries of the process, people with diverse interests—scientists, inventors, artists, and ardent amateurs—sought the satisfaction of actually making a daguerreotype. They quickly learned it required a great deal of human persuasion and skill for "nature to paint herself" or for the "sun to act as a pencil," as the process was widely described at the time. It rapidly became evident that a daguerreotype of the quality of those Daguerre had exhibited was due first to the skill exercised in the operating process itself. True success, however, demanded a sensitive understanding of how the sole medium—light—could be manipulated to produce a seemingly effortless rendering of a natural scene. From Daguerre onward, the eye of the maker is as clear in the finished work as it is in any other artistic medium, and the daguerreotype ultimately would become understood as the result of a human artistic intelligence making choices and decisions.

At the same time the monuments of Paris were being recorded, other amateurs in various parts of the world were also putting views of their native monuments onto their silver canvases. So intense was this activity that, in the short span of three months, Daguerre's manual went through twenty-five editions in five languages. The speed with which the daguerreian art form spread is also shown by the fact that, in January 1840, the optician Noël-Marie Paymal Lerebours (1807–1873) already was offering for sale in his Paris shop original daguerreotype views of scenes taken in Italy.[7]

Contemporaneous with the increase of daguerreian images available in Paris, Daguerre sent a representative, François Gouraud, to America to give lessons and to sell daguerreian equipment as well as individual daguerreotype views of Paris. The cost of both was extremely expensive everywhere. For example, in 1840, the King of Denmark wrote a friend visiting Paris that he was prepared to pay forty francs if a view of the Seine and the Tuileries could be acquired. We do not know if he was successful, but the amount he was willing to pay was equal to two weeks' wages for a middle-class worker.[8] Although much admired by the public who flocked to opticians' windows in Paris, New York, and London to see them, daguerreotypes were unaffordable luxuries except for the few.

The daguerreotype's appeal rested not only in its novelty, but in its amazing ability to set down in miniature form the precise details of a scenic or urban view. Regardless of people's long familiarity with engravings or other prints that reduced views

FIGURE 12
LOUIS-ALPHONSE POITEVIN, French (1819–1882)
View of a House and Garden, about 1847
Sixth-plate daguerreotype plate processed for printing
84.XP.906.2

FIGURE 13
LOUIS-ALPHONSE POITEVIN, French (1819–1882)
View of a House and Garden, about 1847
Engraving made from daguerreotype plate
84.XP.906.1

of enormous subjects to much smaller formats, they found the daguerreotype view—the product of the lens—to be more astonishing. Its ability to include every detail, some not even visible from the distance at which the daguerreotype was recorded, had an almost hypnotic effect. The lens put before them an objective record; for the viewers it appeared that no artist had interceded between what they saw and the subject itself. A daguerreotype became a synonym for truth.

At the same time that daguerreotypes were becoming established as vehicles for the truthful visual depiction of objects or scenic views, travelers, as François Arago predicted from the outset, quickly adopted them as a necessary part of their expeditions. By 1840, travelers to the Near East were recording temples, inscriptions, and ruins and bringing their images back, mostly to Paris, in increasing numbers.[9] The intense push toward finding a manner of making these images more readily, and less expensively, attainable reflected the public's interest in seeing such truthful depictions of foreign lands—an interest far more important to members of the classically trained, mid-nineteenth-century educated class than a photograph of the same site would be today.

To meet the demand for multiple examples of the new process, a simple way of replicating the original daguerreotype had to be found. Although a daguerreotype could be copied by making another daguerreotype of the original, such a solution was not the answer to providing numerous and cheaper copies. The most attractive path was to discover a means for transforming the metal surface of the daguerreotype into a printing plate. As early as September 1839, a process for doing so had been presented to the Academy by Alfred Donné; other similar methods were proposed by Hippolyte Louis Fizeau (1819–1896) and Louis-Alphonse Poitevin (1819–1882).[10] All of these systems attempted, through electrolysis or chemical means, to turn the daguerreotype image into an incised metal surface

that would hold enough ink to allow a paper impression to be taken (Figures 12 and 13). Each method was successful in producing a limited number of copies, but the quality was inadequate; all the original delicacies of light and shade, as well as many of the details, were lost in the process. Daguerre, probably painfully reminded of Nicéphore Niépce's early goal to use his light-sensitive process to make a printing plate, raised a stinging objection to such attempts and wrote to Arago protesting these "supposed innovations" that would destroy the uniqueness of the work of art.[11]

Ultimately, the answer to producing multiple copies of daguerreotype views did not involve physically altering the plate. Instead, somewhat ironically, it lay in first having an artist hand-copy the daguerreian views, then print the drawings by using a traditional graphic process but clearly identify the prints as having been made "from daguerreotypes." The earliest-known examples appeared as lithographs in 1839. They were made by first tracing the image from the daguerreotype plate—a difficult and delicate task, for the image could be destroyed by a stroke of the pencil—then translating the drawings into prints by the lithographic process. The subjects of these first prints appear to be faithful copies of the original plates, enhanced with only a few clouds added to the blank sky of the daguerreotype.[12] While they have value as records of early daguerreotypes, these renderings are even more significant because they reflect how the new visual language of imagery derived from the lens impacted the way the world came to be represented. In the view of the Pont Neuf (Figure 14), for example, the camera angle and the compactness of the objects produce a more immediate and dramatic rendering of the scene than would be found in a traditional drawing of this landmark. The character of the light and dark imagery of the daguerreotype, however, has not been successfully conveyed. The soft, crayon-like strokes of the lithographic medium dominate.[13]

FIGURE 14
L. MARQUIER
French (active 1830s)
Le Pont-Neuf
1839
Lithograph after a daguerreotype
Courtesy of George Eastman House

The Paris supplier of optical, and now daguerreian, equipment, Lerebours, became a major figure in the promotion of the daguerreotype, and his principal contribution was the publication of the series of daguerreian views from around the world, *Excursions daguerriennes*, which he began issuing in 1840. Lerebours commissioned and purchased daguerreotypes in such number that, within a year, he had acquired twelve hundred original daguerreotypes from all over the world.[14] Most of these he apparently sold as individual plates, since only 112 views were ultimately used in his publication. Editions of this work continued to be published for decades, and the accuracy of its views was so respected it came to be used as a geography textbook.[15]

Lerebours first had the original plates traced by artists, just as the earlier lithographic prints copied from daguerreotypes had been; but he chose the aquatint process to reproduce these drawings, employing skilled printmakers to carry out the work. The choice of aquatint as the means of reproduction permitted the quality of light and shade of the daguerreotype to be rendered more accurately than it had been in the lithographs. This process also had a drawback, however, because it did not reproduce the precise detail so valued as part of this new art form, as can be seen in the sketchy sculptural details

depicted in the plate of the Arch of Titus from the *Excursions daguerriennes* (Figure 15).[16] Also, the makers of these prints took more freedom in deleting or adding details in the original daguerreian scenes. In particular, because the daguerreotype still could not capture motion, the scenes were animated by adding a few bystanders, although Lerebours assured the viewer that the added figures conformed to sketches made by observers on the spot at the time the daguerreotypes were made.

A later collection of engravings published by J. B. Chamouin in 1845 is boldly entitled *Vues de Paris prises au daguerréotype*; but here, too, the images were no closer to actual daguerreotypes, since they were the result of the same procedure of tracing daguerreotype plates and turning them into engravings. In this case, were it not for the

FIGURE 15
JOHN CALLOW
British (1822–1878)
The Arch of Titus
Aquatint after a daguerreotype
Published in *Excursions daguerriennes* (Paris 1840)
84.XB.1186.1.33

title we would not associate its engravings with daguerreotypes, as they appear totally similar to the type of engraved views issued long before the daguerreian era.

These engravings present the daguerreian view as if the lens had been able to depict all the gestures and actions of the moving figures. The view of the "Nouveau Louvre" (Figure 16) is animated by a mounted guard galloping across the foreground, as well as by carriages and phaetons carrying their passengers about the square. Fashionably dressed ladies flourishing umbrellas stroll about with their children, and a public conveyance filled with people also enters the scene. Desirable as it may have been to enliven this scene, it was not yet possible to do so with the daguerreotype itself.

Considering the hardship of travel, the bulk of the equipment to be carried, and the many delicate operations to be undertaken, it is amazing what triumphs of photography the explorer-daguerreotypists were able to produce in these early years. At times, working within stifling tents or other make-do shelters, it must have been unclear who was in control—the sun or the maker. Over the next twenty years, the answer became clear as the daguerreotypists produced a view of the world as it had never been seen before.

FIGURE 16
JEAN-BAPTISTE-MARIE CHAMOUIN
French (born 1768)
Nouveau Louvre
Engraving after a daguerreotype
Published in *Vues de Paris prises au daguerreotype*
(Paris 1845)
84.XO.333.1.1

PLATES

Chapter One

PLATE I

LOUIS-ALPHONSE POITEVIN
French (1819–1882)
The Pantheon, Paris
1842
Half plate (reversed)
84.XT.265.12

DUE TO THE MAGIC of the daguerreian process, we are able to hold in our hand an enframed metallic image, only six inches by four inches, that contains an accurate and detailed image of the enormous edifice of the Pantheon—272 feet high and 276 feet wide.[17] The twenty-three-year-old Louis-Alphonse Poitevin was able to record its complete mass on his plate by climbing to the roof of one of the buildings it faced. From this height, he was able to focus his lens on the peak of the pediment, putting that important defining point of the building's design directly in the center of his daguerreotype.

Poitevin's image, therefore, echoes the balance of parts the architect strove to give his design as it rose above its broad base. By adjusting the position of the camera until the central doorway appeared completely surrounded by its white stone frame, Poitevin reinforced the central organization of the building's elements. The doorway initiates a vertical axis that is critical to the translation of the three-dimensional work of architecture onto the flat daguerreotype plate, giving us an image that exactly reproduces the proportions of the monument.

Poitevin enlivened this basic definition of the building by capitalizing on the ability of the daguerreotype to capture the nuances of light. He chose a late summer afternoon when the sun's rays coming from the southwest would penetrate the dark recesses of the porch deeply enough to illuminate the relief sculpture on its rear wall.[18] This same angle of light also formed long shadows behind the columns. Those on the right extend so far as to bend upward as they encounter the side columns.

The same angle allows the sun to strike the inscription and the relief sculpture of the pediment even more brilliantly. What Poitevin has achieved here is an impression of "inconceivable beauty," the term used by the first viewers of daguerreotypes to describe the impact of their incredible detail. Notice how, by positioning his camera, he has been able to illuminate all the sculptures embraced within the pediment, even showing how the head of the center figure is freed from its background. This brilliantly chosen point of view and time of day also sends light into the shallow peristyle of the drum, making the columns stand out as lively objects in their own right, moving in a graceful circle whose motion is picked up by the swelling dome and terminated by the crowning lantern. Such a perfect example of a daguerreotype shows the enormous empathy Poitevin had with this new art form and how adept he had become in its use.

A final touch of perfection, however, was due to chance—the arrival of a group of visitors who appeared before the monument shortly before he exposed the plate. Located far enough away from the camera so their casual movements would not be blurred in the image, this group becomes an exquisite frieze of horses, carriages, drivers, and sightseers whose fortuitous grouping echoes the sculptured figures of the pediment and gives a welcome sense of scale to the scene (Figure 17).

FIGURE 17
Detail, Plate 1

If Jacques Germàin Soufflot (1709–1780), the original architect of this enormous eighteenth-century edifice, had been alive to see this daguerreotype, he would have been astounded that its image had been captured without the aid of a draftsman. The incredible accuracy of detail and correctness of perspective achieved so swiftly by Poitevin could only seem to Soufflot to be a miracle, particularly when he reflected upon the army of draftsmen it had taken to turn the building he could see so clearly in his mind into visual form.

PLATE 2

JULES ITIER
French (1802–1877)
The Ramasseum, Thebes
1845
Half plate (reversed)
84.XT.265.3

"LOOK ON MY WORKS ye mighty and despair" is Shelley's poetic version of the boast chiseled on the base of the mammoth statue of Ramses II, self-proclaimed "King of Kings—Ozymandias." [19] Erected before his vast mortuary temple and palace complex, the fifty-five-foot-high sculpture of the Pharaoh was carved out of a single block of stone weighing over a thousand tons and was without a single blemish. Ancient Greek visitors, amazed by its size and artistic quality, called it an awe-inspiring sight.[20] Jules Itier concentrated his lens upon this shattered monument of vanity, dramatizing the gigantic remains of the statue twenty-five-hundred years after its destruction by the conquering Persians.

The inclusion of Itier's European companion, reclining against a huge slab of rock split off from the statue, is telling evidence of the original grandeur of the Pharaoh's statue as well as of the incredible ability of the daguerreotype to record tiny objects. This one detail convinces the viewer of the absolute accuracy of the scene. Its message of visual truth makes real the poetic imagery spun by Shelley.

Itier fulfilled the possibilities foreseen by Daguerre, Arago, and early writers that the daguerreotype would allow travelers to bring back home the wonders of the world. He made the longest trip of all the early daguerreian voyagers, taking his bulky equipment all the way to China in 1843. He later returned to Europe by way of Egypt and recorded scenes along the upper portion of the Nile before turning toward the port of Alexandria and home. He had an exquisite sensibility for conveying in the daguerreotype's diminutive space the quality of the natural scene he was recording, especially the topographical character of a landscape or the setting of a monument. Both of these talents are at work in this view of the mortuary complex of Ramses II.[21]

Itier was the first person to photograph this site, although artists and archaeologists accompanying Napoleon's campaign into Egypt earlier in the century had visited the monument and identified this confusing mass of architectural rubble as the tomb of Ozymandias. The initial visual record of its remains had been published by Vivant Denon in 1802[22] and in the official report of the expedition in 1809. The illustrations in both these publications show the site from points of view that emphasize the extensive length of the temple complex, but none depict the actual setting of the temple. Instead, the artists added, in their studios, diminutive camels and clumps of palm trees scattered across the sandy expanse.

In contrast, Itier choose to make a vertical view of the site, aimed directly at the ruins of the monumental sculpture but also showing an engaged statue of Osiris and the lotus columns leading back into the distant courtyards. Unlike the earlier engraved views that played down the mass and grandeur of the ruins in favor of their extent, Itier's view conveys scale by contrasting the remains against the distant hills. No topographical rendering so accurately conveyed the setting of this and its neighboring monuments in the Valley of the Kings.

From the shadows cast in the foreground and the outline of the mountains seen against the sky, we can tell that Itier has waited until after the sun was well past its zenith to open his lens. His careful determination of the best time of day to make his view gives a sharp edge to the planes of the foreground rocks, a knife-like delineation to the Osiris piers, and a clear idea of the distance between the ruins and the cliffs. Both Itier's point of view and chosen time of day emphasize the sheer verticality of the cliffs surrounding this area.

Inadvertently, Itier also reveals darkened hollows on these cliffs that ultimately will become known as the tomb of Queen Hatshepsut. This now beautiful combination of terraces, ramps, and gardens would only be revealed through later excavations.[23] Due to Itier's eye, this one daguerreotype possesses, beyond any other visual image, the truth of this site—a truth that lends credence to the imagination of the poet and provides evidence to the archaeologist of sites yet to be explored.

PLATE 2

PLATE 3

SAMUEL BEMIS
American (1793–1881)
Barn in Hart's Location, New Hampshire
About 1840
Whole plate (reversed)
84.XT.180.2

ONE OF THE BOSTONIANS who in the spring of 1840 attended the lectures given there by Daguerre's agent, François Gouraud, was a successful dentist, Samuel A. Bemis.[24] His natural scientific curiosity was so attracted by this new discovery that he purchased a complete daguerreotype outfit and plates.[25] He began to experiment immediately, noting on the back of his first attempt not only the day, April 19, but also the time needed for iodizing and the length of exposure (4:50 to 5:30 P.M.). He also noted the temperature, humidity, and direction of the wind, perhaps because what ensured a successful daguerreotype was still a mystery.

The daguerreotype reproduced here is the result of Dr. Bemis's practice of spending his summers at an inn in Hart's Location, New Hampshire, built along the narrow and barely passable turnpike winding through the Crawford Notch area of the White Mountains.[26] Apparently anxious to continue experimenting with his new equipment, Bemis took it along with him in the stagecoach from Boston so he could try his luck at taking views of the mountain landscape. Thus, less than a year after Daguerre's discovery was revealed, the process was in use some three thousand miles away to record the first photographic views of this isolated part of the New World.

Bemis took advantage of the turnpike and moved his camera along it, taking views of the nearby farm buildings in the areas where the notch widened and where, because the seasonal overflow of the river had created flat plains, idealists were encouraged to try farming.

One morning, judging from the clarity of this daguerreotype, Bemis set up his tripod and camera to record a newly built barn.[27] In this simple scene rests the magic of Daguerre's discovery. It preserves every detail of the structure, not as might be seen in a meticulous perspective drawing, but in a way that reveals its physicality. As a result we are made to feel as if we were actually present at the moment Dr. Bemis let the light fall upon his silver canvas. If we wish, we can count the number of boards across the front or side of the barn; but even more sensuously, we can imagine the feel of the newly cut lumber with its yet-unweathered veins and knots. Equally defined are the rough post and rail fences that divide the land into different plots for purposes still only in the mind of the owner. Now, however, the whole area is covered by stumps of recently hewn trees that must be pulled before the soil can be tilled. There is no artistic reworking here, no choice of what to leave out or to move about; we know we are in the presence of a truth—such was the new world Daguerre had opened up.

The clarity of the scene comes not only because the image was made early in the day, but because Dr. Bemis allowed the light to enter the camera for only about two minutes. Had he exposed it for a longer time, the shadows would have shifted and the brilliant walls of the barn would have become soft and blurred. We can also see in this view the intuitive artistic sense of the photographer, who chose to compose it so the sharp contrast of light between the two sides would define clearly the three-dimensional quality of the building as well as bring our eye to the brightly spotted tree stumps nearby and the white birch trunks in the distant background.

One aspect of this daguerreotype that points to a deliberate awareness of and response to the beauty of the scene is the framing of the entire landscape view. As he looked through the ground-glass viewer of his camera, Dr. Bemis could not be unaware of the crowning beauty of the mountain peaks beyond, and he aligned them behind the barn almost like stage props. The dark mass of the closest mountain—almost totally covered with evergreen growth—slopes behind the barn from the right, leaving the higher peak, clad with bands of light reflecting trunks of leafless birches, to echo the peak of the barn below.[28]

PLATE 3

PLATE 4

UNKNOWN FRENCH PHOTOGRAPHER
Street in Saint Pierre, Martinique
About 1848
Three-quarter plate
84.XT.1581.11

NOWHERE WAS THE INCLUSIVENESS of the new visual language more apparent than in the records brought back of ordinary scenes in distant places.[29] Because of the daguerreotype, the earlier romanticized scenes engraved from artists' renderings of faraway lands started to be replaced by documents of unquestioned veracity. Historians and geographers began to gain a more accurate view of how the rest of the world actually looked.

Certainly no previous scenes of this French West Indies possession would have given what, in the case of this daguerreotype, can be called such a stark view of a street in Martinique. One glimpse of this daguerreotype would have shaken any romantic ideas about the birthplace of Josephine, the glamorous first wife of Napoléon. The delicate artistic decorations of tropical birds, butterflies, and flowers that Parisian artists painted on the walls of aristocratic French houses to remind Josephine of her home in Les Isles are in sharp contrast to this view of a mundane street in Martinique's commercial port city of Saint Pierre.

To make this record of the street, the unknown daguerreotypist chose to view it as if it were the central part of a Renaissance stage set, directing the lens at the pedimented building in the far distance. The edge of the raised sidewalk makes a sharp, dark line on the right that defines precisely the length and perspective of the paved street. Its surface is so clearly delineated that, as had been remarked about some of Daguerre's early images, even the cracks in the pavement are visible. Strong light clearly illuminates the corner of a building standing on the left-hand side, where a cross street interrupts the smooth macadam of the main street by its cobblestone paving.[30]

Above the crossing hangs a lantern, suspended by several wires from either side of the street. Under magnification, two other lamps can be detected further down the street, as well as a flagpole and a sentry box at the side of the distant central building. Along the way to the far end of the street, the camera gives us innumerable details of the haphazard buildings—some three-story masonry structures with modest architectural ornaments, others humble dwellings or shops made of wooden clapboard and overlapping shingles, a feature common to coastal buildings for centuries all the way north to Cape Cod.

Caught by the camera's lens at the right side of the street are two shipping crates, next to which appear two figures whose images are blurred because of the long exposure time. Given the angle of the shadows, the time might well be noon or a bit later, a time for being at home, not on the streets. In any case, the daguerreotypist was intent on recording the stage set, not any actors who might stroll across it.

The diversity of the buildings, the play of different textures, and the irregular projections of the dormer windows all coalesce to make a scene not solely of factual documentation but one that, when viewed today, makes us respond to the abstract artistic qualities of the shapes arranged on the surface of the plate. It is a scene whose contrast between light and dark areas gives it a special reality. The image itself becomes the object; it carries away with it a part of the scene's physicality. To a viewer of the time, it must have been totally convincing.

Unknown to the recorder of this scene, as well as to the first viewers of this daguerreotype, is the fact that history was also being served by this everyday recording; for another descriptive detail shown here reveals that the streets not only were paved in 1848, but were banked to carry away the heavy outbursts of rain common to the tropics. Such minutiae of observation recorded by this daguerreotype became an important historical fact, because when the entire city of Saint Pierre was demolished in 1902 by the eruption of Mount Pelée, all that was left were the paved streets of the city.[31]

PLATE 4

PLATE 5

Unknown Photographer (French or Italian)
View of Pisa
About 1845
Three-quarter plate or cut-down whole plate
84.XT.1580.3

Here, on this daguerreian plate, is preserved an extensive panorama of the Italian town of Pisa. To equal its scope, painters at the panorama in Paris would have needed to use their brushes to cover yards of canvas. Perhaps the maker of this daguerreotype once worked as a collaborator on such vast paintings, for this view is the product of an uncanny eye capable of seizing the complete vista in a single, artful scene.

In this case, the daguerreotypist located the camera on top of the campanile of the Romanesque church of San Piero al Grado, erected around A.D. 1000 at the point where legend says Saint Peter first set foot on the Pisan shore on his way to Rome. From this high vantage point, the artist crafted a powerful diagonal foreground by tipping the camera down upon the buildings lined up along the near bank of the river. This single decision gives the image its impressive strength. Although of no historic significance, these buildings, seen in the early morning light, stand out as if they were cardboard cutouts. The dark, unframed openings punctuating the light walls and the razor-edged rooflines and chimneys create a sequence of architectonic elements that almost suggests the vision of a cubist painter.

Beyond this powerful pattern of light and dark shapes, the placid Arno River reflects a smooth, unruffled surface, not yet turned into a brilliant sparkling stream by a later and stronger sun. The maker has devoted almost half the plate to the foreground play of light on masonry and water, squeezing the subject of this view—the city—into a narrow band stretched across the center. By choosing this point of view and time of day, the artist deftly shows how the city sits between the river and the mountains at the north, beyond which lies Florence.

The monuments, familiar at the time from individual engravings, are now seen absorbed within their urban setting, stretching from the familiar Cathedral enclave on the left (with its famous leaning tower), past the towers of the fortress and the center bridge, all the way to the church towers on the right. This broad cityscape, modeled by light rather than line, presents historians with a single view of the site where events had taken place over the centuries. At the far left is the harbor, where the seven hundred ships of the thirteenth-century Pisan fleet were based during their lucrative trade with Byzantium. Only six miles down the Arno is the beach where Shelley's funeral pyre was built after he drowned in 1822.

The photographer has introduced scale by focusing the camera on the point where the two walls of the fortress meet. One wall, seen in light, runs along the river; the other, in shadow, veers diagonally north toward the cathedral. Suddenly, the monumentality of the famed twelfth-century religious complex, the Plaza of Miracles, is comprehensible. Even though the baptistry, cathedral, and campanile are the most distant objects, in this early morning light their reflective marble surfaces establish their dominance over the entire city. Showing them as an entire religious complex underscores the power of the faith that gave rise to their erection.

This ability to judge a monument in its surroundings was singled out in 1851 by the French critic Francis Wey as a critical benefit of photography.[32] He made the comment in regard to a photograph by Eugéne Piot of Pisa's leaning tower. It demonstrated clearly, he wrote, the superiority of photography because, by showing the entire surroundings, it revealed that the sandy soil of the area also caused neighboring buildings to lean in varying directions. Previously, he said, artists had either suppressed these imperfections or even exaggerated the angle of the tower by depicting the houses around it as vertical.

In the years since this daguerreotype was taken, it has become, like the view of Martinique's Saint Pierre (Plate 4), a precious historical document. A century later, much of what we see here, including all the buildings in the foreground, was destroyed by intensive aerial and land bombardment during World War II.[33] Over this scene of utter devastation, the cathedral complex still rose intact—a true site of miracles. The campanile used by our daguerreotypist, however, was not spared. It was dynamited to keep it from being used as an artillery observation post.

PLATE 5

JOHN JABEZ EDWIN MAYALL
British (1810–1901)
The Crystal Palace at Hyde Park, London
1851
Mammoth plate (reduced)
84.XT.955

SEEING THIS TRIUMPHANT DAGUERREOTYPE, it is easy to understand why John Mayall was considered a master of the new art.[34] Although he was well-known for using unusually large-sized plates, in this case it seems as if it was the only way he could capture the essence of this incredible structure. Because of the impressive size of the plate, which is about twelve by ten inches,[35] the daguerreotype reflects and shares in the incredulity felt by the visitors to this space.[36]

This brilliant view shows the first structure in which an architect used only metal and glass to enclose such an enormous, completely open space. It was as if the vaults of an ancient cathedral had suddenly been stripped of their masonry and opened up to the sky. In this section of the Crystal Palace, even some of Hyde Park's venerable elm trees were enclosed, seeming to underscore the triumph of modern-day technology over Nature.

This engineering feat was considered so awesome at the time that its designer, Joseph Paxton, was commanded by Prince Albert to lead the procession opening the building, even preceding Queen Victoria.[37] It was an unprecedented honor—never repeated—that speaks of how impressed the patron prince was with the Crystal Palace. Its dazzlingly bright presence was the perfect symbol of what the prince hoped to attain by having England stage an exhibition of the world's industrial prowess.

Mayall was well-aware of the effect that entering the hall would produce on visitors. Because of his equal understanding of what could be achieved by a daguerreotype, he has allowed us to share in that experience. He located his camera on the first level of the galleries above the central atrium, encompassing thereby the great extent of floor space and, most importantly, filling the entire upper portion of his plate with the graceful arches of the glass vault. By positioning the camera so it shows both sides of the hall, he has exposed the iron skeleton of the building and the lacy pattern of the vault in a way that imbues the daguerreotype with both a sense of articulation and a liveliness of design.

Despite the mastery of this daguerreotype, Mayall still was not able to convey the total impression of Paxton's creation; since the image is monochromatic, we must imagine the colors that transformed the structure into an even more magical place. The arches of the vault were alternately painted a light blue or cream, making their already delicate form all but disappear into the sky. As one critic at the time said, "Everything corporeal disappears and only the colour remains."[38] In contrast, the vertical elements of the three tiers of railings were outlined in striking crimson red. The glass walls at either end of the barrel vault also seemed to open up to the row of trees that continued into the park. All normal boundaries of space were erased, and the viewers became further transported into an enchanted place as they were simultaneously submerged in an ocean of sound that came from three constantly playing organs and the splashing water of the crystal fountain—this sliver of an iceberg that dominated the center of the courtyard.

Mayall was commissioned to take at least fourteen daguerreotypes, which were subsequently published as lithographs, showing all sections of the Crystal Palace. The impression his works, including this one, made on his contemporaries is evident from critical statements at the time.[39] The entire group was described in glowing terms that praised the daguerreotypes for their extraordinary clarity, vigor, refinement, and delicacy. Importantly, it was said that "Nothing is altered, added, or withdrawn for the sake of effect...they are Nature's own copies of this wondrous scene."[40]

Mayall's abilities as a daguerreotypist were honored in his day, and because of this one masterful work, we, too, get a glimpse of his genius. We are in the presence, in this instance, of the very best the British Empire could offer—a pioneering work of an architect, an exceptional daguerreotypist, and a patron, Prince Albert, who encouraged both.

Chapter Two

STEALING FROM THE MIRROR

———

I F THE SUN'S RAYS could be made to paint views of man's physical surroundings and architectural achievements, could they also be persuaded to depict man himself?

Long before the secret of the daguerreotype was disclosed, Daguerre dreamed about capturing the human face on the silver canvas. If this could be accomplished, he wrote Isidore Niépce in October 1835, they would have no need to market the process because "it would sell itself for us." Over the next three years, this tantalizing prospect was referred to in letters between the partners,[1] with Daguerre consistently raising Isidore's hopes by reporting success in reducing exposure time. Both looked to portraiture as a valuable aid to attract investors, and in January 1838, Daguerre told Isidore that his recent attempt at portrait making led him to hope one or two could be included in the exposition they planned as a marketing showcase. In fact, their prospectus inviting investors to participate held out the possibility that portraits might be attainable but admitted that movement by the sitter might create difficulties.[2]

When first disclosing Daguerre's invention in January 1839, François Arago made no mention of portraiture, but its possibility was of major interest to the art world. Daguerre continued to suggest its feasibility but made conflicting statements about its accomplishment. In an interview on January 24, 1839, with a correspondent for *La Presse*, Daguerre answered simply by saying, "he had not yet succeeded . . . to his satisfaction."[3] Only a few days later, however, the prominent Parisian art critic Jules Janin put Daguerre on record as saying not only that daguerreian portraits would become possible, but that they could be made without requiring the preliminary studies even such celebrated painters as Ingres had to rely upon.[4] Interestingly, Daguerre also was quoted as saying he was at work on a "machine" to keep the subject "immobile."

By July 1839, in his report to the Chamber of Deputies, Arago described daguerreotype portraiture as a possibility requiring only a "slight advance beyond" its current state.[5] He later reversed this optimistic stance when he said in his August 19 address that "there is little ground for believing . . . [it] will ever serve for portraiture." Arago nevertheless added that, since Daguerre had found placing blue glass between the sitter and the sun softened its rays, portraiture might still be possible. These observations about the potential of daguerreian portraiture are the last for which Daguerre is on record.[6]

At the time, scant attention seems to have been paid to these remarks, even by the miniature painters who had the most to lose if the daguerreotype could be used for portraiture. After Daguerre's instruction manual was published, however, other inventors and enthusiasts rushed to try their hand at making daguerreotype portraits, either out of a scientific fascination or because they foresaw how financially rewarding making portraits could be .

In the earliest attempts at portraiture, daguerreotypists were primarily concerned with ways of keeping the sitter immobile during the long exposure time then required. Since the head clamp, long used by portrait painters, proved inadequate to restrain the daguerreian subject sufficiently, new methods were devised to hold the sitter absolutely still. One system, described in an October 1839 report

from Belgium, called for firmly fixing the head between two or three planks solidly attached to the back of an arm chair, and then tightening them further with screws![7] The inventor also prescribed painting the sitter's face dead white and powdering the hair to help the sun secure the image. During the fifteen to twenty minutes that the sitters were required to remain immobile, they also had to keep their eyes shut, both to make the strong light bearable and to disguise any movement by the eyes. A tiny portrait of Henry Fitz of Baltimore, made in late 1839 and showing him with eyes tightly closed (Figure 18), is one of the few images to have survived from this experimental period.[8]

Other innovators sought a different approach to the problem of movement. Rather than concentrating on keeping the sitter immobile, they sought ways to reduce the time the sitter needed to remain still through both chemical and optical means. Almost simultaneously, inventors in both Europe and the United States experimented with different chemical combinations for sensitizing the plate in place of those originally used by Daguerre. In Philadelphia, in late 1839, Dr. Paul Beck Goddard discovered that using bromine as well as iodine to sensitize the plate led to reducing the time required for a sitting from minutes to seconds.[9] In Austria, in 1840, a lens maker, Joseph Max Petzval, succeeded— with the help of skilled mathematicians from the Austrian army—in solving the difficult equations necessary to develop a new type of lens. It proved to be twenty times faster than Daguerre's original lens and was quickly adopted by daguerreotypists everywhere.[10] In France that year, Hippolyte Fizeau discovered that, by rinsing the developed plate in gold chloride, the image became more brilliant as well as more durable.[11] All of these improvements resulted in the commerical viability of the daguerreian portrait.

Even before such improvements were in place the public's curiosity and its willingness to pay for portraits were so strong that, as early as 1840, photographic portrait studios were being opened in Paris and elsewhere in Europe. America also saw daguerreian studios emerge in cities such as New York, Boston, Baltimore, and Philadelphia. Because France had given the process to the world without charge, these commercial establishments could open quickly and develop their business without paying any royalties or license fees to its French inventor. Within months, practitioners in almost all parts of the western world[12] were following and improving Daguerre's original discovery. Together they turned the invention into a force that changed the visual heritage of mankind forever.

Although commercial studios had become feasible, their products were not always joyfully received by their subjects. As one commentator said at the time, "Self-love is not always satisfied by the honesty of the camera."[13] Physical failures were frequent, and account books of some practitioners often bear the words *rejected* or *not accepted*.[14] In fact, the word most commonly used to describe the earliest portraits was *horrible*. One writer, recalling his impressions from this period, used comparisons with historical and mythological figures from the classical past to describe the first portraits on view in the Parisian shops.[15] The earliest ones reminded him, he said, of the Byzantine general Belisarius, who had been blinded as punishment for treason. A subsequent type of portraits, with tearful countenances, he likened to Niobe, condemned to cry eternally over the slaying of her children. Yet a third level in the expressive development of the daguerreotype portrait he saw as resembling the agonized face of Laocoön as he and his sons futilely struggled within the coils of the giant serpents set upon them by the gods. Despite the evidence seen in the shop windows and the disparaging remarks by critics, public demand for these mirror images was so strong that, over the course of the year beginning in mid-1841, the Parisian studio of Lerebours made over fifteen hundred portraits!

Now the miniature painters were in rout; the novelty and convenience of the daguerreotype process had rapidly eroded their business. In fact, the daguerreotypists commonly presented their portraits in cases exactly like those the miniature portraitists had been using. These cases were designed like small books, but now they held a daguerreian image instead of a painted portrait—yet another intrusion of the daguerreotypist into the practice of the artist.[16]

A client no longer had to submit to the inconvenience of numerous lengthy sittings while an artist set down a likeness, but could achieve the same result through a single sitting for a daguerreotype. In place of a small sheet of ivory bearing a likeness created by the delicate brush strokes of an artist, the daguerreotype offered you a metallic mirror that, when tipped at a certain angle, would suddenly disclose a perfect image of yourself. The moment of revelation was, in itself, an intimate and hitherto unknown aesthetic experience.

How could an image painted by the mere hand of man compete with magical portraits drawn by the sun? Or, as one early French daguerreotypist asked, is not an image fixed on the daguerreotype plate "by the person's own shadow . . . more sacred in our eyes than the work of a painter's brush?" A miniature painting, he said, is only "the work of an artist, a daguerreian plate is the work of God."[17]

With each succeeding year, the technical obstacles to achieving a passable likeness disappeared, and during the twenty-some years of the process's popularity, the vast majority of daguerreotypes produced were portraits. These images no longer appeared simply as masks of the individual, but began to convey human expressions suggestive of the sitter's personality. At first, however, only a few makers were successful in encouraging their sitters to relax their facial muscles enough to reveal any glimpse of their inner selves. This lack of expression became the most criticized feature of the

PLATE 7
GURNEY STUDIO
Portrait of Edward Carrington, Jr., 1842
Sixth plate
84.XT.269.14

PLATE 8
JEREMIAH GURNEY
American (1812–1895)
Portrait of Edward Carrington, Jr. ("Uncle Ed"), 1842
Sixth plate
94.XT.55

daguerreotype, and it was quickly seized upon by miniaturists and painters as proof that their work was superior to the new method. Now, having conquered their technical problems, daguerreotypists had to prove they could create works with the same artistic values as those of their competitors.

To do so, daguerreotypists turned to the principles that had been followed by the great portraitists of the past. Instructions on how to succeed were the subject of many manuals.[18] Although such advice varied, it basically set forth several broad goals for the portrait maker. The portrait should be well-lighted and well-composed, the figure should be well-modeled and free from the background, and the person portrayed should seem alive and expressive. Essentially these were the same goals put forth for the portrait painter, but the daguerreotypist had to surmount yet another unique barrier. Unlike the brush, the camera was not a flatterer. Or, as was said in a poem about the daguerreotype in August 1841, "Truth is unpleasant / To prince and to peasant."[19]

Skillful handling of posing and lighting were two ways the daguerreotypist could assuage human vanity. Even so, there were many—particularly women, we are told—who would not submit themselves to the merciless lens of the camera for fear of destroying their wishful ideas about their appearance. The daguerreotypists had to seek other ways to satisfy reluctant sitters, such as placing them before painted views of lovely landscapes or using lofty columns and elaborate drapery, as well as personal objects, to suggest a sitter's respectable standing in society. The final aid in overcoming harsh truth was to borrow the enemy's weapon by employing a brush to add color that would disguise imperfections and add a sumptuous quality to the entire portrait.

These moves to appeal to the customer were also steps toward creating a daguerreian portrait that met the goals of a work of art. In a sense, however, the attempts to soften the actuality that was the very heart of the daguerreian process led photographers to assume a role little different from that of the painter. Recognition of this fact was difficult to achieve, however; the general public and the artistic and scientific communities continued to think of, indeed to refer to, the photographer as an "operator" whose sole act was to encourage the sun to paint the images within the camera.

That such an appraisal was incorrect is clearly set out in the following series of three pairs of daguerreotypes (Plates 7–12). Each example allows us a special insight into how the photographer rose far beyond mere mechanical representation to achieve a daguerreotype that is a superior work of art.

The first pair of portraits, showing a young Edward Carrington,[20] was made in 1842 in the studio of Jeremiah Gurney at the very beginning of what would prove to be one of New York's distinguished photographic institutions.[21] In the first instance (Plate 7), the young boy is placed far to the right of the foreground area, leaving the center of this space occupied by a sharply-lit bench covered by a wrinkled cloth. To the left, merging with the painted foliage of the backdrop, is a partially seen urn,[22] whose sharp silhouette competes strongly with the boy's head as the principal point of interest. The vase's function is shown by the inscription on its base, boldly announcing the name and address of the daguerreotypist. The lettering was painted in reverse to make it read correctly in the completed work, but the painter put the periods of the "N" and the "Y" in the wrong places, thus exposing its contrivance. The landscape background is a typical Hudson River scene made familiar by many prints and folk-art drawings but not common in daguerreian examples.

The lighting of the figure, from the right and forward, picks up rather indiscriminately the brilliant white ruffled collar, the bench cover, the inscription on the vase, and the painted surface of the river. The boy's face, illuminated by reflected light, emerges with difficulty from the painted cliffs, which press against his head. At this point we might

be apt to say that Gurney still had an enormous amount to learn about lighting and composition. The piece presents the subject in an awkward position and pays more attention to the unessential, rather than to the sitter.

Fortunately for our estimate of Gurney, and for our insight into how the daguerreotypist worked, the Getty Museum recently acquired a second Gurney portrait of Edward Carrington made at the same sitting (Plate 8). The difference between the two is so strong that this is likely an instance where the first one was produced by an assistant, the second by Gurney himself. The assistant may not have felt authorized to omit the ingenious Gurney trademark, and was also insufficiently skilled to take advantage of the beautifully painted landscape or to grasp the possibilities offered by the white collar and brass buttons of the boy's outfit.

Studying the changes introduced in the second plate provides a lesson in what a daguerreotypist of keen visual sensitivity could effect. Now the boy is placed clearly in the center of the space, distinct from the painted background yet more harmoniously related to it. The scene has become a carefully balanced arrangement of light and dark, with the subject's face predominating. His head is now brought closer to the source of light, which is allowed to shine full strength on the right row of buttons and the right side of his face. Even though the collar is completely lit, the left side of his face and costume are less brilliant.

A simple but revealing detail between these two records of the same sitting is the way the hands have been arranged. In the first instance, one hand is hidden by the other. In the second, the master, Gurney, also covers one hand with the other, but allows the thumbs to touch, creating with that simple action a strong three-dimensional definition of the sitter. All of the differences between these two images point out the qualities and techniques that an apprentice in the early daguerreian era would

PLATE 9
UNKNOWN AMERICAN PHOTOGRAPHER
Portrait of a Young Man
About 1847
Sixth plate
84.XT.1569.6

PLATE 10
UNKNOWN AMERICAN PHOTOGRAPHER
Portrait of a Young Man ("Brother Willie")
About 1847
Sixth plate
84.XT.1569.5

hope to learn from an already gifted practitioner like Gurney.

Another chance to gain an insight into the artistic process of the daguerreotypist arises because of two works made at the same sitting in an unknown daguerreian studio. This pair of images almost seems to duplicate our previous comparison, for the differences between these two are so significant that they, too, speak of an assistant and a master.

In what we presume to be the first image made during this sitting, we see a portrait of average quality showing a young gentleman in a typical seated pose, his arm placed on a book set upon a decorative table cover (Plate 9). More unusual is the sweep of drapery behind his head. But what a transformation takes place in the second version (Plate 10)! A new eye has come onto the scene, whisking the furniture around and calling for more props. Now the table, with its same figured cloth, has been pushed back against the wall and the gentleman's elegant hat reposes on the book. Above the hat, a heavily framed daguerreotype has been hung upon the previously empty wall.

The sitter himself has been moved left of center, and his plaid-lined cloak has been wrapped around his shoulders and, especially, over his very large hands, which were so unpleasantly evident in the first version. The drapery on the wall has been slightly shifted so as to place his entire head against its uniformly colored background. In addition, the camera has been moved slightly back from the sitter, giving him the appearance of being more comfortably placed within his surroundings. The uniform lighting used in the first version remains unchanged, but now it is used to emphasize the contrasting texture and geometric shape of the cylinder of the hat and the rectangles of the frame, as well as the pattern of the sitter's clothes—all of which combine to make the portrait a superior work of art.

A third fortunate pairing again brings before us two portraits of the same sitter shown in the same

PLATE 11
JAMES M. FORD
American (1827–about 1877)
Portrait of a Boy with Gold-Mining Toys
About 1854
Half plate
84.XT.406.1

PLATE 12
JAMES M. FORD
American (1827–about 1877)
Portrait of a Boy with Gold-Mining Toys
About 1854
Half plate
84.XT.269.22

setting. These two portraits were made by the Western daguerreotypist James M. Ford about 1854.[23] Families who had taken the long trip to California, far from family and friends, often wanted portraits to send back east to their far-off relatives. This seems to have been the purpose of these daguerreotypes, as they show a boy in Western garb wearing boots and a pistol, surrounded by wooden toys representing the gold-mining equipment of a forty-niner—pick, shovel, wheelbarrow, and rifle. It would make clear to the folks back home that children in California preferred playthings other than hoops or hobby horses. Even the youngest of the Wild West had their eyes set on the big prize.[24]

What we see in these two examples of daguerreian art is unlike, however, what we found in the other comparisons. Those images gave us a glimpse into the makers' artistic vision. This comparison demonstrates how the daguerreotypist used the power of light to evoke the personality of the sitter. In one (Plate 11), the boy is brightly lit from above. No part of his body or toys is outside the fairly strong light that brilliantly illuminates a circle of the carpet around him. Seen against a completely neutral background, the youngster stands out in sharp silhouette, expressing an extreme vitality. By these means, the maker has produced a stunning, life-like image of a young boy.

In the other version (Plate 12), Ford shows a different aspect of the boy's personality. Clearly his approach in this instance is a bit theatrical. The brilliant light of the previous image has been reduced and made to focus more dramatically upon the subject, whose pose complements the theatrical feeling. Light from one very selected beam falls on the feather in the boy's hat, the side of his face, and his neck, and reflects off the barrel of the rifle. The mood created by this light is enhanced by the pose of the figure, no longer an erect image of gleaming youth but a soulful, perhaps vulnerable, young boy. Dramatic, even obvious, in their presentation, these two portraits again demonstrate the goal of the daguerreotypist: to create a work of art that would transform traditional ideas of portraiture by introducing a degree of realism not previously imaginable.

PLATES

Chapter Two

PLATE 13

WILLIAM LANGENHEIM
American (1807–1874)
Portrait of Frederick Langenheim
About 1848
Quarter plate
84.XT.172.3

INTELLECTUAL FERMENT CHARACTERIZED an important group of Philadelphia's citizens in the first half of the nineteenth century. Unlike Boston, where equal intellectual intensity centered about political, literary, and philosophical pursuits, Philadelphia's vigor sprang from the Franklin Institute, a society that encouraged the scientific bent of its members. News of Daguerre's discovery and reports on the process stimulated many there to experiment on their own. Their knowledge of chemistry and metallurgy immediately led to ways to improve and enhance the new process.[25]

Into this center of "daguerreomania" came the two Langenheim brothers, William and Frederick, emigrants from Germany. A relative of theirs, the German optical manufacturer Peter Voigtländer, sent them one of his new cameras with a Petzval lens, which soon inspired their fascination with photography and led to their opening a studio for making portraits in 1842.[26]

Adept at marketing, they opened their studio in the Mercantile Exchange, the center of Philadelphia's commercial activity, and along its halls they displayed examples of their work to induce a still-hesitant public to sit in front of the camera. If this portrait of William by his brother Frederick is an example of the type used to lure the uninitiated into their studio, there is no question why they succeeded so quickly in their new profession.[27]

This daguerreotype shows that the Langenheims followed the dictum in their advertisement that proclaimed: "Light, the first created Element, draws the picture." A total mastery over light is evident in this portrait; coming from above and the left side, the light is most brilliant along the image's central axis. Its greatest intensity occurs on Frederick's white shirt, elegantly outlined by the two dark ends of his neckpiece. From this point, the light spreads out into the soft gray of the finely checked vest, which, from its creases, buttons, and lapels, is responsible for giving the metal plate of the daguerreotype a depth of tone that yields the feeling of a rich, painterly surface.

Frederick Langenheim's head is lit in a manner that contrasts with the bright central area; the lower portion of his face is bathed in a softer light. This weaker illumination infiltrates the texture of the mustache and goatee to create a subtly different area of light and dark on the plate. His nose and high forehead emerge almost stridently, lit by a skylight, a source even reflected in the pupils of his eyes, as can be seen with a magnifying glass. Staring directly at the lens of the not-distant camera, this man, so subtly and complexly defined in light and dark, totally dominates the format in which he is contained. No sense of the space in which the figure sits is defined, for that would weaken his powerful presence. Compressing his subject into the limited area of the oval mat, the artist draws from him a sense of vitality and force that few other daguerreians achieved.

Advertisements from the mid-1840s indicate that the Langenheims well understood the quality of their own work. One newspaper ad stated that they "excel not only in the mechanical treatment of the plates," but that their posing of the sitters ensures that "they are artistical in the highest degree." Understandably the brothers soon rose to prominence among the other Philadelphia daguerreotypists. In 1844 they were second in honors given at the fair of the Franklin Institute, but in succeeding years they were judged superior to all other contestants.

In 1851, at London's great international exhibition, their work was praised, along with that of other American exhibitors. The general comment by the jury about the superior quality of all American portraits seems to be exemplified by the work of the two Langenheim brothers: "America stands alone for stern development of character: her works with few exceptions reject all accessories, present a faithful transcript of the subject and yield to none in excellence of execution."[28]

PLATE 13

PLATE 14

JOHN JABEZ EDWIN MAYALL
British (1810–1901)
Portrait of Caroline Emilia Mary Herschel
About 1853
Half plate
84.XT.1574.1

THIS BEAUTIFULLY POSED PORTRAIT combines two important names in photography. The subject is the oldest daughter of Sir John Herschel, an astronomer with wide scientific interests, particularly in the reproduction of images. He was a close friend of Talbot and, at the invitation of Arago, had visited Daguerre to inspect his work. The daguerreotypist is John Mayall, who first worked in Philadelphia with other pioneers there and then returned in 1846 to his native England, where he became one of its foremost daguerreotypists.[29] In 1847 he opened his own London studio, which he proudly called the American Daguerreotype Institution. Over the next few years, his work came to be considered the finest in London, and at the Great Exhibition of 1851, in addition to being commissioned to record the Crystal Palace itself (Plate 6), Mayall also displayed seventy-two daguerreotypes, winning an "Honorable Mention." He was known as the "American Daguerreotypist" because his work was believed to surpass that of his fellow English makers in its polish, clarity, and size. One journal cited Mayall's superior work as proof that the English failure to procure images as clear as those made in America could not be blamed, as had been claimed, on the fog of London.[30]

It is no surprise, then, that Sir John Herschel would have sought out Mayall to have his own portrait made[31] as well as that of his eldest daughter. As is clear from many of his portraits, Mayall was particularly skilled at choosing a pose for the sitter that both animated the figure and concentrated attention upon the face. In this case, Mayall provided Caroline Herschel with a setting following the formula used by seventeenth-century Dutch painters—introducing only a minimal number of objects to set off the figure against a modulated background.

Although basically creating a pyramidal composition, Mayall used light to divide its base into two distinct but related parts. The brilliantly illuminated arabesques of the table cover are sharply contrasted with the folds of the sitter's skirt, but because those folds remain so distinct within the overall dark skirt, the two sides actually echo each other. Only a highly buffed plate, as Americans were noted for using, would allow such details to be so sharply recorded.

Above this solid base, multiple shifts in the position of the body animate the figure. The light falling on her lower hand stresses the center point to which all other objects are related—the books, her elbow, the space seen between her raised arm and side, and particularly the space between the chair's curved back and its single visible support. Each of these elements contributes to making a strong horizontal platform from which the upper part of her body rises in an upward twist. This motion is crowned by her elaborate white embroidered collar, whose strong contrast and shape form a separate base for her head, which is turned in yet another direction.

A subtle light falls upon her face while a stronger light picks up each strand of her hair with its fashionable coiffure. Collectively, Mayall's arrangement and lighting of her body give an inner vitality to the person of Caroline Herschel, while at the same time creating a beautiful three-dimensional form set in front of the harmonious silver shades of the daguerreotype's background like a piece of sculpture displayed against a museum wall.

PLATE 14

PLATE 15

MARCUS AURELIUS ROOT (attributed)
American (1808–1888)
Portrait of a Gentleman
About 1846
Half plate
84.XT.1571.35

THE ALMOST SHOCKING IMMEDIACY of this unknown person and the brilliance of the light tell us we are seeing a subject who submitted himself to the demands early daguerreotypists made upon their sitters. This gentleman is firmly seated with a strong light coming from a high window on the left side—perhaps tinted blue to reduce some of the glare—but his eyes show us he cannot sit in this bright light much longer. In fact, the brilliance of his eyes makes them appear as if they were beginning to water.

That the daguerreotypist has been able to show so successfully the textural difference between the lightly checked vest, the starched white shirt, and the elaborately knotted, striped cravat probably is due to his holding a dark cloth over this part of the sitter during a portion of the exposure time. Had he not done so, these bright areas would have turned blue, an effect caused by the daguerreotype's extreme sensitivity to the light reflected from totally white areas. In this case, however, the preventive measure also reduced the shadows that would usually be seen in the folds of the sitter's neckpiece and shirt. Without such subtle gradations, the abrupt light and dark contrasts exaggerate the nearness of the subject as well as under-score his immobility. No doubt this stoic sitter was also held firmly in place by a head brace and severely cautioned not to move his hand, whose fingers were safely and immovably hidden under his waistcoat.

Despite the discomfort this gentleman had to endure, he and his family must have judged the effort worthwhile, for the daguerreotypist has produced a striking portrait in which bold juxtaposition of light and dark endow the sitter with an heroic aura and clearly etch his individual features.

Although this splendid portrait is not marked by the name of its maker, certain characteristics strongly point to Philadelphia as its place of origin. Several daguerreotypists there, such as the Langenheims and Plumbe, favored this type of paper mat with an ornamented border. In this instance, however, the design in the corners duplicates exactly the one used by Marcus Aurelius Root,[32] one of the prominent members of the exceptional group of daguerreotypists operating in the Quaker City during this period.

Many of the characteristics of this portrait, including the manner of lighting, resemble those described later by Root in his lengthy book *The Camera and the Pencil*, published in 1864.[33] Not intended as a technical treatise but as a guide to the artistic aspects of photography, Root paid special attention to the ideal goals for portrait photographers. He encouraged them to think of the human face as the mirror of the soul, comparing it to the face of a clock, which represents only its internal mechanism. To make a portrait reflect the intellectual and moral character of the sitter, he instructed the photogra-pher to concentrate on the changeable features of the face—the eyes and lips. He specifically urged that the eyes be directed to the side and every attempt be made to capture small spots of reflected light within them. All these qualities are achieved in this stunning daguerreotype, which meets Root's goal of creating a portrait that gives the "semblance of *life* instead of a mere *shadow* of life."[34]

PLATE 15

PLATE 16

CHABROL
French (active 1840s)
Portrait of Paul and Hippolyte Flandrin
1848–49
Half plate
84.XT.265.17

RARELY DOES A DAGUERREOTYPIST achieve in a double portrait an interplay between the subjects as intimate as in this work. How this came about, however, is not due to the maker—known to us only from a label on the back as Chabrol, of Lyon—but to the sitters themselves. In keeping with a practice of many years of posing together, it is the two brothers who have arranged themselves in a way that gives this daguerreotype its expression of brotherly familiarity.

The subjects are two well-known academic painters—the younger Flandrin brothers, Paul and Hippolyte—both of whom were trained and worked in the studios of Ingres in Paris and Rome.[35] An older brother, Auguste, also trained as an artist, but remained in their native home of Lyon as a professor at the School of Fine Arts. This daguerreotype probably was taken when the younger brothers left Paris during the troubled days of the Revolution of 1848.

Even if the daguerreotype bore no label, it would be clear from its appearance that a provincial, rather than a Parisian, studio was its origin. The most revealing provincial characteristic is the sloppily hung backdrop, with its wrinkles and creases left untended. The setting also lacks any subtlety of lighting—only a single light source off to the right side appears to have been used, and no assistance or control from reflectors is indicated. The operator's lack of technical and artistic skills was more than compensated for by the sitters' tradition in depicting themselves as we see them here.

The unusual bond between these two brothers, even after Hippolyte was married, had long been observed by their friends. During their years together in Rome as part of Ingres's circle of admirers, they were considered so inseparable that Paul was jokingly called the shadow of Hippolyte. Their fellow artists often addressed the two of them as if they were one person. They themselves expressed this fraternal intimacy over the years by posing together in double portraits with each brother painting or drawing the other (Figure 19). In this case, they have used the daguerreotypist to achieve the same interplay of figures and personalities.

FIGURE 19
PAUL AND HIPPOLYTE FLANDRIN
French (1811–1902; 1809–1864)
Portrait of Hippolyte and Paul Flandrin
1835
Pencil drawing
Musée du Louvre, Cabinet des Dessins;
Photo © R.M.N.

PLATE 16

PLATE 17

WILLIAM CONSTABLE
British (1783–1861)
Self-Portrait with a Recent Invention
About 1854
Quarter plate (reversed)
84.XT.266.13

PROUDLY POSING FOR THIS DAGUERREOTYPE is William Constable, showing off his most recent scientific invention, an improved regulating device to increase the efficiency of steam power. The inscription cast into the wheel's rim—*COMPENSATING FLY-WHEEL Invented by WILLIAM CONSTABLE Photographic Institution Brighton Model M O Patented*—records the link between his mechanical ingenuity and his work as a daguerreotypist.[36]

Constable became fascinated with the daguerreotype as soon as news of its invention was announced. In his long career as a civil engineer, he had been primarily involved with another marvel of his time, the steam railroad. As a surveyor determining where roadbeds should be laid out and as a designer of the bridges they required, he was familiar with a variety of optical instruments, including the camera obscura. Out of this background sprang his interest in mastering this new process. The chemical, mechanical, and artistic challenges of making a daguerreotype opened up an exciting new world to this self-made civil engineer.[37]

Constable's success as a daguerreotypist was due, first of all, to his location in Brighton, a fashionable English seaside town that was the site of one of the royal villas, the outrageously fanciful Turkish-style Pavilion erected in the 1780s. Visits by the royal family and their guests provided an enviable list of potential clients for the portrait studio Constable opened there in 1841. His great stroke of luck occurred on March 5, 1842, when Prince Albert chose Constable's studio in which to pose for a camera for the first time in his life. From then on, Constable's posing room was filled with the nobility of Europe; his list of clients became a miniature "Almanach de Gotha" and included the Grand Duchess of Parma and Ferdinand, the Duke of Saxe-Coburg.

When he added a studio to his seaside home along Brighton's stylish Marine Parade, Constable used blue glass for the walls. This was done to cut the glare from the direct sunlight, following a principle first suggested by Daguerre, but on a larger scale than other practitioners, who generally used blue glass only in skylights or movable partitions. Constable's studio soon became known as "The Blue Room," and the subtle shading of light that he achieved in the small close-ups of his subjects was the result of the glareless light in his studio. This filtered light also allowed him to capture a natural, sometimes even relaxed, expression on the sitter's face, very different from the stiff faces seen in early portraits taken by others.[38]

For making full-length portraits, Constable designed a special posing device, a low, square platform containing a revolving circular area about four feet in diameter. This allowed him to rotate his subjects into the position he desired. For the proper lighting effects, heavy velvet hangings surrounded the platform on three sides. Both of these variables allowed Constable to model the figure almost like a sculptor, choosing the type of light and pose he thought would best bring out the sitter's character.

Constable often preferred a profile view for his subjects, as we see in this self-portrait. Here Constable has seated himself within his posing cubicle, with the drapes pushed back to either side so the wheel and his figure are clearly visible against a backdrop showing a painted balustrade. The pose of the artist and the arrangement of the objects within the format are in perfect sympathy with each other. Together they present a harmonious and peaceful composition, one that conveys a clear feeling for the man pictured, who is probably near the end of an amazing and productive career.

PLATE 17

PLATE 18

CORNELIUS JABEZ HUGHES
British (1819–1884)
Portrait of a Yeoman
About 1853
Quarter plate with applied color
84.XT.1566.2

A MILITARY UNIFORM is in itself enough to create an aura of strength and a commanding presence for its wearer. Cornelius Hughes[39] has taken advantage of that fact to place this young bare-headed sergeant in a ramrod position, set at an angle to the picture plane. He has further emphasized the tension in the body by showing it sharply twisted at the waist while the details of the uniform accent the sitter's soldierly bearing. The stripes along his legs lead to the brightly lit spot of his glove and then, through a sequence of ornamental insignia, to the polished epaulet on his shoulder, which in turn points in the direction of the high, stiff, decorated collar. The bright sash at the waist and the curve of the leather strap across the chest stress his stiff military mien and, more importantly, give us a sense of the contained tension in the figure.

This tension is made even more palpable by the contrast Hughes has introduced by countering the active side of the young man's body on the left with a stable object on the right—the shako held so firmly in his other hand. The play between the soft fullness of the helmet's gleaming plumes and the smooth flatness of his chest takes full advantage of the daguerreotype's ability to convey distinct textures, a feature further heightened by the subtle coloring of the surface.[40] The brilliant contrast between these elements also enhances the vitality of this yeoman, who is probably seeing himself for the first time in the new uniform adopted in 1852 for the Scottish Lanarkshire Yeomanry regiment.[41] Despite all the pompous details of the uniform, the individuality of the sitter still emerges. The softer light that illuminates his face, set apart by his textured beard and hair, also accentuates his slightly downward glance and barely open mouth. This young gentleman appears very aware, and perhaps slightly amused, by the impression he makes in his new uniform.

PLATE 18

PLATE 18

PLATE 19

UNKNOWN AMERICAN PHOTOGRAPHER
Portrait of Edgar Allan Poe
Late May or early June 1849
Half plate
84.XT.957

DURING THE LAST YEAR of his short life, the poet, critic, and playwright Edgar Allan Poe sat four times for his portrait. Of these daguerreotypes, only this example gives us such an intimate portrayal of the man, one so immediate that it seems as if no photographer intervened between the man and the camera's lens. The other images taken of Poe during these last months lack the passionate intensity expressed here, primarily because they are more artfully composed, looking more like traditional portraits where the light is evenly controlled and the composition more balanced. As a result, these daguerreotypes show him more relaxed, but the man himself is distant, less an individual than the man who haunts us here.[42]

In this portrayal of Poe, there seems to be no question that he wished his inner soul to be bared, to appear like one of the characters of both intense beauty and vivid horror that he created in his own stories. In fact, during this last year, 1848–1849, his life had become a horror tale of its own; a tale that told of the empty wanderings of a desperate man who, after the death of his young wife, futilely searched for other romantic companionship and support, and, unable to escape from his dependence on drugs and alcohol, came to a mysterious death.

All of these conflicting emotions are painfully set before us in this portrait as deliberately as Poe would have gone about describing the macabre forces that permeated his stories. In sharp contrast with his other portraits, here he presents himself as a brooding and exhausted man, dramatically lit to emphasize his enormous eyes, his perhaps purposefully uncombed hair and disarranged clothes—all of which combine to make him seem a disturbed figure seeking help.

This daguerreotype's beseeching appeal must have been clear to Annie Richardson—one of the two women to whom he looked for support—at whose desire and expense this portrait had been made. Years later, she described it as unflattering, blaming its quality on the fact that it was the best that could be achieved at that time in Lowell, Massachusetts, where it was taken. In contrast, today this mesmeric portrait appears as an achievement rarely found in the work of even the best daguerreotypist.

PLATE 19

PLATE 20

UNKNOWN FRENCH PHOTOGRAPHER
Portrait of an Elderly Woman
About 1853
Sixth plate with applied color
84.XT.403.19

THE UNUSUAL HEADDRESS worn by this elderly woman identifies her as living in a French province, possibly Normandy or Brittany, but regardless of its specific origin it serves to associate her with a special place in a society of which she has long been part.[43] Probably born about 1770, while Louis xv was still reigning, she has seen a stream of rulers and revolutions come and go, the most recent change having taken place only a few years previously. Despite her age and reflective mien, she nevertheless remains a figure of authority and command. Her dress of satin, the corded belt with the bag of household keys, and the luxurious furnishing of her surroundings clearly identify her as the head of a well-to-do household in which she remains firmly in charge.

Some of our speculation concerning the subject of this portrait is due to the potential of the daguerreotype to record every detail of her appearance and surroundings. However, we are also given a sense of her character because of the art of the daguerreotypist, who posed her surrounded by a number of decorative objects and colorful areas that accentuate the surface of the plate. On the upper right side, the artist has daringly enlivened the surface by adding with a brush three zigzags of color unrelated to any depicted object. To the left, the intricate patterning of the oriental table covering, the loosely brushed bouquet of flowers, and the delicate, reflective framework of the flower container provide a context in which her hand appears strikingly alive, its fingers cramped by age, looking as detailed as the studies of hands done by Leonardo.

Despite the brilliance of her white turban, it does not overwhelm her face beneath, in part because the stripes of color to the right break up a sense of deep space behind her and because, by completely enveloping her face, the two objects become one, both creased and wrinkled as in a minutely detailed drawing by Dürer.

As a result of this careful composition, the daguerreotypist has created surroundings for this woman that give it a character unlike that of the usual studio setting. The maker has evoked an environment in which this woman has withdrawn from the events of the moment, more absorbed and reflective of the events of the past, caught in a segment of time afforded by the daguerreotype.

PLATE 20

PLATE 21

JEAN-GABRIEL EYNARD
Swiss (1775–1863)
Self-Portrait with Daguerreotype of Roman Forum
About 1845
Half plate (reversed)
84.XT.255.38

WHEN THE ELEGANT GENTLEMAN posed here, the brilliant financier and diplomat Jean-Gabriel Eynard,[44] became infatuated with the magical art of the daguerreotype immediately after it was revealed, he did not simply admire or acquire works by others; he learned for himself how the process worked. We do not know from whom Eynard received instruction, but his status easily ensured him access to the most skilled operators in Paris, probably even to Daguerre himself.

Evidently he became highly skilled, for we find his work praised in two of the earliest French manuals on daguerreotypy.[45] Unfortunately, none of his earliest works taken on his travels throughout Europe have been identified. Instead, we must judge the excellence of his daguerreian work primarily on those he made at his homes in Switzerland, where roughly one hundred images were preserved among his family's vast archive of documents and letters. These images show that he trained his camera—seemingly on an almost daily basis—on his mansion in Geneva; his nearby country houses; his family, visitors, and household staff; and, especially, himself.

The self-portrait we see here was probably made around 1845, when he was seventy years old. Like practically all early daguerreotype self-portraits, this one was made with the help of an assistant.[46] The clarity of the image and the beautiful balance of light and shade in this outdoor setting tell us immediately why Eynard's colleagues considered his work superior. The composition also reveals his mastery of presentation, with the weight of his figure almost totally set off to the left of the scene and enclosed by the drape of his coat. His long, outstretched leg crosses a still-life arrangement of a table's pedestal and rustic bentwood chairs.

This spread of objects across the frontal plane also emphasizes the most important element in this portrait— the pose. Eynard had a precise idea of how he ought to be pictured, and the same sinuous curve of his crossed leg here predominates in other portraits of him, whether painted or photographed. His belief that pose was a critical artistic quality was spelled out in his sharp objections to an 1831 portrait painted of him by Horace Vernet.[47] It was a particularly bad portrait, he believed, because the pose the artist chose was wrong—it did not display his body in a way that revealed his personality.

Eynard deliberately turned the self-portrait we see here into an autobiography by including at least two objects that call attention to important aspects of his life. The central and most obvious of these is the large daguerreotype of the Roman Forum, perhaps one of his own earlier works, thereby establishing his role as a pioneer in this new art form.[48] The other distinctly personal element in this self-portrait is the large pamphlet propped against the chair on the right. Although the bent cover does not allow us to read the complete title, the bold capital letters spell out the name *CAPODISTRIAS*. This pamphlet is likely one written by Eynard himself in memory of his close friend, the martyred first president of Greece.[49] Its presence in this self-portrait recalls one of the most important goals of Eynard's life, his passionate devotion to the cause of Greek independence.

The installation of Joannis Capodistrias (1776–1831) as the head of the new republic of Greece was due directly to Eynard's considerable diplomatic skills, as well as to the expenditure of an enormous portion of his vast personal wealth. Capodistrias's assassination was a tremendous blow to Eynard's hopes for the fragile Greek republic, but he continued to fight for it for the rest of his life. His devotion to this cause was so intense that he became known throughout Europe as the Father of Pan-Hellenism.[50]

Eynard was the political and financial force working to realize the Romantic dreams and desires expressed by so many poets, like Byron, and artists, like Delacroix, to free the Greek people from the chains of Turkish tyranny. Alas, we have no record of whether Eynard ever saw the sculpture of *The Greek Slave* in Hiram Powers's Florence studio (see Plate 51), but if he had, it seems reasonable to assume that a version of it—or at least a daguerreotype—would have joined his rich art collection in Geneva.

PLATE 21

PLATE 22

Albert Sands Southworth and Josiah Johnson Hawes
American (1811–1894; 1808–1901)
Portrait of a Young Girl
About 1852
Quarter plate
84.XT.837.3

As master painters from Michelangelo to Picasso have individual styles that mark their work as their own, so do certain master daguerreotypists have their unique styles. Only Albert Southworth and Josiah Hawes could have created this portrait of a little girl. Supreme practitioners of their art, they were able to combine reality with a sympathetic insight into their sitters. Their primary tools were the sensitive use of light and shade and a brilliant and original approach to posing their sitters. The fame of their portrait work was recognized by other pioneers in the field even though they never submitted their work to juried exhibitions outside of the Boston area. Their attitude toward their profession was clearly expressed by their insistence that their place of work at 5½ Tremont Row be referred to as the "Artists' Daguerreotype Rooms."[51]

Portraits of children by Southworth and Hawes particularly reveal their ability to relate immediately to the character of their sitters. They seem to have had an instinct for knowing how best to draw out the potential of such still emerging personalities. For this small, slightly chubby girl, whose face had not yet assumed distinctive features, they probably seated her on the low, soft stool they used in other children's portraits; and they placed her against an abstract background of light and dark undefined except for the dark shadow line on the left, which serves to accent her head. They manipulated the light so it fell most brilliantly on her exposed shoulder, the lace edging, and the puffed up fabric of her dress and sleeve. This area reflects the light coming from above and gives, within this portrait, an active surface of folds and shadows that emphasizes the delicacy of her arm and hand on the left. Even the position of her fingers speaks of her age and tenderness.

All of these details are subsidiary to the isolation this lighting creates for her face. The brilliant light emanating from her bare shoulder illuminates one side of her face, concentrating our attention on the individual characteristics of her eyes, nose, and mouth. The particular quality of light Southworth and Hawes obtained also allows her curly, slightly mussed hair to create an interplay of light and shade about her head that suggests a halo.

The subtle tonal gradations of the entire plate intensify the pictorial space of the image, but at the same time that this illusionary space is made so palpable, Southworth and Hawes, in an almost contrary manner, also allow a multifaceted play of light to enliven the mirror-smooth surface of the plate.

PLATE 22

PLATE 23

THOMAS M. EASTERLY
American (1809–1882)
Portrait of a Father, Daughters, and Nurse
About 1850
Quarter plate (enlarged)
84.XT.1569.1

THOMAS EASTERLY WAS SO CONVINCED of the superiority of the daguerreotype over other processes that he continued making them long after his contemporaries had turned to newer techniques. During his lifelong career in Saint Louis, he always practiced as a daguerreotypist, whether portraying the Native Americans who visited his city in their colorful tribal garb or recording the architectural projects that turned Saint Louis into a booming mid-nineteenth-century metropolis. This group portrait shows us why he found the process so rewarding. He was a master of the language of the daguerreotype—its clarity, its brilliance, its depth of tone—and was able to speak it with a particular sympathy to the character and personality of his sitters.[52]

What is most apparent about this family is the absence of a wife and mother, whose loss Easterly clearly conveys. He seems to understand the mixed emotions within the family; and through his arrangement and poses of the figures, Easterly allows the personality and role of each member of this group to be transmitted to us. The bulk of the father—its downward weight stressed by the slope of his shoulders—the descending loop of his watch chain, and the lifeless drape of his hands against the dark trousers of his spread legs all speak of a lack of spirit. Continuing this mood, the standing daughter clutches her father's coat with one hand, while her forearm supports her other, almost lifeless, drooping hand. The vertical drape of her dress and her ruffled sleeve cut her off visually from her younger sister, making her father and herself into a unified group whose sorrowful gazes are directed toward us. The apparent pain of the father and tearful eyes of the daughter reinforce the somber and poignant feeling of the image. The seated daughter, whose ornamented dress sets her apart from the rest, looks downward, slightly away from her sister and father, concealing from us any sense of her inner feeling.

Almost like a member of a Greek chorus in a play, sitting a slight distance behind, is the black mammy, on whose shoulders have fallen the responsibility of caring for these children. Her body is erect, her hands crossed, while a bright white shawl and cap starkly outline her stern visage. Hers is the strength that keeps this family together, and her respected role as a member of that family is stressed by her inclusion in this piece. As if to mark her pivotal role in this family's life, the photographer directs the light across the group so that it shines most brightly on the one figure whose strength is crucial, then subtly decreases in intensity as it moves across the other figures.

Easterly exhibits in this one piece all his insight into the capabilities of the camera for creating an artistic work; it displays a confident manipulation of light and focus on the silver canvas by one who also was able to sense and convey the characters of his sitters.

PLATE 23

PLATE 24

James Earle McClees and Washington L. Germon
American (1821–1887; 1823–1877)
Portrait of a Young Lady
About 1848
Half plate
84.XT.1565.30

When this gracious young Philadelphian went to visit the well-lit daguerreian rooms of McClees and Germon (Figure 20), she was seeking out one of the finest and most fashionable firms in the city.[53] When James McClees and Washington Germon formed their partnership in 1846, they each brought to it previous experience as daguerreotypist and engraver. Only a year after it was founded, the firm began receiving awards, perhaps due to Germon's training as an artist. Not until a fire destroyed their gallery in 1855 did they dissolve the partnership; McClees later pursued a successful career as an art dealer.

It was probably in the early years of their partnership that this young lady arrived in their studio dressed in a style fashionable throughout the 1840s.[54] She is wearing an off-the-shoulder evening dress—most likely of red silk—covered by a light muslin garment known as a "pelerine." She has enriched her outfit with a collar embellished with lace covering a black velvet band and bow that are held in place by a brooch. A fashionable bracelet adorns each arm. Her attire shows she intended to obtain an impressive portrait that would enhance her natural beauty, perhaps a portrait to be sent to the parents of her betrothed.

That she clearly wanted to project an image of beauty and wealth in this portrait is also suggested by the large porcelain vase, about two feet high, which is of such rarity and quality that it surely was brought to the studio by the subject herself.[55] Such a family treasure was not a normal studio prop like the paisley cloth and column upon which the vase stands. By its position and lighting, the daguerreotypist suggests a relationship between the classical character of the vase and the graceful figure of the young lady. Both are counterparts within the otherwise dark and finely polished surface of the background.

Whether or not the sitter intended to endow her portrait with the poetic imagery suggested by this vase we can only guess, but an association with the one in Keats's *Ode on a Grecian Urn* makes that suggestion probable. Although written in 1819, the *Ode* still appeared in popular ladies' magazines in the 1840s, and its message was a familiar figure of speech. What could be more fitting for this subject than to recall Keats's words: "Beauty is truth, truth beauty"?

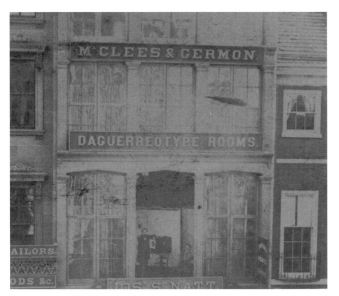

FIGURE 20
James Earle McClees (attributed)
American (1821–1887)
McClees & Germon Daguerreotype Rooms (detail)
1853
Salt print
The Library Company of Philadelphia

PLATE 24

PLATE 25

JOHN PLUMBE, JR.
American (1809–1857)
Portrait of a Man Reading a Newspaper
About 1842
Quarter plate
84.XT.1565.22

THIS SITTER'S CHARACTER is so clearly delineated by the clever—even inspired—lighting that we immediately understand the type of man portrayed. Absorbed in reading *The Philadelphia Ledger*, he is the very model of a mid-nineteenth-century American entrepreneur: a man whose inventive mind and tenacity for accomplishing goals promotes success but also courts failure. John Plumbe, Jr., was also such a person, and this probably accounts for his ability to express so sympathetically the personality of this sitter.

Plumbe had two professional passions in his life.[56] One was to convince Congress to endorse the construction of a cross-country railroad, an interest that grew out of his experience as a surveyor during the early years of railroading, when he worked to lay out and extend the tracks from the Eastern seaboard to the middle of the country. His other passion was to create a worldwide photographic enterprise that would embrace all aspects of the daguerreotype. As early as 1840 or 1841, he had invented an "improved" camera and was beginning to distribute equipment and supplies to daguerreotypists. At the same time, he began to open an ever-increasing number of photographic studios. These studios not only provided low-cost portraits but, by offering instruction, also enlarged the market for his products. His advertisements stressed the enjoyment amateurs—particularly women—would find in this new art and subtly pointed out that this practice could also be a respectable means of making a livelihood.[57]

To encourage would-be daguerreotypists, Plumbe emphasized in his advertisements that his improved camera allowed images to be produced without elaborate lighting equipment. He boasted that, by using his system, only the light of a single window was needed to make a fine portrait, of which this daguerreotype is an example.[58]

Plumbe has positioned the sitter at an angle to the window, placing his dark frock coat and trousers in the brightest rays of light. The wrinkles in his sleeves and trousers break up the light to create a richly textured area of the plate, making a strong contrast with the sharply defined planes of the window's sill and frame.

The direct rays of light gradually diminish while passing over the sitter's dark clothes; but, on striking the broad sheet of the diagonally placed newspaper, they are reflected back onto his plaid neckpiece and up into his face. Both the incoming and the reflected rays of light meet at the upper part of his hat, emphasizing it as a tangible object. It stands out so sharply that the flat wall behind the figure is transformed into atmospheric space. Simultaneously, the hat serves as the apex of the basic pyramidal composition originally conceived by the maker. The artistic excellence of this daguerreotype makes us realize that Plumbe's boastful ads were not without truth.

The number of Plumbe's studios spread rapidly until, at the peak of his career in 1846, sixteen locations in the United States and abroad bore his name. In each city, Plumbe hired operators to perform the work; thus, even though daguerreotypes bear the Plumbe name on their brass mats and cases, they are not necessarily by Plumbe himself. Since these operators were trained by Plumbe, however, it is not surprising that many of their images often display the same high artistic principles and quality that we see in this example.

Plumbe gradually retreated from this peak of power in the photographic world. He sold off his studios between 1847 and 1849, when he left for California. He probably went in search of gold, but also to continue seeking support for his railroad plans; he found neither. His life ended by suicide in 1857 after his return to the Midwest, the home of his dream for a transcontinental railroad. To this extraordinary man, the development of the daguerreian enterprise in America owes a tremendous debt. He not only trained and promoted many highly skilled daguerreotypists, but more than any other single practitioner, he made the daguerreotype an object everyone could hope to possess.

PLATE 25

PLATE 26

UNKNOWN AMERICAN PHOTOGRAPHER
Portrait of a Young Sailor
About 1848
Quarter plate with applied color
84.XT.1571.2

WEARING FRESH, NEW CLOTHES large enough to grow into during his first sea voyage—a trip that could last as long as several years—this young mariner had his photograph made by one of the many daguerreotypists who set up their studios at America's expanding ports. The barrel—with its multiple uses for holding rope for the sails, provisions for the crew, and whale oil during a successful return—next to which the lad is posed, is a prop provided by the photographer to serve as an appropriate reference to nautical life.

Appearing to be about twelve years old, this young lad probably has just been signed on to serve as a cabin boy and is having his photograph taken to leave behind with his family. He appears firm and resolute, his pose stiffened by the posing stand we can detect between his legs. Although the red shirt was a personal choice, as no uniform dress code existed at this time, he is proudly wearing his new symbol of manhood, the broad straw hat covered with a tar-soaked canvas that sailors wore when on shore leave.[59]

The tar stains on his fingers are only a small hint of the hazardous and rigorous life he will lead during the months or years before he returns to his home port. Without realizing it, the daguerreotypist provided us with visual evidence of the young seagoing men who overcame innumerable dangers to build up the maritime power of our country.

PLATE 26

PLATE 27

ANTOINE FRANÇOIS JEAN CLAUDET
French, active in England (1797–1867)
Self-Portrait with His Son Francis
About 1856
Stereograph, right plate of two sixth plates (enlarged)
84.XT.266.10

POSED IN THE STUDIO SETTING that is a trademark of his stereographic portraits, Antoine Claudet is pictured here with his son Francis. Probably taken when Claudet was in his late fifties, he was by then one of the most respected daguerreotypists in the world. He had gained this prominence not only because of his many technical inventions that advanced the art, but also for the superior artistic quality of his own photographs, which totally justify Claudet's expressed desire to be known as a "Photographic Artist."

Claudet's background was not that of an artist, but of a successful industrialist who supervised the English branch of his family's glass business. Because of his close ties with French glass manufacturers and opticians, Claudet was one of the first to learn about Daguerre's discovery. Immediately recognizing its significance, he returned briefly to Paris to learn the process from Daguerre himself. From that moment on, Claudet's life became completely intertwined with this new art form and he constantly contributed to its progress.[60]

Almost immediately, Claudet made a significant improvement in Daguerre's invention by formulating a new chemical solution that increased the sensitivity of the plate, thereby decreasing the time needed to expose the image. He announced his discovery at a Royal Academy of Sciences meeting in June 1841, the same time he opened his first portrait studio.

Claudet's primary concern during most of his career was to find ways to ensure the sharp definition of objects. Through experiments, he determined that, since the lens did not see what the human eye saw, it was impossible to tell just by looking on the ground glass whether the image would appear in focus on the finished plate. He solved this problem in 1844 by designing what he called a "focimeter," a circular device with ornamented fan-like blades.[61] When looking at the blades of the focimeter through the ground glass, the photographer could select—by a complex system—the correct adjustment to the focus. In normal practice, the focimeter would be removed before the plate was exposed, but in this double portrait it was left to sit prominently on the center table to indicate its role as an important invention by Claudet.

Claudet's work in theories of perception grew out of his experience behind the camera, and his particular interest in the arrangement of objects in space led him to become an immediate supporter of the new stereographic process as soon as it became available in 1851.[62] When seen through a special viewer, two similar images merged into a single picture whose contents were seemingly transformed into solid objects existing in a three-dimensional space. By this means, Claudet could obtain an image that fit perfectly with his own concept of an ideal photographic work of art.[63]

Claudet's purpose in inventing the focimeter—to permit photographers to have better control over the clarity of the image—also led him to devise a comparable system for taking stereographs. The portrait we see here is itself part of an experiment to attain that control. It is one of four similar stereographs,[64] each of which has a prominent white card in the lower left-hand corner. The small numeral *22* at the bottom stands for the number of feet between the sitters and the stereo cameras. Each stereograph in the group also has a larger numeral representing the number of inches between the lenses of the two cameras when that particular stereograph was made. For this version, that distance is eight inches. The other versions show the cameras as being two, four, or twelve inches apart. From these results, Claudet could detect the changes such differences would cause in the illusion of three-dimensional space when the image was seen through a stereo viewer.

In later years, Claudet's thinking about photography underwent a fundamental change. Rather than encouraging photographers to achieve sharp definition in their work, he proposed in 1866 that they should aim for a soft focus. His proposal for works with softer edges and obscure, hazily lit settings pointed toward the work of the later Pictorialist photographers. Claudet's abilities to formulate ideas that were not realized until much later reveals his innate understanding of photography as an art form—an ability that had guided all of his life's work.

PLATE 27

PLATE 28

RICHARD BEARD
British (1802–1885)
Portrait of a Young Gentleman
About 1852
Sixth plate with applied color
84.XT.1572.3

PLATE 29

ANTOINE FRANÇOIS JEAN CLAUDET
French, active in England (1797–1867)
Portrait of a Girl in a Blue Dress
About 1854
Sixth plate with applied color
84.XT.833.17

THE EARLIEST PORTRAIT STUDIOS in London—those of Richard Beard and Antoine Claudet—both opened in late spring 1841. Immediately each sought ways to improve the somber appearance of their pioneer daguerreotypes.[65] In December 1841, Claudet introduced painted canvas backgrounds depicting rows of books to suggest that the portrait was taken in the interior of a library, thereby replacing the otherwise overall metallic sheen of the daguerreotype's plain background with an image of illusionary space. Later Claudet, and also Beard, adopted exterior landscape scenes and cloud-filled skies as backdrops. Soon both were hiring miniature painters to add color or even to paint imaginary scenes on the plate. By 1843, London daguerreotypists were known for their delicately hand-tinted silver portraits. Even though others railed against hand-coloring as an intrusion into the realm of pure photography, Claudet defended it as a proper and laudable practice. In his mind, the addition of color turned the photograph into a genuine work of art.

Claudet particularly enjoyed creating a relationship between the three-dimensional objects in a setting, the pose of the figure, and the illusionistic, painted background. In this example (Plate 29), where all these elements have been controlled, Claudet introduced an amazingly cluttered variety of shapes and forms in the lower half of the portrait that crowd against the young girl's body. The different hues of these decorative objects make the single color of her dress stand out to emphasize her body. Her full sleeve and her slightly twisted waist mark the point where her body begins to free itself from the still-life objects and ascends into open space. The column and drapery on the right, as well as the horizontal line of the couch, mark off a rectangular area behind her head that serves as a picture frame, creating a beautiful miniature painting of her delicate face within the daguerreotype.

In contrast to the complex posing and setting Claudet created for the girl, Richard Beard's presentation of a young gentleman is simple and straightforward (Plate 28). The relaxed pose of his figure, with one arm and hand resting on a plain table top and the other placed across his leg, is set within a minimally defined space by the balustrade at the right. The light, falling on the collar that sets off his head and on the cuff, is attuned to the other details of this carefully balanced composition. All of the details recorded by the camera are enveloped in a harmonious whole because of the gifted painter who has responded so well to the photographic base of the portrait. The miniaturist applied the color discretely, enhancing the scene rather than overcoming it, as some frustrated miniaturists were apt to do. In this case, the restraint of the colorist—for example, in avoiding the temptation to ornament the table cover—makes this daguerreotype a superior example of the quality obtained by the blend of the painter's brush and the camera's eye.

PLATES 28 and 29

PLATE 30

CHARLES WINTER
French (1821–1904)
Portrait of a Seated Man
About 1852
Half plate
84.XT.403.7

THERE IS NO ESCAPING the steady gaze of this French gentleman: he appears to be waiting patiently for an answer to a question he recently posed. It seems as if we have been deep in conversation with him, a conversation still going on. The daguerreotypist, Charles Winter of Strasbourg, has been able to suggest such a relationship between viewer and sitter because he has arranged the sitter in a pose that makes him appear especially alert and engaging.

The intimate presence of this elegant man stems from the clarity Winter has given to the diagonal thrust of the low chair, precisely setting out the depth the figure occupies by the contrast between the chair's highlighted side on the right and its darker counterpart. The chair acts to encompass the sitter in this daguerreotype much in the way a niche in a wall encompasses a free-standing sculpture.

Above the chair, the body's twist at the waist is strongly marked by the brilliant area of light centered on the man's hands and the movement of his arm across his body, which leads us smoothly to the dark velvet collar below his face. The dark coat enclosing the upper portion of his torso is gently set off from the plain background, but enough light falls upon it to bring out its texture, making an area of the rich and deep tonality distinctive to the daguerreotype. The direction of his body is further defined by the light caught along the buttons and the edge of the gentleman's coat.

The triple arcs made by the coat's velvet collar, the dark cravat, and the shirt's white collar all underscore the change of direction the sitter's head has taken. Framed by his dark hair, his face is tilted, turned against the rising direction of his torso and brought into the brightest area of light. Through this complex pose and skilled lighting, Charles Winter has provided the sitter with a distinctive portrait, one of great strength and animation.

PLATE 30

PLATE 31

UNKNOWN AMERICAN PHOTOGRAPHER
Portrait of a Man with Crossed Hands
About 1845
Sixth plate
84.XT.270.22

PLATE 32

UNKNOWN AMERICAN PHOTOGRAPHER
Portrait of a Father and Smiling Child
About 1855
Sixth plate
84.XT.1578.3

SOON AFTER IT BECAME POSSIBLE to make daguerreian portraits, a stream of would-be photographers began to course through the American countryside following trails already taken by itinerant portrait painters. Curiosity stirred by the new wonder of the daguerreotype promised both a wide audience and a new way of making a fortune without requiring a large investment. Traveling with a special studio wagon, or renting rooms in one town after another, members of this new profession covered wide areas of the country, announcing their arrival with broadsides hailing the quality of their work.

Both of the images seen here have the characteristics of the work of itinerant daguerreotypists, whose minimal training did not allow them to absorb the subtleties of portraiture from which more experienced daguerreotypists benefited. The face of the tall, lanky man (Plate 31) is lit by such a strong light that the portrait was probably made outdoors using direct sunlight. The light is so bright that his face is sharply divided by the prominently lit ridge of his nose, as in a Picasso-like depiction of the face that combines both profile and full-face. The deep folds allowed to disturb the background are further evidence that this image is by an itinerant artist, as is the placement of his hands. Isolated by his rumpled cuffs, they are picked out by the light in a way that mercilessly emphasizes every bony finger. The only difference between this and the primitive paintings being offered by itinerant artists of the period is that the painted portrait would have been garnished with bright colors. In comparison, this sitter paid far less, and suffered posing for a much shorter time, than did those of his contemporaries who sat for painters.

What no primitive painter could hope to achieve, however, is the joyous, instantaneous image of father and child (Plate 32) the other daguerreotypist was able to capture. The child's delightful smile probably is a response to an antic of her mother, standing off to the side. Here, feeling at ease with her father, she is caught at a time when she found her world a joyous place. Her father sits stiffly, clasping her tightly on his knee. His face glows with a warmth of pride, his slight smile clearly expressing his feeling for the child.

The wonderful picture this family was able to take away with them shows that, even in the hands of a not-very-skilled daguerreotypist, this medium was able to capture the intimacy of loved ones. As with the other image, this daguerreotypist made no attempt to set his subjects in special lighting and even allowed the father's hand to be so close to the lens that its size is exaggerated. The father's ill-fitting dress shirt and crudely knotted tie, as well as his sunburnt face and working man's hand, give us the impression that the family has come in from their farm to the daguerreotypist's temporary studio for this special occasion. The unknown daguerreotypist, while lacking artistic skill, was lucky enough to capture a fleeting moment of familial love.

PLATES 31 and 32

UNKNOWN AMERICAN PHOTOGRAPHER
Portrait of a Girl with Her Deer
About 1854
Quarter plate
84.XT.172.5

WHAT A GREAT CHANCE for the itinerant daguerreotypist who discovered this earnest girl with her pet deer and was able to capture them in his camera! Although the girl is restraining the fawn by holding a rope around its neck, its ears are upright and alert, suggesting it may bolt at any moment from the photographer's presence. Packing a portable tent and camera equipment, the daguerreotypist has come to a homestead area in the western part of the continent, where the black-tailed deer ranged. Beyond the fence, the silhouette of the barn also suggests an area of northern California or parts of the North-west that only recently had been settled by pioneers from east of the Mississippi.

The girl's clothes were designed to protect her from the sudden changes in the weather common to this area. The long ribbons of her hat could be used to tie it securely to her head, and its veil could surround her face to protect her from dust. Beneath her knee-length overgarment she wears a long dress that descends almost to the ground, but a small part of her white pantaloons are still visible. Even though this farm girl is far from a daguerreian studio, she has been able to have her portrait made. Her personal image and evidence of her lifestyle were preserved through the miracle of Daguerre's invention at the same moment that naturalistic and topographic surveys were being sent out by the federal government to discover what was contained in the newly expanded nation.[66]

PLATE 33

PLATE 34

Warren T. Thompson
American (active about 1840–about 1860)
Self-Portrait as a Hunter
About 1855
Stereograph, left plate of two sixth plates with applied color (enlarged)
84.XT.838.1

FROM THE SCANT INFORMATION available about Warren Thompson we never would imagine him to be the flamboyant and exotic person revealed in this self-portrait. In addition to this pose as a hunter, he also pictured himself in other romantic roles, such as that of a heavily cloaked Arab stealthily withdrawing a silver dagger. Without this series of stereographic self-portraits—all taken in his adopted city of Paris—the facts about his life would suggest he was more a scientist and technician than an artist.[67]

Thompson was a member of the group of Philadelphia pioneers who were introduced to the miracle of the daguerreotype in its infancy. He conquered the process so completely that, by May 1843, he was granted a patent for inventing an electrolysis process for coloring the images, but since he immediately assigned the patent to another Philadelphia daguerreotypist, it appears he already had plans to move elsewhere.[68] His activities remain unknown, however, until 1849, when he was announced as the winner of one of only two medals awarded in the daguerreian category of the Industrial Exposition in Paris. Reviewing—not all favorably—the entries in this exhibition, the respected French critic Léon de Laborde praised Thompson's work for its large size and concluded that the clarity, size, and overall accomplishment of his work surpassed most of the other daguerreotypists in Paris.[69] Unfortunately, since only a few of his works are known today, it is difficult to match the enthusiastic words of the critic with actual daguerreotypes. We do know, again only from written sources, that he continued to carry out photographic feats that added to his fame.

In 1851, Thompson's skill in handling oversized plates enabled the Italian astronomer Ignazio Porro to obtain the most successful pictures yet produced of an eclipse of the sun. The following year, as one of the two official photographers chosen to record a great military festival staged by Napoleon III, Thompson easily surpassed his competition by constructing an enormous apparatus that used daguerreotype plates as large as two by three feet.[70] One of the contemporary journals, speaking of these mammoth records of the event, praised them as "monuments to the glory of photography."[71]

Soon, however, Thompson's passion to create increasingly impressive daguerreotypes no longer had to be accomplished physically by using larger and larger plates. With the advent of the stereoscope, he could create the impression of immense scenes on a physically small object. An entire world could be contained within the limited size of a stereograph, yet appear more real because of the intimate way one viewed the image. With eyes pressed tight against the twin apertures of the viewing apparatus, cut off from the outside, a viewer was brought directly into a three-dimensional world. From then on, all of Thompson's portraits were stereographs.

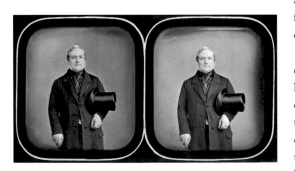

PLATE 35
Warren T. Thompson
Portrait of a Gentleman with a Top Hat
About 1855
Stereograph, two sixth plates (reduced)
84.XT.405.2

Thompson, like so many of the early daguerreotypists, had a mind capable of combining the most innovative and daring ideas with the keenest and most sensitive artistic vision. The other work reproduced here (Plate 35) also gives us a glimpse into the kind of man he was, for the sense of fun and parody apparent in his self-portraits occasionally slips out in portraits of his clients, as in the way he posed this very trusting gentleman, who, placed directly in the center of the scene, is frozen in place by his hat. Thompson has made this work not simply a portrait of the man, but an image of the relationship *between* the man and the hat. We can sense here that a bit of the caricaturist Daumier lurked in Thompson's personality.

PLATE 34

PLATE 36

UNKNOWN AMERICAN PHOTOGRAPHER
Portrait of Three Women
About 1849
Quarter plate
84.XT.1577.2

THE POWER OF THIS DAGUERREOTYPE comes not only from the way the three figures are so harmoniously grouped, but from the photographer's keen sensitivity to the subtle effects achieved by combining textures and light. No single detail in the scene appears to have been left to chance—not the strikingly different hair styles (which seem to have been partially arranged by the photographer), nor the multiple directions of their glances, nor their uniquely independent stances. By these means, the artist—as such the daguerreotypist should be called despite remaining unknown—clearly identifies for us the markedly different personalities of the women, perhaps a mother with her two daughters. They are woven together into a beautiful, harmonious whole by the rhythmic interlacing of their arms and hands. The three are bound together in an emotional relationship we are unable to define, in part because each has also been given her own space and independence.

The figure at the left is set against the flutes of the column rising behind her. The central figure is almost solely restricted to the background, but her finger touching the crest of the chair ties her psychologically to the other two. The seated body of the third woman claims the corner space. Even though they are firmly settled in their own space, the dominant rhythm of their hands and arms entwines them, a subtle linking of the group further heightened by the play of light on the fabric of their gowns. We are first attracted to the plaid stole wrapped around the woman at the left. Its pattern acts to soften her figure in relation to the architectonic quality of the column, but it also serves as an accent to the lively surface of the shiny cape worn by the central figure. The bare shoulder of the seated young woman is another strong foil to the other active areas of light, and the fringe on her sleeve enriches the surface quality of the image. The three women probably had been informed that dark clothes and plaids were preferable for having one's portrait taken, but it was the maker who was responsible for the way the different materials were draped and contrasted, and who directed the play of light that turned the textures and values of each gown into a lustrous setting that creates the uniqueness of these three women.

Despite allowing us to enjoy the sensuous aspects of this portrait, the artist denies us a full understanding of the group. A sense of mystery exudes from the poses and gestures of the three women. The two side figures extend their arms toward the center, where one finger of the girl on the left is held by the net-covered hand of her sister on the right. Immediately beneath this point is an enigmatic assemblage of grapes, sharp-edged leaves, and a basket handle that throws a strong reflection, as if made of metal. Perhaps this still-life arrangement is intended to unite this group or to give us some other message, but it remains indecipherable. We are left only to admire the amazing visual effects this daguerreotypist has achieved and to wonder if the content of the portrait has been raised to a metaphorical level—as if its title should read *"The Three Fates."*

PLATE 36

PLATE 37

UNKNOWN AMERICAN PHOTOGRAPHER
Portrait of a Nurse and Young Child
About 1850
Sixth plate with applied color
84.XT.172.4

ON SEEING THIS IMAGE TODAY, we first are conscious of it as a social document reflecting a shameful period of our past. As a work of art, however, this beautiful daguerreotype becomes a meaningful and truthful memorial of a long-gone relationship. In the daguerreian era, young children of wealthy families often were raised by slaves or freed black women, and the bond between the two could become very strong, lasting throughout their lives.

This daguerreotype is probably a record of the early stage of such a relationship, one that could become a deep and loving substitute for a familial tie. The emotions that emanate from this portrait are primarily due to the expression and gesture of the nurse. The maker must have suggested that the little girl stand on the nurse's lap, thus raising her face to the same level as the nurse's. This position allowed the child's face to be fully lit, defining clearly her large eyes and rounded cheeks.

The angled light falls more softly upon the striped headdress of the nurse, but with sufficient strength to model the dark features of her face. Her nose, cheek bones, and lips are strongly defined, and she stares out of the scene in a way that declares her individuality. Her physicality and expression give us a sense of a specific personality that, when combined with the power of her huge hand holding the tiny one of the child, clearly expresses the importance of her presence for the little girl. In this daguerreotype, there is a contrast of light and dark, of small and large, but there is no contrast of expression; both are solemn for this important event. We realize we are in the presence of the powerful emotions such relationships generated.

PLATE 37

PLATE 38

UNKNOWN AMERICAN PHOTOGRAPHER
Portrait of a Man
About 1854
Sixth plate
84.XT.441.11

ALMOST EVERYTHING ABOUT THIS PORTRAIT indicates that its daguerreotypist was aware of the daring effect it would achieve. What daguerreotypist would have been so bold as to use pose and light in a way that seems to break all the accepted rules for a perfect likeness? Where was this daguerreotypist when the etiquette of proper portrait making was proclaimed? It seems almost impossible to believe that a daguerreian artist would have been so bold in the presentation of a figure, yet not one element in this portrait appears to have been accidental.

The principal effect of this portrait comes from the placement of the subject within its frame. All the parts of the figure that touch or are cut off by the mat—the elbow at the left, the hand at the right and its open book, and the edge of his hat at the top—have been deliberately arranged.[72] This figure is positioned just as the daguerreotypist wished us to see him.

By being confined within the space chosen by the daguerreotypist, the positions of each part of the figure take on a heightened impact, like the figures compressed within a Greek relief panel. The relaxed angle of his heavy forearm on the left is countered by the diagonal of his vest, thrusting up from below. From here, the arm holding the book extends across the back and spindles of the chair. All such movements culminate in the sharply lighted head and top hat. The well-defined contour of the man's face isolates his striking eyes, set in the shadow cast by the brim of his hat, whose pronounced downward thrust anchors our attention even more keenly on his eyes. They seem to stare directly at us—almost rudely; not simply regarding, but as if inspecting.

Regardless of the impression of the sitter this portrait conveys, the daguerreotype seems to be more a work of art than a simple attempt to capture a personality. The careful composition of the figure within the pictorial field plays up the amazing modern feeling this work possesses, an observation strengthened by the highly unusual pattern of window light falling on the back wall. It seems impossible to believe that the daguerreotypist was not conscious of its effect. This area of light appears to have been a deliberate device to weave the figure and the surrounding area into a single field, a play between solid objects and flat surfaces that we might expect to find in works by Manet or Degas.

Even if we relate the unusual shadow of the window to the similar devices used by earlier artists like Rembrandt, whose etchings and paintings often show such a light cast on a wall, their intent was different. The older masters used it to define the presence of a figure or the spatial extent of a room. In this daguerreotype, however, the device serves a reverse purpose; rather than enhancing the spatial definition, it emphasizes the shallowness of the space between figure and background.

Who was this daguerreian artist? Who was the sitter for this portrait? How did this maker prefigure the candid snapshot? We have no answer to these questions, but there is ample evidence here that the vision of future photographers was already present in the art of the daguerreotypist.

PLATE 38

Chapter Three

THE ARTIFICIAL RETINA

———

A T THE CONCLUSION of François Arago's January 1839 announcement about the daguerreotype process, the eminent physicist Jean Baptiste Biot (1774–1862) rose immediately to add his own words of praise for Daguerre's discovery. For Biot, the potential for illustrating monuments was secondary to the impact he saw the daguerreotype would have on the acquisition of scientific knowledge. He considered the daguerreotype a valuable new research tool, one that would serve, he said, as an "artificial retina." Every observation could now be made with a completely neutral eye, and recorded with absolute fidelity. In his own field of physics, Biot prophesied that the daguerreotype would lead to uncovering the true nature of the primary element of the universe—light.[1]

Astronomers were among the first to extend their research with the aid of the daguerreotype. They immediately combined the telescope and the camera to increase vastly their basic information. Together, these tools allowed them to keep more accurate records of the constellations at any given time. Now their observations of the skies could be preserved, and precise comparisons could be made, as the heavenly bodies changed their positions. As early as 1843, it was reported that an observatory in Rome had succeeded in "combining the power of

the telescope and the daguerreotype" to produce a perfect celestial atlas, a "map of the heavens."[2] If all of these separate views could be pasted together, the reporter added, they would require a domed space as large as the interior of London's Saint Paul's Cathedral. The author's forecast of such a view of the heavens was not realized until eighty years later, when, in 1923, the world's first planetarium opened in Dresden.

Successful views of solar eclipses and studies of the moon also were obtained in the early years of the daguerreotype, both in Europe and America. Not until 1851, however, was a finely detailed view of the moon's surface produced. This was accomplished by Boston daguerreotypist John A. Whipple (1822–1891), who was able to work with the world's largest telescope at the Harvard College Observatory. His achievement, for which he was awarded a prize, attracted enormous attention at the London Crystal Palace exhibition.[3]

During those early years, the daguerreotype also became an indispensable companion to the microscope. Previously, scientists complained that artists working directly from the microscope could not attain the rigorous fidelity the minute details demanded, and one writer described this work as being executed "in the same manner as that in which

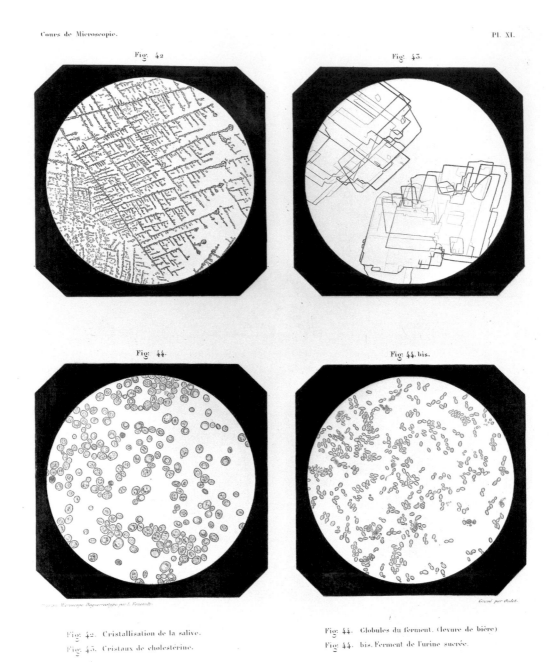

Cours de Microscopie.   Pl. XI.

Fig. 42   Fig. 43.

Fig. 44.   Fig. 44. bis.

Fig. 42. Cristallisation de la salive.

Fig. 43. Cristaux de cholestérine.

Fig. 44. Globules du ferment (levure de bière)

Fig. 44. bis. Ferment de l'urine sucrée.

FIGURE 2I
Engravings after Daguerreotypes Made by Léon Foulcault
French (1819–1868)
Published in Alfred Donné, *Cours de microscopie*
(Paris 1845), pl. II
84.XB.950.8.II

a portrait-painter produces his effects." To make the drawing absolutely accurate, he said, it must be "independent altogether of those impulses which imagination and taste never fail to impart to the pencil, even of the most conscientious artist." Now these details "have been happily supplied by photography," and the writer praised the work of the French scientist Alfred Donné, who in 1845 had engravings made from daguerreotypes taken through the microscope's lens (Figure 21). The daguerreotype supplied the long-desired absolute accuracy.[4]

What the physical sciences had gained in the daguerreotype was an accurate reporter whose newly available exactitude required no intermediary. Science was not alone, however, in benefiting from the daguerreotype, although its contributions to other disciplines of knowledge were not always so direct or immediately grasped. This was particularly true for historians, whose work depended solely on their interpretation of the written texts of the past. Until then, the visual records available were the result of an artist's interpretation of an object, or often, simply an illustrator's fanciful vision of the past. Now, with the daguerreotype as their own artificial retina, their knowledge of the past was amplified by the facts provided by the photographic image.

The visual memory created by the daguerreotype also had a direct personal effect on the relationship between people of the world, not just by showing them as subjects of anthropological or anatomical studies but by providing famous names with actual likenesses. Daguerreotypists all exhibited and sold original and copy portraits of famous people—elected leaders, monarchs, principals of the stage, inventors. Primarily, however, their work was in providing portraits of family members to an eager public. No longer was a list of birth and death dates written in the family bible adequate, now albums containing visual histories of the family were the goal. If no previous image had been made, a postmortem daguerreotype became the record, like that of the deceased man in his coffin (Plate 39). Such views provided daguerreotypists with one of their earliest sources of income, for although postmortem paintings had long been made, the belief in the truthfulness of the daguerreotype gave an image like this one an objectivity a painting would have lacked.[5]

The difference between the evidence derived from the daguerreotype and the information pro-

vided by the artist can be clearly seen in a comparison of a daguerreian view (Plate 40) with an engraved view of the same site taken from the highly regarded publication by James Stuart and Nicholas Revett of ancient Greek monuments (Figure 22).[6] These monuments were considered in the West to represent the highest degree of classical architecture, despite their being known only from ancient descriptions and fables, as the Turkish masters of Greece had long excluded foreign visitors. When, in the mid-eighteenth century, a few travelers were permitted to visit the original monuments and produce drawings made at the site, their results were widely accepted as finally providing accurate representations.

The engravings by Stuart and Revett were the most respected of these depictions, but, as we can see, the setting they created for their view of the

PLATE 39
UNKNOWN AMERICAN PHOTOGRAPHER
Postmortem of a Man
About 1855
Sixth plate (reduced)
84.XT.1569.10

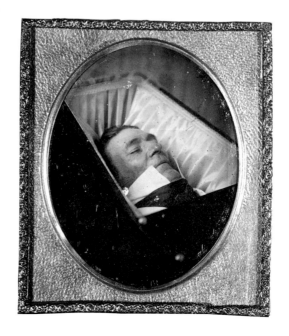

PLATE 40
PHILIPPOS MARGARITIS AND PHILIBERT PERRAUD
Greek (1810–1892); French (born 1815)
The Arch of Hadrian, Athens
1846–47
Reversed quarter plate (enlarged)
90.XT.65.9

Arch of Hadrian was completely different from that shown in the daguerreotype. Originally erected in Athens by the Roman Emperor Hadrian in the second century A.D. to mark the distinction between the original Greek city and its Roman expansion, this urban monument has been transported by the draftsman into a fictitious pastoral landscape. Its archway has become a passage for a shepherd driving his flocks, followed by a horse bearing a woman carrying a swaddled baby—a clear reference to the traditional biblical image of the Holy Family's flight into Egypt. As this rhythmically arranged procession passes to the Roman side of the city, it comes onto a vast plain, empty except for a few ragged columns of the temple of Zeus, even though its actual ruins were then far more complete than the engraver has indicated. The artist's pencil has ignored the other

FIGURE 22
The Arch of Hadrian, Athens
Engraving published in James Stuart and Nicholas Revett,
The Antiquities of Athens (London 1762, reprint, New York
1968), vol. 3, ch. 3. plate 1
Courtesy of The Research Library,
Getty Research Institute

remains of the city in favor of a dramatic landscape, placing over this relic of the past a picturesque veil to spark our imagination.

In the daguerreotype the arch is not seen as a monument enveloped by a delightful pastoral scene, but as a remnant of a lost urban setting, the remains of the most admired city of the ancient world. Because of its incredible ability to depict detail, the daguerreotype permits us to see beyond the arch, into the original Greek part of the city, to the distant mount of the Acropolis, demonstrating how it towered above the city as a separate place, truly a sacred site for the gods. There, the silhouette of the giant temple of Athena—the Parthenon—dominates the entire sanctuary; a new reality is given to the poetic descriptions by the ancient Greek bards. No painterly effects are needed to embellish this outcropping with awe; its existence on the silver canvas accomplishes that. Between these two representations of the Arch of Hadrian lies the invention of Daguerre. On one side is the romantic aesthetic of the past; on the other, the realism of the present, which is his gift to the historians of the future.

If the historian wished to accept it, the daguerreotype had the potential of being, therefore, a direct opening to the truth. For some historians, however, its evidence was seen as a threat to their future usefulness, as a Boston newspaper pointed out when describing daguerreotypes taken of the Crimean War: "The historian may now break his tablets and throw away his pen—he is left entirely in the background, eclipsed and buried by the daguerreotypist."[7]

The acquisition of exact visual knowledge encouraged historians to write a more comprehensive type of history. With an ever-increasing amount of visual documents, a new social and anthropological interpretation of cultures developed. In a short time, photographic copies of works of art made it possible for historians to compare the visual expres-sions and preferences of different cultures; and although they were supplemented much later by many other reproductions of works of art, these early contributions of the daguerreotype were the true beginning of André Malraux's *Museum without Walls*.

One writer keenly aware of the effects this powerful new tool of observation could bring about was Edgar Allan Poe. As early as January 1840, Poe noted in a brief newspaper account that, like all new philosophical discoveries, the consequences of the daguerreotype's invention could not "even remotely be seen."[8] What impressed him immediately was that because the daguerreotype was "infinitely" accurate, it would disclose, unlike a painting, a "more absolute truth." He described this quality of the daguer-reotype as having a "perfect identity" with what it represented, and as such it became a way of accumulating unalterable facts, a tool that would forever change how history would be recorded. It is appropriate that Poe was one of the first to sense immediately how the daguerreotype would lead to a new truth, one that would shape a new visual language; an observation that reflected his own poetic vision.

PLATES

Chapter Three

UNKNOWN FRENCH PHOTOGRAPHER
Study of Rocks
About 1845
Half plate
84.XT.183

HOW WAS THE EARTH FORMED? Geologists in the early nineteenth century were in a ferment over this question. European scientists advanced a number of opposing theories, some of which diverged from the six-day answer given by the Bible. Speculation about the origins of the earth was thus already intense when the daguerreotype appeared and provided a new tool to record physical evidence for fresh hypotheses.[9]

One theory developed by the Swiss scientist Nicholas Sassure (1767–1845) explained the existence of the huge, isolated boulders of granite found on the slopes of the Jura Mountains. He baptized them *erratics*, as they appeared to him to be unrelated to surrounding geological formations. He postulated that they could only have been deposited there by great torrents of water, like those of the biblical deluge. In 1837, another Swiss scientist, Louis Agassiz (1807–1873), saw these boulders as the remains of retreating glaciers. He continued to develop his theory by field studies in several parts of the world, despite what was then called a "glacial" reaction to his theories.[10]

Our unknown daguerreotypist must have had the goal of recording one of these erratics, a massive boulder that testified to the tremendous force with which it had been rent apart. The daguerreotypist deliberately chose to aim the camera from below, allowing part of the boulder to remain unseen, thus emphasizing, within the same view, both the detailed physical actuality of the rock as well as its surface characteristics. Many photographers sought to obtain accurate geological records during the years after this daguerreotype was made, particularly the French photographers Bisson frères (active 1840–1864). An 1855 article in *La Lumière* described their attempts to record earthquakes and avalanches immediately after they happened so they could document the newly opened chasms and the boulders that had fallen from inaccessible peaks.[11] As a result, geologists and historians obtained objective visual evidence on which to base their theories. Man's knowledge of nature's catastrophes was increased by the daguerreotype's factual images, which were probably far different from the illusionistic avalanche Daguerre created at the Diorama.

When writing about the Bisson photographs and their great value for science, the *La Lumière* author also remarked that they were art works of great merit filled with beautiful detail and "picturesque effect." Although today we may use different terms to describe what makes this daguerreotype a work of art, there is no question that we share this earlier writer's conviction that such images *are* works of art. In this daguerreotype, the overwhelming, palpable presence given to the boulders by the shadowy recesses and the sharp ridges of the overhanging ledges make the image more than a descriptive record of their appearance. The image is also a memory of the impression these distinctive, solid forms had on the eye of the artist. The dual nature of the daguerreotype process thus makes this piece both a remembrance of the visual experience of the maker and a scientific record of the objects depicted.

Ever since the time this daguerreotype was made, photographers have been fascinated by the unmoving reality of rocks. This daguerreotypist's work would feel at home with such images as the river studies by Carleton Watkins from the 1870s and Aaron Siskind's studies on the shores of Martha's Vineyard in the 1950s. It is rare that a work intended to inform also becomes a work of art, but as we will see in other examples in this book, information and aesthetics are sometimes hard to separate in a daguerreotype.

PLATE 41

PLATE 42

JULES ITIER
French (1802–1877)
Portrait of an Egyptian Water Bearer
1845
Half plate
84.XT.184.1

So INTENSE WAS the Egyptian desert sun when Itier made this daguerreotype that his camera found enough light to operate in the dark cavern beneath the large foundation stones of an unidentified ruin across the Nile from the Temple of Kom Ombo. Covered over with palm fronds for additional protection from the heat, this cave-like place, adjacent to a water wheel, served as a stable for the donkeys and as a protected place for water jugs, as well as a refuge for the native helpers who accompanied Itier on his excursion along the Nile. An identical, or similar, place must also have served Itier as a darkroom where he could prepare his plates.[12]

One aspect of this scene that makes it unusual among the growing number of images then being taken in from Egypt is that this daguerreotype is an anthropological record, not an archaeological one. Itier clearly intended the subject of this scene to be the turbaned, heavily robed figure with a distinctive face—a portrait of an Egyptian native. Other photographers included natives in their views of monuments, but primarily to serve simply as human yardsticks to provide scale for the scene. Maxime Du Camp (1822–1894) told in his journal how he used one of his servants, Hadji Ismail, for this purpose and contrasted his personality with Fergally, another of his helpers. His interest in them, however, was piqued by the difference in their attitudes, rather than by their racial distinctions.[13]

Itier was not alone, however, in using the daguerreotype to make this type of cultural observation, for at the same moment, in different parts of the world, two other French daguerreotypists were recording the appearance of the natives they encountered. Theodore Tiffereau (active 1842) was photographing the inhabitants in Mexico, and E. Thiesson (active 1844) was doing the same in Mozambique. Already, in 1845, the idea of a museum to house these new documents showing different members of the human race had been proposed by Antoine Serres, a professor of comparative anatomy at the Jardin des Plantes in Paris and the president of the Academy of Sciences.[14]

In a later article entitled "Photographie Anthropologique," Serres specifically described the key role played by the daguerreotype in determining "the truthful representation of human types." He pointed out that, with few exceptions, previous representations of natives had been idealized and that, in fact, almost all of the illustrators had simply shown native costumes being worn by European-looking types. "Art shone" in those representations, he said, "at the expense of reality." What anthropology needed, Serres asserted, was the reality—naked and without art—that the daguerreotype could provide.[15]

Itier's record of this Egyptian native is, therefore, more than just a remarkable daguerreotype. It is an initial step toward providing the visual records of racial types on which future ethnographic studies would be based.

PLATE 42

PLATE 43
_____

UNKNOWN FRENCH PHOTOGRAPHER
Lottery Announcement
About 1852
Two half plates and six quarter plates (reduced)
84.XT.265.21

THE FACES STARING OUT from these eight daguerreotypes of residents in a French asylum exert a powerful impression. Their peculiar expressions immediately attract our attention, but they remain elusive, lost within themselves. The portraits have been brought together in an unusual presentation, assembled on a cardboard mount covered by a paper mat inscribed at the top with the mysterious title *"Galerie Historique,"* whose meaning only becomes apparent when placed in a broad context.

The concept that facial expressions were the key to an individual's mind and soul was an ancient idea that had gained new currency in 1775 through the work of Johann Lavater (1741–1801).[16] His illustrations of different types of facial expressions and his explanations of what each indicated about a person's mental state became the subject of serious debate in Europe. Regardless of whether Lavater's ideas were accepted or rejected, they led other scientists to make their own observations, particularly the physicians who were supervising the increasing number of asylums being opened for the insane.

Drawings and engraved portraits had been used to record the appearance of asylum patients, but such representations were very generalized. They did not adequately record, for example, the specific facial distortions that were thought to reveal the state of the inner mind. Such depictions of each minuscule emotion were, however, provided by the daguerreotype. The scientists, as they themselves declared, could now move beyond the generalized primitive suggestions of Lavater to observations based on the factually recorded facial expressions of specific individuals. By accumulating such accurate records of a patient's visual appearance, a system could be developed to classify types of mental illnesses. The invisible could be revealed by the visible.[17]

The collection of daguerreotypes presented in this unusual poster-like assemblage reflects this approach. It shows different types of demented persons—ranging from monomaniacs to alcoholics—sheltered in an asylum. The purpose of this presentation, however, was not concerned with scientific theory; the individual daguerreotypes of these patients were gathered on this display board to serve a more practical end. The hand-lettered inscriptions at the bottom, *"La Loterie"* and *"au bénéfice des originaux,"* make its purpose clear—a lottery was being held to raise money to assist the asylum in caring for patients like these. Although used in France for centuries to raise money for special building projects or to enrich the royal coffers, all national lotteries were officially banned in 1838. Exceptions were made, however, for local lotteries that raised money for the fine arts or for philanthropic charities, as was done with this lottery.[18]

The institutional character of this grouping is evident from the uniform manner in which the daguerreotypes were taken. Each person was placed in an identical setting with similar harsh illumination, and each was crowded within the photograph's edges, thus intensifying the patient's apparent condition. Given the crudeness and execution of both the design and the quality of the daguerreotypes, this presentation was probably of provincial origin, displayed in a local tobacco shop or post office. The title in the upper part of the piece—*"Galerie Historique"*—is probably intended to be a sardonic comment, since such a title was generally used to describe published collections of biographies of famous monarchs and statesmen. The phrase *"au bénéfice des originaux"* also probably has a double meaning. *Originaux* can refer simply to the original subjects of the photographs, but *originaux* was also an expression used for people whose behavior was out of the ordinary.

Prizes would have been offered to encourage ticket buyers not motivated simply by the desire to support good causes. From what we can learn from other sources, these prizes apparently were not of great intrinsic value, but the novel use and powerful imagery of these daguerreotypes must have made an unusually strong appeal.

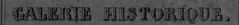

GALERIE HISTORIQUE.

EN LOTERIE

AU BÉNÉFICE DES ORIGINAUX.

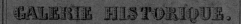

GALERIE HISTORIQUE.

EN LOTERIE

AU BÉNÉFICE DES ORIGINAUX.

PLATE 44

UNKNOWN FRENCH PHOTOGRAPHER
Man with Open Mouth
About 1852
Quarter plate
84.XT.402.4

WITHIN THE DAGUERREIAN IMAGERY created in the mid-nineteenth century, this example makes a startling impression. We are brought so suddenly and immediately into the presence of this man that we are momentarily confused by the experience. It is rare for a daguerreotype to have such an effect, yet this work lacks all the subtle gradations of light and dark or the gentle contrasts of texture so typical of the art. These effects have been passed over in order to take advantage of only one thing—the daguerreotype's ability to record fact. Clearly this is not an image sought by the sitter but one made to record a physical condition.

Even that distinction is not adequate to describe this obtrusive image, for within the tight space into which the head is forced, the area most brightly and brilliantly lit only occupies the very center part of the face—the eyes, nose, and mouth. But these are not singled out here as if to define a type of human expression an artist might be called upon to paint. This is not an illustration, like those from the collections of engravings published at the time, to instruct painters how to depict human emotions, nor is it the face of an actor practicing how to express inner emotions. Instead, this is an image only the daguerreotype could produce—a direct record unaltered by the pencil of the artist—showing the distorted face of a man forced to assume this position. His unfocused and strangely asymmetrical eyes offer us a vision of pain, but no windows into his soul. His face might well have been included with the asylum patients portrayed in the previous example (Plate 43).

Something else, however, is responsible for our fascination with this image, for even within the unusual face, the focus is clearly directed to his open mouth, which seems to be open not in a scream of protest nor an expression of agony, but by command. He had been directed to open his mouth widely, pulling back his lips, to expose the deformities of his teeth and diseased gums. If his appearance suggests he was an inmate of an institution, he could well have been available to the staff for research. This photograph probably was not intended to guide any treatment of his condition but, instead, to help record different types of dental disease.[19]

Research into this area began in the mid-eighteenth century, particularly after oral surgeons became independent from the general surgical guilds. Publications appeared at that time in France, England, and Germany detailing and classifying the different types of dental afflictions. In the early nineteenth century, there was an increasing interest in determining the causes of such disease, including the problem of gum disease. The lower right side of the patient's mouth displayed in this daguerreotype shows the ravages of this disease. With our broader understanding of what this daguerreotype represents, we can look upon its subject as one whose afflictions contributed to future scientific knowledge. This record also exemplifies why scientists in all fields embraced the daguerreotype for the new factual information it could provide them.

PLATE 44

HORATIO B. KING
American (1820–1889)
Seth Eastman at Dighton Rock
July 7, 1853
Half plate (reversed)
84.XT.182

PHOENICIAN VOYAGERS, Viking warriors, Portuguese explorers, or American Indian record keepers? All were said to have been responsible for the mysterious markings carved into the face of this boulder, located in Massachusetts some ten miles up the Taunton River from the open sea. Dighton Rock's existence was first noted in 1680, after which descriptions and illustrations of its pictographs and inscriptions appeared in both the old and new worlds, ranging from accounts in the popular press to a scholarly folio issued by the Copenhagen Society in 1790.

As none of the interpretations of these markings agreed with one another, the New-York Historical Society asked Henry Schoolcraft, a historian of Native American tribes, to visit the site.[20] His account of his trip in 1847 reveals the obstacles faced by anyone wishing to record the markings. First of all, the monolithic rock was totally exposed only at ebb tide, and even then the markings were covered with "a light marine scum" deposited by the several feet of water that partially covered it at high tide. Only by removing all this deposit, Schoolcraft pointed out, could any scientific examination take place.

Schoolcraft related, in great detail, his experience in deciphering the inscriptions. He approached the rock in a skiff rowed across the river by a young boy, who, he tells us, had gone over earlier that morning and highlighted the figures with chalk, even turning one into a fanciful image of a deer. Schoolcraft made sketches of the inscriptions from his shaky seat on the boat, while the lad rowed it about to get the best light on the markings. He published his report four years later in the first of his impressive six-volume work, *The Indian Tribes of the United States*. There he stated his conclusion that, despite the difficulties of carrying out his observations, "it was evident . . . that there were two diverse and wholly distinct characters employed, namely, an Algonquin and an Icelandic inscription."

In 1853, Schoolcraft decided to have a daguerreotype made of the rock and commissioned the illustrator of his book, Captain Seth Eastman (1808–1875), to obtain one.[21] Eastman was a talented artist who had taught drawing at West Point and spent many years at frontier outposts, where he both painted and made daguerreotypes of Native American tribal life.[22] For the Dighton Rock photograph, Eastman called on the services of the daguerreotypist Horatio B. King, from the nearby town of Taunton, to assist him. Probably recalling Schoolcraft's remarks about chalking the inscriptions, Eastman prepared the surface to be photographed by deepening and whitening the markings. (Under magnification the tool Eastman used can be seen in his hand.) To be able to include the full eleven-foot length of the rock, King had to set up his tripod and camera in the river. Apparently he used only a portrait lens, since the distant landscape is blurred but the inscription is sharply defined.[23]

When Schoolcraft published a reproduction of this daguerreotype in the fourth volume of his history (1854), he had no hesitation in reversing his earlier identification to accord with what he saw in the daguerreotype. The new visual evidence, he said, was proof that the inscriptions were "entirely Indian." His previous belief that part of the markings were Icelandic was now rejected. In subsequent references to Dighton Rock, Schoolcraft cited the daguerreotype as "correcting" any previous illustrations, including the drawing he had published in the first volume of 1851. For Schoolcraft, the visual evidence of the daguerreotype even supplanted his own personal inspection of the site. For him, its image was a welcome and incontestable demonstration of the truth.

PLATE 45

PLATE 46

Jean-Gabriel Eynard
Swiss (1775–1863)
Scene at Eynard's Country House
1846
Quarter plate
84.XT.255.46

From the moment the world began to record itself by means of the daguerreotype, the Muse of history, Clio, had to expand her attributes from only the quill and scroll to include the lens of the camera. Not all historians were able to encompass this new reality immediately. They had no experience in receiving visual information that had not come through an interpreter: the natural scene transformed by the brush and pen of an artist or by the burin of an engraver. Now the daguerreotype provided them with raw data, and they had to become familiar with what Poe had praised as "the new visual language."

Although this new language might not be readily understood or practiced, it was building a vast new vocabulary that would, in future years, be used to write history. Particularly in these early years of visual documentation, details of everyday life were being recorded unconsciously. It is unlikely, for example, that when Jean-Gabriel Eynard took this daguerreotype of several workers on his Swiss estate he intended to provide material for a history of his time. He was primarily interested in making a successful composition, showing a rhythmical grouping of figures in the stable yard.

Nevertheless Eynard did provide historians more than a century later with specific facts about the workers, their clothes, their relative status, and their tools—an infinite number of details were unknowingly documented for the future. Oliver Wendell Holmes especially appreciated this aspect of photography, and he chose as an example of this unconscious heritage one of the most strikingly visible elements recorded in this view. Holmes mused about the benefit future historians would gain by being able to look back at old photographs and discover such an accidental detail as a clothesline. Seeing the laundered sheets that had been hung out to dry would, in his view, bring to life the people who had used them.[24]

PLATE 46

THIS SENSITIVE POSTMORTEM of a child is a factual record of a lost life turned into a hauntingly beautiful image through the artistic talent of the daguerreotypist.[25] Charles Durheim's abilities are clearly evident from both the quality of the composition and the way he handles light almost as if it were a pen or pencil. Indeed, his advertisements spoke not only of his skill as a daguerreotypist but also as an artist making drawings in ink and crayon. It was his experience in both these arts that guided him in making the sensitive artistic decisions that produced this beautiful portrait.

To begin with, Durheim built up a pattern of soft drapery folds across the foreground, rising diagonally to the right where the folds become deeper and fuller. He further softened the entire foreground by allowing it to be slightly out of focus. As a result, the body of the child is softly enfolded and appears already to be in a place apart. Within this enclosing space, Durheim focused his lens sharply on the child's face, which, beneath the dark cap of hair, is turned toward the viewer. Each feature—eyebrows, lashes, cheeks, nose, mouth, and chin—is clearly delineated and delicately colored, creating an indelible image of this child.

These features are further emphasized by the light, falling first on the scalloped collar around the neck, then on the thin but crisply etched folds of the gown. This area in the center of the plate almost appears to be an artist's study of white drapery rather than a covering for the body, an impression that adds to the peacefulness of the scene. Its effect is so successful that its disturbance by the bent elbow and arm is startling and almost seems to be a sign of movement, but the tranquillity is quickly restored by the delicate play of lace that leads to the folded hands. The bent arm is only a recollection of the life that is gone.

Through such a careful arrangement of the child's body and the bedclothes, Durheim has shown his artistic awareness of the value of a skillful composition. His reliance upon light to create simultaneously the effects of reality, individuality, and remoteness reveals his abilities with the camera. Used together, he has provided the family with a moving visual record of the child taken from them.

PLATE 47

PLATE 48

UNKNOWN FRENCH PHOTOGRAPHER
"Cherubini and the Muse of Lyric Poetry," by Jean-Auguste-Dominique Ingres
1841
Quarter plate (reversed)
84.XT.265.26

As soon as the first daguerreian studios opened, they offered their services to copy works of art—paintings, engravings, or sculpture. Because it gave a precise reproduction in infinite nuances of light and dark, the daguerreotype was welcomed by artists and patrons who wanted a copy of their work. This new machine was said to make mirror images of great works of art without artistic pretensions of its own. Send your camera to the Louvre, suggested critic Jules Janin, and you will shortly receive copies of paintings by Raphael or even a portrait done by the master hand of Ingres.[26]

This daguerreotype of the portrait of Luigi Cherubini (1760–1842) by Jean-Auguste-Dominique Ingres (1780–1867) was made when the canvas still was on its easel in late 1841.[27] It was probably photographed immediately after the artist had completed certain changes made to satisfy the sitter.[28] Only by virtue of this daguerreotype can we recapture the original appearance of Ingres's painting, even though it is without color. Today the painting's condition has deteriorated so severely that, despite sophisticated restoration attempts, the meaning Ingres wanted the painting to convey can no longer be fully understood or appreciated.

Essentially, the painter's intention was to depict Cherubini, the renowned Italian composer, director of the Paris Conservatory since 1822, and longtime friend of Ingres, in a setting that would underscore the musician's genius by showing him accompanied by the Muse of poetic inspiration. It was a novel and daring concept that required joining the worlds of realism and idealism. Ingres appears to have deliberately emphasized the difference between the two by presenting the portrait of Cherubini in an unusually realistic way and rendering the painting of the Muse in a distinctly classical style, giving her, in addition, a separate setting reminiscent of Pompeiian wall painting. By attempting to bring these two approaches together in a single painting, Ingres apparently wished to pay homage both to the composer and to his genius as an inspiration to other musicians, a view widely shared by nineteenth-century composers, especially Beethoven and Brahms.

Unfortunately, Ingres chose to depict these two worlds by physically joining two separate pieces of canvas. The portrait of the composer at our right was originally a completely independent painting, executed by Ingres in 1834 and taken later that year to Rome, where he began a six-year term as director of the French Academy. He did not begin work on his concept of the expanded painting until near the end of his Roman stay in 1840, when he glued the earlier portrait of Cherubini onto a new canvas large enough to add the poetic imagery. Over the years, the physical joining of the two parts has progressively become more visible. The paint of the two sections has aged differently, making the separation between the two independent parts of the canvas even more evident and thus also removing the union Ingres had hoped to depict between the composer and his inspiration.

Shortly after the painting's completion, it was purchased by King Louis-Philippe. Following the practice of the time, a painting of this status would have a reproduction issued by a printmaker granted this privilege by the artist. In this case, Louis-Henri Brevière (1797–1869) was chosen to make the official lithograph. This 1843 print displays, by its unusual accuracy and its strong contrasts of light and dark, the influence of the new daguerreian process. Brevière himself had taken up this new art form immediately after it was announced, and he may well have been the maker of this daguerreotype, intending it to serve as a model for his graphic reproduction.[29]

Ingres would not have objected to using the invention, for he was an early advocate of the benefit daguerreotypes would give to painters. In fact, Ingres had in his possession two daguerreotype portraits of Cherubini, and although he said they were "horrible" images,[30] a description often used about portraits taken in those initial days, he might have used them while painting the 1841 version of the portrait of the musician, for the realism shown in the head of Cherubini strongly suggests such an influence.

PLATE 48

PLATE 49

UNKNOWN FRENCH PHOTOGRAPHER
Engraving after Franz Xaver Winterhalter's 1853 Painting, "Florinda"
About 1857
Half plate
84.XT.835.7

THE PAINTER OF THE SCENE represented in this brilliant daguerreotype, Franz Winterhalter (1805–1873), normally confined his talents to meeting the enormous demand by European royalty for his flattering portraits. For the Paris Salon of 1853, however, instead of portraits of nobility, the artist decided to display a vast narrative painting (six by eight feet) to show off his painterly skills more vividly. His choice was this lively and rhythmical grouping of seminude female figures within a verdant landscape. Through their flesh tones and the lustrous hues of their silk and satin draperies, Winterhalter created a vibrant pattern of color across the entire width of the painting.[31]

Except for the painting's title, *Florinda*, there is slight indication that the scene illustrates the key moment in an ancient Spanish legend when the Visigoth king Rodriguez saw the beautiful Florinda at her bath and, falling violently in love, seduced her. Her noble Spanish father, seeking revenge, invited the North African Moors to help him defeat Rodriguez in battle. Their success, according to the story, led to the Moors' eight-hundred-year rule over Spain.

Whether many viewers at the Royal Academy exhibit of 1852 in London, where this painting was first displayed, recalled this obscure legend is doubtful. Regardless, the romantic tale provided a veil of respectability for the eroticism of the painting. One critic even spoke of the "Miltonian purity" of the artist's vision. Surprising as it seems today, Queen Victoria so admired this painting that she bought it as a birthday present for her Prince Albert, thereby requiring Winterhalter to paint a second version for display in the 1853 Salon in Paris. Amusingly, when it was on view in London, a critic deplored the "Frenchness" of the models, while a Parisian critic at the Salon objected to their "Englishness."

Four years after the 1853 Salon, this giant work by Winterhalter[32] had not found a purchaser but was in the possession of the prominent Parisian art gallery, Goupil et Cie., which often promoted its paintings by commissioning engraved reproductions.[33] Although a daguerreotype copy, like the one made after the painting of Cherubini by Ingres (Plate 48), could be made in far less time, Goupil et Cie. probably first chose to have an engraving made of the Winterhalter work because, unlike today's black-and-white film, the daguerreian plate was not equally sensitive to all colors. A daguerreotype taken directly from the painting could not convey the varied hues radiating from the flesh tones and silky draperies.[34]

However, translating the colorful painting into the brilliant lights and darks of an engraving provided an object from which a daguerreotype could then be made that conveyed all the brilliance and nuances of the artist's palette. Indeed, because of the daguerreotype's own remarkable sensitivity to light and dark, its silver canvas could transform the engraved image into a work of even greater richness of brilliant whites and velvety blacks. In this instance, an especially superior daguerreotype was created because the photographer was working from an early state of the engraving, when its richness would have been at its peak.[35]

With the intensity added by the daguerreotype, the photographed engraving appears so lush it seems as if we were seeing the original painting reflected in a mirror. In fact, it is just this scintillating aspect of the daguerreotype that brings it closer to Winterhalter's original work. Its reduced size, along with the monochromatic depiction of the colorful painting, emphasize the erotic density of the original work; the maidens taking part in the legendary scene now appear more forthrightly as nudes. Overall, the daguerreotype rendering conveys a more sensual nature than the original painting, particularly when reduced to this intimate size, enclosed like a jewel in a rich, daguerreian case. Held in the hand, such a presentation of the painting could powerfully convey to a potential purchaser the true nature of the original painting.

PLATE 49

PLATE 50

UNKNOWN FRENCH PHOTOGRAPHER
Nude Model
About 1855
Stereograph, left plate of two sixth plates, with applied color (enlarged)
84.XT.405.13

IN ADDITION TO PROVIDING COPIES of their creations, artists received another gift from the daguerreotypist—the possibility of acquiring permanent factual images of the human figure to guide their work. Such photographs of nudes, or "academies" as they were called, became available in London as early as July 1840, when Antoine Claudet advertised daguerreotypes showing "figures from the living models." The models, who were accustomed to holding lengthy poses for painters, now began doing the same for photographers. Also in 1840, the Parisian optical firm of Lerebours, which already possessed a large stock of daguerreotype views of monuments, began offering sets of nude studies for use by painters. Such studies quickly became widespread because, in contrast to living models, they were less expensive, more convenient,[36] and completely surpassed the previous lithographic examples (Figure 23).[37] These photographic studies were even more sought after because, until the late nineteenth century, female models were prohibited in the classrooms of the École des Beaux Arts.

A leading proponent of the use of these studies was the renowned painter Eugène Delacroix (1798–1863), who called the daguerreotype more than just a tracing of an object, but a mirror of one. In 1850, he pointed out to his students that these studies displayed details of the human body that often went unseen when an artist drew from a living model. By studying and copying daguerreotypes, he said, an artist would gain fuller understanding of the body's structure. In addition, the daguerreotype's gradations of light allowed the true surface qualities of the body to emerge, showing exactly their solidity or softness. Delacroix acted on his belief by collecting and using daguerreian studies of the human body and even commissioned photographs to be made of models in positions he was considering using in his paintings.[38]

FIGURE 23
BERNARD ROMAIN JULIEN
French (1802–1871)
Study of a Nude
Lithograph published in *Cours des Dessin* (Paris 1833)
Cliché Bibliothèque Nationale de France

The daguerreotype reproduced here exemplifies one such study taken after the introduction in the 1850s of the stereographic camera. In this form, the nude photographic studies resembled a living model even more strongly and led to a greater number being produced. What makes this piece so distinctive is the position the model was required to hold, as well as the daguerreotypist's ability to light the body so the articulation of its parts is clearly defined. At the same time, shadows are used to convey the different qualities of the body's surface in relation to the underlying musculature. The daguerreotypist also has sharpened our sense of the tension exerted when the body is held in this position by contrasting it with the inert folds of the cloth covering the posing support, a comparison that became even more evident when the image was delicately hand-colored.

Even though the stereographic nudes might be substituted for living models, they did not serve the purpose for which Delacroix had praised the earlier two-dimensional photographic images, because the stereographs did not transform the three-dimensional body onto a flat surface. Whichever form was chosen by an artist, it became clear that both were extensively employed, for as the Parisian critic Théophile Gautier said of the paintings on view at the 1861 Salon, "the daguerreotype, which has neither been given credit nor medal, has nevertheless worked hard at this exhibition" and "spared much posing of the model."[39]

PLATE 50

PLATE 51

ALBERT SANDS SOUTHWORTH and JOSIAH JOHNSON HAWES
American (1811–1894; 1808–1901)
"The Greek Slave" by Hiram Powers
1848
Quarter plate (reversed)
84.XT.1582.1

A UNIQUELY LIT VIEW of the sculptural masterwork *The Greek Slave* by Hiram Powers is transformed by this daguerreotype into a dazzling image of light and shadow. We owe its impact both to the singular presentation that the sculptor designed for displaying his work and to the supreme skills of the Boston daguerreotypists, Southworth and Hawes. The record they made of how the sculpture appeared when it was on view in Boston in the summer of 1848[40] allows us to comprehend the viewers' astonishment at how a marble statue could convey such a sensuous quality. That effect is recaptured for us in this exceptional daguerreian record of the event.

Hiram Powers, a native of Vermont, was one of the most successful members of the American group of sculptors who, in the mid-nineteenth century, had established their studios in Italy, seeking that country's more receptive attitude toward artists as well as the skilled workers who could translate their plaster models into marble and stone—of which Italy had an incomparable variety. *The Greek Slave* was the first work by Powers that brought him world fame and established America as a nation where, despite its reputation as a wilderness, first-rate artists could be produced.

After his arrival in Florence in 1837, Powers's studio became a magnet for all important visitors whose praise for his work resounded in their letters home. *The Greek Slave* was, therefore, the first chance America had to see an actual work by him, and its arrival in the cities on its tour was highly anticipated. By the time *The Greek Slave* arrived in Boston, it—and another version of it—already had been on view in New York, Baltimore, and Philadelphia in a triumphant tour begun the previous year. That a completely nude statue could have been successfully put on public view in mid-nineteenth-century America was due to the context in which its subject was placed. Protests over its nakedness were raised by some church leaders and their congregations in every city where it was shown, including Boston, but other religious and civic dignitaries made strong statements in its support. The rationale of their defense rested in the subject matter of the piece, for it does not represent a classical Venus—as we might believe from this view—but a Christian martyr. Her true meaning is only revealed when viewing the front of the sculpture, where the cause of her nudity is explained. A heavy chain shackles her wrists, and suspended from her garments, discarded on the post, is a small cross. She represents a subject from recent history familiar to the audience—the fate of Greek Christian women captured by the Turks and exposed in the public market place to be sold as slaves. By casting his nude sculpture in this role, Powers drew a veil of innocence over the erotic white marmoreal splendor of the sculpture.[41]

The experience of viewing *The Greek Slave* was masked, therefore, as a spiritual experience, although the managers Powers had hired to supervise the tour apparently trod a prudent path by scheduling afternoon showings exclusively for ladies and families. The tour was a great financial success, since at some exhibition sites, if handbills are to be believed, over fifty thousand visitors arrived daily to stand or sit before her. The silence of the huge crowds impressed many who recorded their experience; most described the hush of reverential awe that overcame the viewers as soon as they stepped into the statue's presence. Her purity of character, they remarked, was enforced by the dignity of her stance and by the way she defiantly averted her eyes from examination by her Turkish captors. Journalists never failed to point out this feature, ascribing it to the inner strength of character derived from her Christian beliefs.

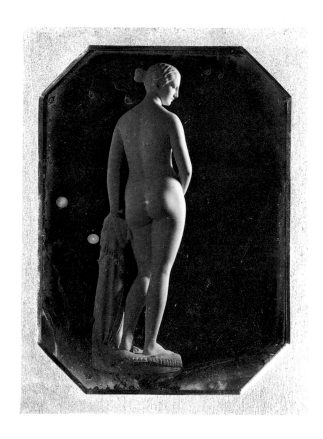

PLATE 51

FIGURE 24
Re-creation of a Lost Daguerreotype by Southworth and Hawes
Showing Three Views of "The Greek Slave by Hiram Powers"
Original 1847 marble in the collection of the Newark
Museum, gift of Franklin Murphy, Jr., 1926

When the sculpture finally appeared in Boston in June 1848, it was displayed in Horticulture Hall, mounted on a pedestal designed by Powers so it could be slowly rotated before the viewers, exposing each side in succession. This presentation recaptured the original vision of Powers, who had conceived of the statue as a series of parts flowing in continuous movement throughout the body of the figure. This effect was heightened by his further demand that the sculpture be seen within a canopy of full-length, crimson velvet hangings, illuminated from above by a hanging gas lamp. This lamp was designed so that its rays fell only upon specifically selected areas of the marble.[42] The warmth of praise for the piece, as well as the cash receipts, varied in proportion to each location's ability to provide the conditions Powers had specified for its display.

The limitations under which Southworth and Hawes had to make this daguerreotype underscore why their accomplishment is so remarkable. Perhaps their willingness to undertake the assignment was the reason the manager of the tour gave them an exclusive right to photograph it on its viewing in Boston. The city's other prominent daguerreotypist, John A. Whipple, was not permitted by the tour manager to photograph the sculpture until the day before the exhibition closed, almost three months later.[43]

One daguerreotype by Southworth and Hawes of the sculpture was singled out for special mention in a Boston newspaper as a particularly beautiful artistic achievement (Figure 24). What so amazed the reporter was that the photographers had been able to depict three separate representations of the statue on a single plate—a back, front, and side view— "each conveying a very perfect idea of the original."[44] Another tour-de-force accomplishment by Southworth and Hawes was reported by them in an 1851 advertisement, in which they singled out for special praise an enormous single plate (13 ½ by 16 ½ inches) that they had made of the sculpture. Not only did Southworth and Hawes boast of the daguerreotype's unusual size, they also described the very special way it was displayed in their gallery: it was illuminated and magnified so that it projected a life-size image of the sculpture. Visitors to their studio were bewildered—how could the sculpture they knew to be on view at Horticultural Hall also be seen here in the daguerreotypist's studio? Using their own skills, Southworth and Hawes could match Powers in the presentation of his work![45]

In addition to these unusual examples, Southworth and Hawes would have made individual daguerreotypes for sale to viewers, a practice the tour manager is reported to have encouraged without Powers's knowledge. The daguerreotype shown here is special because it documents the sculpture as it appeared in its distinctive setting under artificial light and because it shows the sculpture as the side flows into the back of the figure—a view that many critics considered the most beautiful of all its aspects.[46]

Chapter Four

AN INTRUDER IN THE REALM

PRAISE SHOWERED ON the daguerreotype process by scientists was not necessarily echoed by artists, who exhibited a disdainful, even fearful, attitude toward the new invention as yet another intruder in their field. To them, the daguerreotype joined an army of devices that had invaded their profession during the last quarter-century. Although described as aids to artists, these inventions also were touted as devices that allowed people who lacked natural artistic talent to produce satisfactory works of art. Such new processes and their claims reinvigorated centuries-old arguments over what could properly be claimed as the realm of art.

Most threatened by these mechanical developments were the graphic artists—engravers and etchers. The first shock to this often closely linked group of artists had come in about 1806 with the introduction into Paris of lithography, a reproductive process that particularly affected copyists of paintings or drawings.[1] Through lithography, artists could draw directly on a smooth stone surface to produce a printing plate. While professional pressmen made the final prints, lithography no longer required the services of the skilled engravers or etchers who previously would have transcribed the artist's work. Because the lithographic process encouraged very large editions, inexpensive popular prints soon began papering even the walls of garrets and workers' quarters. The bins of Parisian print sellers overflowed with lithographic representations of hazily lit landscapes, studies of flowers, historical scenes, and caricatures, all providing a vast increase in the visual imagery available to the broad public. In this sense, lithography paved the way for the even more extensive world of images the daguerreotype would soon unleash.

Like the daguerreotype, the lithographic process removed the need for an intermediary between an artist and the production of a work of art. Lithography threatened the livelihood of some traditional graphic artists, but it was not as direct a threat to their skills as were other machines introduced during these years. One of the earliest and most widely applicable of these was invented by Nicolas-Jacques Conté (1755–1805) in 1803 to speed production of the over eight hundred mammoth plates needed to illustrate the official scientific and archaeological report of Napoleon's Egyptian campaign.[2] Many of these plates were to depict large, uniform expanses of sky or desert. Before Conté's machine, such areas of undifferentiated texture were obtained by ruling by hand identical indentations on the plate to hold the ink. This task required an engraver with a completely steady hand capable of sustaining even pressure. Skies had always been particularly difficult to depict, although minor errors in their execution could easily be obscured by introducing clouds. Such a solution was not feasible, however, when representing the perpetually cloudless skies of Egypt. Conté's invention solved these problems by mechanically controlling the engraving tool. When the enormous project was completed, it was estimated that the Conté machine accomplished in two or three days what an artist working by hand would have needed six months to create. Conté's machine was soon adapted for other engraving projects, further undermining the makers of handmade prints.

Mechanical tools of all types intended to aid artists and amateurs were constantly being announced in the journals during the years preceding the introduction of the daguerreotype, but none created as much controversy as the diagraphe, a drawing machine invented in 1830 by Charles Gavard (born 1794).[3] Operating through a complex mechanical system that established points and interconnecting lines, the diagraphe facilitated copying the most intricate designs. The significance of Gavard's machine was of great concern to the artists of Paris, and its contribution was fiercely debated in 1831. Although it was agreed that the diagraphe might aid an artist in accomplishing certain mechanical tasks, artists could not resolve the volatile question of whether it stifled or encouraged genius. When, in 1836, Gavard was given permission to use his diagraphe to reproduce engravings of all the sculpture and furnishings of Versailles, another uproar among the artists occurred. One even wrote to L'Artiste, claiming that the diagraphe was destined to kill art.

Not only were the fields of the graphic arts and drawing being invaded by machines, but mechanical devices had also entered into the realm of sculpture. Just when François Arago announced the discovery of the daguerreotype, the press reported that a new machine by Achille Collas (1794–1859) allowed copying a work of sculpture to any desired scale without the assistance of an artist.[4] In August 1839, London's Literary Gazette, probably still in a pique about the success of the daguerreotype, went so far as to propose that the Collas copying machine would prove to be as remarkable a discovery as Daguerre's.

The appearance of the daguerreotype led the critic Jules Janin to write an essay encompassing all of the new mechanical innovations in what he called "this singular epoch."[5] He foresaw the sphere of the arts being invaded by the same mechanical transformations that already had taken place in the industrial world. He cited as an example Gavard's diagraphe, amusingly describing it as an instrument that commanded even the ceilings of Versailles to do its bidding. He also singled out the miraculous machine Collas had invented that could produce a perfectly reduced three-dimensional copy of the Venus de Milo. All these amazing devices, he said, were now joined by the daguerreotype, a machine he predicted would replace both drawing and engraving. He went even further to suggest that, before long, there would be machines that could dictate the comedies of Molière and the verses of Corneille. He did not foresee, however, that workers would become so threatened by machines that, during the Revolution of 1848, they would attack and destroy them in the textile and printing factories.[6]

Placing Daguerre's discovery within this context was, unfortunately, a natural consequence of all the other mechanical innovations that had recently entered into the production of works of art. Regardless of Daguerre's desire simply to capture the images seen in the camera obscura, his success became embroiled in the fierce aesthetic duel that was being waged by those who believed that anything produced by a machine must inherently lack the essence of the creative spirit.

On first hearing about the daguerreotype in 1836, the future restorer of France's medieval monuments, Eugène-Emmanuel Viollet-le-Duc, then a young student on his first tour of Italy, discounted all

such devices, saying that our souls will always pre-
fer the work of the hand to that of the machine.
He even suggested that Providence had built into
all such mechanical processes a certain imperfec-
tion that led us to reject the "slave" in favor of the
"idea."[7] Viollet-le-Duc's hostility to even the possibility that such a thing as a daguerreotype could exist
reveals the depth of the emotional opposition with
which one part of the artistic community greeted
the daguerreotype.

Daguerre surely anticipated such a reaction to
his invention, which would make it unnecessary to
employ copyists and more importantly threaten the
widespread use of artists to produce a convincing
representation of a scene from nature. Arago also
probably foresaw the potential negative reaction by
artists and tried to forestall it by consulting the academic painter, Paul Delaroche.[8] This artist's first
reaction was more positive than Arago perhaps
expected, for in the official report of April 3, 1839,
Delaroche is quoted only as saying that daguerreotypes would be of immense service to the fine arts
and that even the most skillful painters would find
them worthy of study, an endorsement reassuring
to painters.[9] In fact, nothing in Delaroche's official
endorsement explicitly addressed the potential painterly qualities of the daguerreotype; the qualities he
stressed were the same as those the scientists had
singled out for praise—the daguerreotype's amazing
capacity to precisely define the object before it.

This capacity, however, was only one aspect
of what Daguerre believed he had invented. The
daguerreotype was not seen by its inventor merely
as a substitute for making preparatory drawings
or as an aid for those who could not draw. His own
definition of the daguerreotype had been stated
simply and directly in 1838, in the preliminary
announcement he made of its discovery. It is not,
he said, merely "an instrument to be used to draw
nature," but a process giving nature the ability to be
her own artist.[10]

FIGURE 25
LOUIS JACQUES MANDÉ DAGUERRE
French (1787–1851)
Dessin Fumée—Fantasie
1826–27
Graphite and vaporized ink
84.XM.1019.1

That Daguerre should see his invention primarily as the creation of a new art form is not surprising, given the fact that his entire life had been
spent as an artist. Testimony to his attitude exists in
many forms. A particularly ironic one occurs in a
letter sent to Talbot in 1840 by the French scientist
Jean Baptiste Biot, one of the earliest admirers of
the daguerreotype process. In it Biot lamented how
unfortunate it was for science that Daguerre always
considered his results from the artistic view, never
from the higher purpose of contributing to the
progress of discovery in general.[11] In contrast, Samuel
Morse, the American inventor and painter who had
visited Daguerre's studio in 1839, later declaimed
"Honor to Daguerre, who has first introduced
Nature to us in the character of a *Painter*."[12]

Although Daguerre's fame and honors were
due to his gigantic illusionistic works at the panorama, Opèra, and Diorama, he also had produced,

FIGURE 26
LOUIS JACQUES MANDÉ DAGUERRE
French (1787–1851)
Still Life with Drape and Sculptures
1838–39
Whole-plate daguerreotype
Collection of the Musée Hyacinthe Rigaud, Perpignan,
France; Photo P. Jauzac, Perpignon

along with many other artists, lithographic prints for the enormous travel series of thousands of scenes produced by Baron J. Taylor, Charles Nodier, and Alphonse de Cailleux between 1820 and 1878.[13] All of Daguerre's lithographs show his skill at choosing favorable points of view and in employing light and dark to define the subjects. He also made individual drawings and sketches, almost all of which are directly related to scenes he was preparing for the

Diorama. Daguerre also executed several oil paintings, one of which, an interior scene of a Parisian chapel, was purchased by the state from the Salon of 1814 and has recently been installed in the new galleries at the Louvre. The most well-known, *Ruins of Holyrood Chapel*, which appeared in the Salon of 1824, is actually a reduced version of one of the enormous Dioramas.[14]

One unique form of drawing Daguerre invented about 1826 is specifically linked to his large-scale illusionary work. These small architectural renderings appear as if emerging from a cloud of mist or smoke and were called *dessins fumée*, or smoke drawings. (Figure 25). They represent scenes comparable to the canvases he was preparing for the Diorama at the same time, and the two art forms

FIGURE 27
LOUIS JACQUES MANDÉ DAGUERRE
French (1787–1851)
Still Life
About 1839
Whole-plate daguerreotype
Collection of the Société Française de Photographie

appear to be reflections of the same problem that Daguerre was then wrestling with—the insubstantiality of visual imagery.

Soon after their relationship began, Daguerre sent such a drawing as a gift to Niépce and described it in an accompanying letter as a "fantasy."[15] Niépce was seemingly puzzled by its relevance to their mutual interest. It is an early indication of the distance between the two men—Niépce was essentially concerned with the technology of multiple

images; Daguerre with the illusionistic quality of the object. Arago appears to have understood this difference of approach between the two, and it would seem to form the basis for his remark referring to Niépce as the "natural philosopher of Chalôns" and Daguerre as the "painter of Paris."[16]

Daguerre's desire for the daguerreotype to be accepted as a new art form is evident by the examples he chose to present to European heads of state as proof of his invention's potential. In each case, Daguerre always included a still-life composition, the same type of image he consistently had exhibited to studio visitors before the secret was disclosed and to the Assembly at the time they were considering his pension. He also chose to send a still life to the curator at the Louvre as proof of his dis-

FIGURE 28
LOUIS JACQUES MANDÉ DAGUERRE (attributed)
French (1787–1851)
Still Life
About 1839
Daguerreotype
© Musée des Arts et Métiers-CNAM,
Paris / Photo Studio CNAM

covery and gave Arago a still-life composition as a gift in gratitude for his support. To understand these curious and unique creations and the importance he gave them, they should be seen as statements by Daguerre of how this new art form did, indeed, invade the realm of the painter.

Actually, the still-life compositions are the second demonstration of the incursion of photography into the fine art of painting. The first was the most obvious—the absolute ability of an image produced

in a camera to depict objects in perfect perspective. Since the fifteenth century, any painter of quality had to master the rules of perspective, whether a work exhibited such knowledge directly, as in a painting of a city view, or indirectly, through the organization of a landscape or a group portrait. Each of Daguerre's Parisian scenes made clear that such expertise in perspective had now been supplanted by a machine that could make no errors, and some of the scenes went beyond the simple placing of objects in space to also locate them in time-of-day and weather. Importantly, like a painting—but unlike a print—each was unique.

The early still-life compositions (Figures 26–28) were even stronger statements by Daguerre regarding the status of this new art. Given the fact that only a few other artists in his immediate circle

FIGURE 29
HUBERT
French (d. 1839–40)
Still Life
1839
Daguerreotype
Collection of the Société Française de Photographie

(Figure 29) also produced them, and then only in the first years of the daguerreotype, it seems clear that Daguerre selected them to serve a specific purpose. If we look at these still lifes in the same light in which we considered his views of monuments—as exemplifying a principle of painting—it is apparent that they, too, were made with this aim. The still life embodied all the crucial challenges for the painter, requiring the artist to show visual sensitivity and skill in numerous ways: the choice of objects for their forms, textures, colors, and shapes—all care-

fully arranged and lighted within the space they filled, defined, and activated. In a small compass, all of these tests challenged the artist's ability to perform within an illusionistic format.

It was a long-held belief that a painter's ability to achieve pictorial unity could be judged by the skill in rendering, through light and dark, one particular object—a single bunch of grapes. A successful depiction of this one subject required a complete mastery over the use of light and dark to create the illusion of the separate, but clustered, orbs of the grapes. This observation, believed to have first been made by Titian in the sixteenth century, was repeated through the seventeenth and eighteenth centuries; even in the 1830s it was still a popular shorthand criticism of an artist's ability. Art dictionaries of the period defined "bunch of grapes" as a term used to express a perfect grouping of numerous objects through the effects of shadow and light.[17]

Daguerre met the "bunch of grapes" challenge head-on. All of the still lifes offer, in different degrees of complexity, a daring exhibition of how flawlessly the daguerreotype could define a group of diverse objects through minute shadings and complete control over light and dark. In almost all of the examples he also introduced sculpture by way of statuettes. None of the numerous art students who had spent hours drawing from casts could escape the comparison. These still lifes are, in effect, Daguerre's deliberate challenge to the skill of painters, and his success must have been apparent to artists for what it was: an invasion of their field. All of the work Daguerre had done in the theater, the panorama, and the Diorama had been conceived as creating objects of illusion. There is no reason to believe that his

FIGURE 30
SAMUEL F. B. MORSE and WILLIAM DRAPER
American (1791–1872; 1811–1882)
Still Life
1839–40
Quarter-plate daguerreotype
Photographic History Collection, National Museum of
American History, Smithsonian Institution

FIGURE 31
LOUIS JACQUES MANDÉ DAGUERRE
French (1787–1851)
Landscape, 1850–51
Finger painting on reverse of glass with separate brown velvet backing
Photographic History Collection, National Museum of American History,
Smithsonian Institution

FIGURE 32
Showing Figure 31 with half of velvet backing removed

personal interest in making these still-life daguerreo-types was any different.

One observer of Daguerre's still lifes who clearly understood their message and took it away with him was Samuel Morse. Although he does not specifically refer to the still lifes when reporting on his visit to Daguerre's studio, some of his published observations appear to derive from a reaction to such pieces. The most compelling evidence, how-ever, of Morse's recognition of their meaning and importance comes from a daguerreotype still-life composition he himself made with his close friend and coworker, William Draper (Figure 30). Probably dating from 1839 or 1840, it is the only known Amer-ican example comparable to the still-life daguerreo-types originating in Paris.[18]

The image depicts drawings by Morse casually pinned to a textured hanging similar to one appear-ing in a still life by Daguerre (Figure 26), in front of which is arranged a series of three-dimensional objects. In the center appears a chemistry book and laboratory utensils. Apparently Morse and Draper thought of this daguerreotype as symbolizing a col-laboration between art and science. If so, this piece certainly would have pleased Daguerre, who had spent so many years to bring about such a union.

Daguerre never lost his fascination with how the thin line between appearance and reality could be conveyed by a work of art, for in his later years, as described by early biographers, he continued other projects emerging from this obsession. One example is the painting given to the American daguerreo-typist Charles Meade by Daguerre's widow (Figure 31).[19] The dark and eerily lit landscape whirls as if caught in a raging storm, its topography barely visi-ble; only a building on a hill at the left suggests the presence of civilization. Looking closely at the sur-face, we can see that Daguerre used his thumb, not a brush, to create this scene. The paint swirled around by his bare hand has modeled the forms. On even closer examination, we discover that Daguerre had executed it on the reverse of a glass plate and that the medium he used was a transparent substance, prob-ably related to a material used in the Diorama paint-ings. Like a scene at the Diorama, this landscape only becomes visible under special lighting conditions—in this case when seen against a dark brown velvet cloth (Figure 32). Daguerre was revisiting his earlier creations but still inventing new forms of art.[20]

The possibilities of the visual language pro-vided and encouraged by the daguerreotype were explored by Daguerre's followers. On their own, they developed this new art form following indi-vidual concepts and sensibilities. The potential of daguerreian art first set out by its inventor became the inspiration and guide for those who practiced photography in the future. Almost a century later, the noted photographer Edward Weston (1886–1958) stated, "For beautiful image quality, the best of the old daguerreotypes have never been equaled."[21]

PLATES

Chapter Four

PLATE 52

JEAN-GABRIEL EYNARD
Swiss (1775–1863)
Self-Portrait with a Folio Volume
About 1845
Half plate
84.XT.255.62

WHILE SOME PRACTITIONERS of the new art of daguerreotypy had taken the style of famous portrait painters of the past for their inspiration, particularly those whose fame rested on their brilliant handling of light and shadow, the maker of this daguerreotype went so far as to imitate a favorite subject of one of those masters. Here, the Swiss daguerreotypist Jean-Gabriel Eynard has placed himself in the pose of a saint similar to those portrayed in paintings by seventeenth-century Dutch artists. Many such paintings represent saints reading—a frequent choice being Saint Jerome in his study. The image of a man reading occurs frequently in the list of Rembrandt's paintings, etchings, and drawings, sometimes without any specific religious connection. Eynard certainly was familiar with them and may even have owned one, as we know that a Rembrandt painting is listed in an early inventory of the works that made up his large art collection.[22] If this is indeed the case, we are in the presence of a very special self-portrait that reveals how Eynard pictured himself as the subject of a painting by a master artist, a choice that also discloses a facet of his own personality.

It is almost irrelevant to the meaning and power of this image to point out how beautifully Eynard has recreated the rich surface of a Rembrandt painting or print by his choice of a fur collar and the long, twisted fringe on the edge of the table. Both can easily be imagined as strokes of a brush or the scratch and rubbing of an etching tool. Yet both are achieved here by Eynard's understanding the abilities of the daguerreotype to produce such effects through the control of light and dark. Eynard's bent head is given a special sheen by the light from above that transforms the hair—even though precisely portrayed—into a sweep of paint by the artist's brush. Controlling the light source so that it appears to emanate from the open book is Eynard's secret for the beauty and accuracy of this daguerreotype, but the effectiveness of this illusion is a trick he learned from the artist he set out to imitate.

PLATE 52

PLATE 53

Unknown French Photographer
Sister of Charity Serving a Patient at the Hospice de Beaune
About 1848
Half plate with applied color
84.XT.404.6

THE MAKER OF THIS DAGUERREOTYPE clearly desired to stage a moment occurring in real life. An artist wanting to make a painting of a similar scene probably would have made pages of studies detailing the costumes, the space, and the poses of the figures. The daguerreotypist would also have made preliminary studies for depicting this moment in real life; but rather than making drawings, the daguerreotypist would have made frequent visits to the famous fifteenth-century hospital in Beaune, France, to study its light, become familiar with its architecture, observe the routine of the Sisters of Charity who served in it, and learn the characteristics of its indigent patients. Then, instead of taking sketches off to a studio, as an artist would, to combine them into a completed work, the daguerreotypist would return to the hospital itself and use his observations to guide the work with the camera.

By that time, the daguerreotypist would have chosen the spot within the beautiful cloister where the figures could be posed effectively and would have selected the moment when light would best serve the preconceived image.[23] In this case, the choice would be when the sun fully lighted the arcades of the courtyard at noon, allowing the subjects to be posed so they were sheltered from its direct rays but sufficiently illuminated to convey the distinctions between them. A primary concern would have been the danger of overexposure, easily possible because of the flowing white garment of the nun. The maker also would already have chosen these subjects, deliberately contrasting the beautiful face of the young nun with the time-worn face of her aged patient. Having made these artistic decisions, it only remained to pose and direct the two figures within the closed space.

The old man was placed slightly back from the open cloisters against the corridor wall, his cane set between his legs. The nun stands in pictorial isolation. Her white habit stresses her erect posture and leads up to the white Flemish coif, isolating her within the dark background. Her beautiful, serene face is completely framed, underscoring her relationship to the observer. Although she supports herself by placing one hand on the patient's shoulder, her other hand moved slightly as she held out the metal bowl to the patient. This slight blurring of the image does not take away from the tender genre scene the maker set out to portray but, in fact, increases its reality. The added color heightens the gentleness of the image and locates the figures securely in the space defined by the simple, but rich, contrasts between light and dark that the daguerreotype medium so readily creates. A maker as skilled as this one knew how to use the daguerreotype's new visual language in a work of art, combining the long-established ideals of painting with the new verities of the daguerreian process.

PLATE 53

PLATE 54

JEAN-GABRIEL EYNARD
Swiss (1775–1863)
Portrait of Two Servants
About 1845
Quarter plate
84.XT.255.31

BY RIGOROUS CONTROL of all the visual elements, Eynard has made this view of two servants in his household into a timeless work of art.[24] The human figures have been incorporated into a still life; the carefully considered relationship between their bodies is the bonding element that transforms them into a single composition. The clarity and precision that the daguerreotype gives to the folds and pleats of their aprons create a surface of light and dark that also imbues these two sunlit figures with the plastic nature of relief sculpture.

The stolidity of the seated figure, so strongly emphasized by her firmly folded arms, is also stressed by the deft break in the difference between the patterns of the fabrics in her apron and her dress, giving added physicality to her upper arms and bosom. The static quality of her body makes the turn of her head especially forceful, strengthened by the intensity of her gaze to our right.

Her round figure is complemented by her erect, standing companion, whose pose is emphasized by the vertical pattern of the lath work behind her, which Eynard has carefully located within the composition so it ends exactly between the two figures and leaves a dark undefined space behind the seated worker. The edge of the white bonnet and collar around the head of the standing woman and the slight turn of her face to our left ensures her individuality within this composition, even while the link between the two servants is made explicit by the angle of her arm on the shoulder of her seated companion.

Eynard has further personalized both women by the way he placed them in the outdoor light, fully illuminating the seated figure while casting the upper portion of her companion into half shadow. This light also emphasizes the natural folds and creases in their garments so they resemble the painted draped figures of late-eighteenth-century neoclassical painting. As a collector and patron, Eynard was familiar with such works and the table placed next to the draped figures probably also derives from that tradition, its choice a rustic echo of the simple forms and delicately decorated surfaces of the furnishings depicted in such paintings. This work testifies not only to the artistic qualities inherent in the daguerreotype process, but also to Eynard's ability to recognize and employ them to a degree that brought him high regard from his peers.

PLATE 54

PLATE 55

UNKNOWN FRENCH PHOTOGRAPHER
Portrait of a Laundress
1848–50
Three-quarter plate (oval cut)
84.XT.403.21

THE DELICATELY BALANCED composition of forms and nuances of light and dark Eynard aimed for in his depiction of two servants (Plate 54) contrasts sharply with the approach taken by the maker of this figure study of a domestic worker. In place of the disengaged, artistic perfection that Eynard aimed for, this daguerreotypist sought to bring us into direct contact with the subject, allowing no background details to distract from the powerful presence of the solitary figure. In essence, the difference between these two works is the same as the inherent distinction between a painting and a work of sculpture.

The effect achieved by the maker of this daguerreotype makes us more aware of this figure as an individual; we become conscious of her as a human being rather than merely as a posed subject. Here we are given a realistic portrayal of a woman similar to those Gustave Courbet and his followers would paint some fifteen years later. Courbet's paintings, however, appear less realistic than this daguerreotype because they can never escape the sensuous, tactile quality of the oil paint in which they were created. By choosing a subject whose life actually was spent in the role portrayed, this photographer also employed what would later become a principle of the realist school of painting. The daguerreotypist's principal artistic choices in presenting this image of a laundress were the pose and placement of the figure within the confines of the frame. The image's oval format was apparently preconceived, since the metal plate was crudely cut to fit this form. The definition of the space within this format is also determined by the lighting, which allows the figure to dominate its murky surroundings easily, rising from an undefined base.

The clear, sculptural definition of this figure also derives from her position behind the worktable on which she labors. By its placement, the area her body occupies is carved out of the otherwise amorphous background. The diagonal backward thrust of the table is muted by the garments draped over it and is firmly stopped by her hand grasping what to our modern eyes might appear to be an iron, but is in fact a wedge of soap.[25] This object acts as a clue for the entire piece, almost like a symbol in a Balzac tale or the subject of a Daumier cartoon. Her body rises from this point, built up by the bulge of her apron and the diagonal fold of her richly decorated vest.

The daguerreotypist directed the laundress to turn her head straight toward the camera, giving us full opportunity to see her expressionless face, slightly animated by her eyes that squint into the light. The side of her body closest to us is lit along the full length of her sleeve, which stretches to her enormous hand placed before the wedge of soap and emphasizes again the subject of the study. The contained posture and the required immobility of the figure underscore her resignation to her role in life. The artist has succeeded in creating not a portrait of an individual, but a universal portrayal of servitude.

PLATE 55

PLATE 56

UNKNOWN FRENCH PHOTOGRAPHER
Woman at a Mirror
1850–52
Sixth plate with applied color
84.XT.1582.31

ALTHOUGH THE SUBJECT of this striking piece is a nude figure, the daguerreotypist has created a setting for her that enhances her beauty by making her part of a work of art, a painting composed by using the language of the daguerreotype.[26]

The principal element, light, wielded as if by brush, strikes brilliantly on the standing mirror angled behind the subject to allow a side view of her figure, but most importantly to reflect the French door, its daylit panes, and a hint of sky beyond. The light rays reflect from this distinctly defined rectangle, passing through the net of her garment and merging imperceptibly with the reflected light from another source that the photographer has directed toward her. So subtle is the daguerreotypist's control over the lighting that we almost are unaware that the discarded garment on the curved chair in the lower right, as the brightest white area, anchors the scene and directs us back to her body, which also is softly lit from above.

No sculptor could have better modeled the female body than did this daguerreotypist, using light alone to form the figure. Adding the subtle, momentary gesture of adjusting an earring has given her a pose worthy of classical sculpture. Of the many daguerreotypes taken for the active pornographic trade in Paris, the level of quality seen here raises this piece above that genre. Instead, the sensitivity of this daguerreotypist to the use of light and an understanding of the effects to be gained from the reflective surface of the metal plate suggest a body of work where such insights could be best expressed.

Finally, the beauty of this piece also derives from the delicate manner in which the color is applied. Once again our artist reveals an aesthetic understanding of the visual language Daguerre had created.

PLATE 56

PLATE 57

Unknown French Photographer
Woman Reading to a Girl
About 1845
Quarter plate (double elliptical cut)
84.XT.404.I

This French daguerreotypist was certainly one of the most creative and skilled practitioners operating in the mid-1840s. The unknown photographer also must have been one of the small circle of art lovers in Paris who were just beginning to discover and admire the rich effects of light and dark used by seventeenth-century Dutch painters. These artists modulated the brilliant, stark contrast of light and dark Caravaggio had developed in the sixteenth century into a velvety darkness that produced a distinct sheen and shimmering surface. Their style only began to be appreciated in France in the early nineteenth century. In understanding hands, the daguerreotype was a perfect medium to achieve the same effects since its light and dark qualities were enhanced by the glow and gleam of its mirror-like surface. This artist seems to have sensed these possibilities and excelled at achieving them, accentuating their effect by covering the daguerreotype plate with a convex glass that magnified the depth of the image and increased, at the same time, the surface texture.

These visual qualities are brought to the fore by the scene the maker has staged, which may or may not have been intended as a portrait. The pose emphasizes the tenderness of feelings expressed by the figures and their intimate gestures. These qualities are further impressed upon us by the soft focus in which the two figures are seen.

The exquisitely soft shadows that model the faces of the two figures are delicately balanced, with the lower part of the child's face cast in a gentle shadow out of which rise her glowing cheeks, her shadowy eyes, and her brightly lit forehead, while her dark hair is softly undefined. All the subtleties of Vermeer's lighting exist here, giving her an intensity of concentration that simultaneously defines her gaze but keeps us from feeling we know her intimately. A certain degree of mystery surrounds her. By the position of her arms, she remains physically attached to the older woman; but whether she is psychologically involved with the lesson seems questionable.

The perfect oval of the woman's inclined head is accented by her head scarf, which becomes, along with the girl's collar, a solid, sharply defined object within the otherwise amorphous grouping of the two principals. This solidity and the almost complete lack of lighting on the expressive features of the woman's face make the direction of her gaze her principal visual role in the setting. Her glance travels directly to her pointing finger at the center of the scene, which also transfers our attention once again to the younger girl, leaving the open book—the source of radiating light—to become part of a still-life arrangement occupying the lower right hand side. The illuminated edge of the circular table and the turnings of its central post deftly define the circumscribed space in which the scene takes place. This lower area, connected to the figures by the diagonal of the woman's gaze, adds to the calmness of the scene and reinforces the elusiveness of the standing child. This example is so singular in the brilliant handling of the medium that it would seem reasonable other works by this artist should emerge.

PLATE 57

PLATE 58

UNKNOWN FRENCH PHOTOGRAPHER
Two Nude Women Embracing
About 1848
Half plate with applied color
84.XT.172.6

THIS HUSHED MOMENT of tender intimacy between two people would have appealed to Fragonard or Boucher, the most sensuous eighteenth-century French painters of female nudes.[27] Neither could have painted such an image, however, for the pensive beauty of this scene is due to the qualities the daguerreotype was uniquely capable of rendering through the eye of a gifted maker. Even in its slightly damaged condition, the superiority of this daguerreotype is obvious. This successful composition demanded an incredible understanding of how these two reclining women had to be posed so that the fullness of their figures and the erotic touching of their bodies could be clearly indicated on the daguerreotype's flat surface without breaking the tenderness the scene required.

The more we analyze the arrangement of the bodies, the more admiring we become of the maker's inventive and daring posing. The upper figure reclines on the couch, with her limbs arranged to display the silhouette of her upper torso while her other leg is crossed beneath her to fully expose the rounded abdomen and the clearly lit pubic area. More conspicuously, her companion is posed reclining on a lower chaise longue, fully displaying an even more supine body that creates a sinuous line that brushes against the bent leg of her partner and continues beyond her waist to the point where her lover touches the fully exposed breast.

The breasts of the upper woman, framed by her arm, lead downward, heavier and shadowed by the light, while the arm of her partner stretches behind her head and thrusts her face upward in what seems to be a loving regard, although the damage here prevents us from fully understanding the all-important glance between the two. But the daguerreotypist further explains the relationship between the two by arranging a mirror behind them, so that the welcoming embrace of the lower woman, whose arm is stretched backward, is clearly shown.

The rest of the surface that makes up their surroundings is filled with indeterminate areas of textures and light and dark, suggesting the secret haven of these lovers. Only a daguerreotype, with its capacity to define the nature of the scene precisely while placing the participants in an atmosphere suggested by gentle and soft lighting contrasts, could become a beautiful work of art that, at its time, would nevertheless have been considered socially unacceptable.

Such photographic images became quite common in France during the stereographic era of the 1850s, but pornographic imagery already had a long history in the graphic arts. The recent introduction of lithography, with its greater ability to make cheap, multiple copies, had vastly increased the availability of such material.[28] Although the subjects were often disguised as illustrations of literature, the principal purpose of the depiction was evident. Merchants often ran afoul of censorship laws, but they continued to issue thousands of lascivious prints, including lesbian scenes.[29] These prints were only partly supplanted by the more expensive daguerreotypes, but the latter gradually became more sought after because the realism of the scene made the imagery more salacious.[30] Although such daguerreotype examples profited from their sensuous combination of actuality and art, few examples reached the quality of this scene.

This particular example must have been an exceptionally costly production, given the beauty of the two models and the risks involved in making it. The piece probably was not made to be sold in the trade but was a special commission[31] for a particular person—most probably a man, since men were the patrons who delighted the most in such lesbian scenes. In this sense it is a prototype of *The Sleepers*, the most celebrated painting showing two entwined nude women, painted by Courbet in 1866 for a Turkish male patron.[32]

PLATE 58

PLATE 59

UNKNOWN FRENCH PHOTOGRAPHER
View of Pisa along the Arno River
May 1844
Half plate
84.XT.265.20

AWAKING EARLY ONE May morning in 1844, this French daguerreotypist[33] looked out the window of his hotel and immediately took the image we see here, which captures the golden light spreading across the line of palaces reflected in the Arno River. The location of the hotel, at the southeast end of this fashionable promenade in Pisa, provided a perfect opportunity to record a scene that appealed to the artist's pictorial sensitivity.[34] No famous monuments of Pisa are present in this view; its only subject is the splendid morning light.

Our daguerreotypist's response to this scene is like that of the French painter Corot, who only a few years earlier, on his trip through the Italian countryside, made oil sketches that recorded his joy in this same kind of light. The thought of a painter recording this light makes us realize how differently and uniquely the daguerreotype acheived the same artistic end. From this window, the photographer sought not only to capture the light but also to create a beautiful composition. The artistic choice lay in limiting the lens's view so as to make the banks of the river create a sweeping and graceful arc.

Although a painter could have achieved the same compositional success, the additional descriptive quality the daguerreotype provides was not easily achieved by other means. Along with the artistic composition and the glorious sheen of light, this daguerreotype provides a network of accurate detail made up of minute shadows and reflections that seem to exist within, or behind, the overall sheet of early-morning light. It is the peak of pictorial expression and one that was, and continues to be, unique to the daguerreotype process. The photographed light—the actual image—is again reflected in the metallic surface of the silvered plate, almost as if the light itself of that May morning so long ago still exists within the object—a holographic image that only the daguerreotype could produce.

PLATE 59

PLATE 60

THÉOPHILE GAUTIER (attributed)
French (1811–1872)
The Escorial, Spain
1840
Quarter plate
84.XT.265.24

A PAINTER MIGHT READILY have created with his pigments and brush this view of a moisture-laden sky moving toward the vast, gray stone edifice of the Escorial.[35] For the daguerreotypist to make this massive building seem to float within a sky, however, required waiting for just the right moment for the building to become tangible, because it was being washed with changing light as a weather front approached. The two bands of light that make up the sky are in movement, the dark upper area spreading out and descending quickly toward us. Of all the visual processes available at this time, only the daguerreotype could have produced such an exacting image. The maker was able to create this picture under these conditions because, in the moments before a thunderstorm, the darkening sky allowed him to record the details of the entire building without, at the same time, overexposing the sky, a condition which on a bright day would turn the sky into a dark mass.

The subject of the daguerreotype is the Escorial, a gigantic building that slowly rose into place about twenty-five miles outside Madrid between 1563 and 1584 to satisfy a vow made by the Spanish King Phillip II in 1550. Within the eight acres covered by its masonry are encompassed a monastery, a church, and a palace.[36] Its grandiosity was the principal cause of renown; severity and uniformity of style were its most frequently cited faults, underscored by the bleak, unpleasant countryside in which it was located.

Luck seems to have brought the daguerreotypist here at just this moment, for this image gives an unusually attractive, even flattering, view of the Escorial. Seen in this light, from the top of the hills of Saint Damascus immediately behind the building's western front, the dome and towers of the monastery are blessed with an airiness that few critics of the time accorded them. Indeed, in this case it is ironic that although the quality of the daguerreotype in delineating each and every part of the building in its view is clearly present, its sensitivity to the gradations of light have made the monument far more attractive than foreign visitors considered it.

Called by its supporters in the eighteenth century the "eighth wonder of the world," the Escorial was rarely visited at the time this daguerreotype was taken because of the dual hazards of bandits and barely passable roads. The only known travelers from this time who came to Spain equipped with a daguerreotype camera and who visited the Escorial were Théophile Gautier and his companion, Eugène Piot (1812–1891). Although no daguerreotypes taken by Gautier have been uncovered so far, this example may well be by him. It accords in date with his 1840 trip to Spain, described in his book *Wanderings in Spain*, in which his visit to the Escorial is related in detail. Gautier praised the building's effect from a distance, standing out from a "vapoury background" as in our daguerreotype, almost looking like "an immense Oriental palace, the stone cupola and balls which terminate all the elevated points" adding to this effect. Close at hand, however, his impression changed radically. "Aside from the pyramids of Egypt," he wrote, it is "the largest heap of granite upon the face of the globe." Nothing in this "Pharaoh-like assemblage" pleased him. He wrote that only when he left did he feel "restored to life."[37]

Gautier's critical opinion of the Escorial was echoed by later nineteenth-century visitors, but our daguerreotype preserves a moment in which it became a more fantasy-like creation due to the artistic qualities of the new daguerreian process.

PLATE 60

PLATE 61

SAMUEL A. BEMIS
American (1793–1881)
View within Crawford Notch, New Hampshire
About 1840
Whole plate (reduced)
84.XT.818.14

THE RUGGED WILDERNESS in which the early settlers of North America lived could not have been more dramatically presented than in this daguerreian scene taken in the White Mountains of New Hampshire. Had this example been seen in Paris or London, it would have caused enormous excitement, both for its subject and for its quality as a daguerreotype. Imagine how Claudet or any of the premier daguerreotypists of Paris might have praised it! Painters, too, would have been in awe of this romantic landscape of daring and exotic truth.

America's own early daguerreotypists would also have been surprised, for the work of this pioneer of landscape photography was unknown at the time. Its maker is Boston dentist Samuel Bemis, whose work we have seen earlier (Plate 3); the image was taken with the daguerreian equipment Bemis had purchased in the spring of 1840 from Daguerre's agent, François Gouraud.

During his leisure months, Dr. Bemis stayed at an inn near Crawford Notch, where he experimented with his new camera, taking close-up views of the inn and its out-buildings. He also began to venture further south along the turnpike,[38] making broader views of the landscape and nearby farm buildings. At one moment, however, Bemis followed the turnpike further north to this area of harsh beauty. He took this view facing northeast, with only a low spring sun behind him. Had the season been more advanced, the now leafless trees would have blurred the rocky terrain, masking its truly rugged aspect, which the remains of snow serve to define. The image required a very long exposure, which darkened the sky but not sufficiently to blot out the ridge lines of the surrounding hills or to diminish the daguerreotype's detailed delineation. The trunk and branches of the trees in the center appear so crisply defined they would not be out of place in German Renaissance engravings. The foreground, filled with contrasting boulders and foliage, completes the scene in a manner that gives it the character of a picturesque painting.

Two facts probably were responsible for Bemis's choice of this scene: its rugged beauty and its legendary fame as the site of an August 1826 avalanche. The location achieved its renown because of the fate of a farm family named Willey, which, in trying to escape, left its cottage to seek shelter on a nearby rise. Ironically and fatefully, the roaring torrent of water and boulders divided into two paths, bypassing the house but sweeping the family away to its death. The Willeys' fate captured the imagination of the press worldwide, and thrill-seekers sought out the cottage, where the open family Bible still rested on a table and where, immediately after the disaster, a fire still burned on the hearth and candles still glowed from the windows.[39]

Although scenic beauty was what attracted Bemis, it seems appropriate that the subject of this outstanding early American daguerreotype should also be associated with a story of pioneer hardship.

PLATE 61

PLATE 62

PLATT D. BABBITT
American (active 1853–1873, d. 1879)
Niagara Falls
About 1855
Whole plate
84.XT.866

THE GLORY OF ONE of nature's mightiest wonders is splendidly conveyed in this daguerreotype, whose dark, undefined foreground plays up the sweeping diagonal of the river's edge leading to the silhouetted viewers standing in awe of Niagara's force. The dark boundary underscores the broad, gliding plane of the streaked and swollen torrent as it plunges into the turbulence below with a deafening roar. Beyond, the foaming mist rises and brilliantly illuminates the center of the image, defining the density of the air and indicating the great height of the distant falls. Because of the photographer's ideal location and his placement of the figures in the scene, this daguerreian view appears to be one of harmony, a compositional unity imposed upon a scene of unleashed energy. It gains an even greater degree of placidity by the length of the exposure and the lustrous silver surface of the plate.

The classical beauty that the daguerreotype has given to this scene is at odds with the effect this natural wonder had upon its earliest discoverers.[40] Chronicles of the seventeenth-century French explorers spoke with awe of its power and savagery. Early visitors stressed the frightening roar of the falls and the suddenness with which the flat terrain opened out before them to reveal the awesome chasm. Later, mid-eighteenth-century visitors would delight in these same qualities but associate them with attaining a peak of aesthetic emotion. Visitors of this period viewed the cataracts of raging water from the rugged boulders on the Canadian side, looking up from below at the thunderous falling water—an experience that produced a state of mind they equated with being in the presence of the sublime.[41]

None of this awesome character is present in our daguerreotype view taken in the mid-nineteenth century. By then, because the American side had become more accessible after the opening of the Erie Canal in 1825 and the Buffalo Railroad in 1836, painters had been able to discover a more favorable viewpoint, one that fit their aesthetic attitude toward nature as an example of God's majesty. Prospect Point, as the site became known, hung over the edge of the river immediately before the American Falls and allowed the Horseshoe Falls on the Canadian side to be centered within the scene. Both falls seem to blend together naturally, with a clearly defined foreground that met the ideals of a truly "picturesque" painting.

Concurrent with this shift in the desired viewpoint of the falls was a change in attitude toward nature. By the middle of the nineteenth century, terror of the sublime was replaced by reverence, and natural wonders increasingly became examples of God's majesty. Niagara's visitors now came as pilgrims who passed several days viewing each of the prospects that made up the totality of this matchless scene. As one visitor of 1850 described it, "One becomes utterly Niagarized" as the "great cataract goes sounding through all one's soul and heart."[42]

Our daguerreotype comes from a time when a quest for a transcendent experience was more likely to be fulfilled by visiting natural wonders than by studying the monuments of the past. According to one guidebook, the ruins of Balbec or Palmyra, the pyramids, or the temples of Greece and Rome are "but the toys and foot-ball of time" when compared to Niagara.[43] The falls became a sacred place; a journey to it became a holy quest, a status recognized by the Catholic Church when Niagara was consecrated in 1861 as a "pilgrim shrine" equal to Rome and Jerusalem.[44] An 1858 visitor, Anthony Trollope, instructed visitors how to attain the emotional and religious experience they were seeking. Position yourself at the edge of the precipice, he said, and stare down at the waters until "at length you will be at one with the tumbling river before you."[45]

This is the moment our daguerreotype represents; we see the backs of the pilgrims as they contemplate the waters below. They gaze down on the torrent because their reason for having a daguerreotype made was to obtain a permanent

PLATE 62

FIGURE 33
FERDINAND RICHARDT
American (1819–1895)
Niagara (detail)
About 1855
Oil on canvas
Heckscher Museum of Art, Huntington, New York
August Heckscher Collection

remembrance of the reverence they experienced during their visit. These visual records would change in the near future, however. As tourists replaced pilgrims and positioned themselves to face the camera, what they desired was simply a souvenir of their presence at the site.

The daguerreotypist Platt Babbitt ensured the success of his work by permanently installing his camera beneath a canopy he had erected on leased land, thus gaining a monopoly of this unique view. Amateurs or competitors who tried to invade Babbitt's space were frightened off by assistants waving open umbrellas.[46] An 1850s painting, *Niagara*, by Ferdinand Richardt (Figure 33) shows people waiting at Babbitt's canopy for their turn to be photographed.[47] The camera can clearly be seen in profile under the canopy. The space at the edge of the cliff where Babbitt's customers will pose is currently occupied by other visitors who will be forced to leave before the photographer takes his next daguerreotype.

Not all thoughts about Niagara Falls at this time were reverential in nature, for, after recovering from his first reaction to the falls, at least one observer looked at their power from a technological bent. An 1839 English visitor was led to comment that he wished he were a magician so that he "might transport the falls to Italy, and pour their whole volume of waters into the crater of Mount Vesuvius, witness the terrible conflict between the contending elements, and create the largest steam-boiler that ever entered into the imagination of man."[48]

Chapter Five

CAPTURING THE MOMENT

———

DESPITE THE MAGICAL powers of the daguerreotype, its inability to record a clear image of a moving object was a failing immediately pointed out by the first viewers of Daguerre's process. The occasional unforeseen results of this limitation not only provoked amazement, but sometimes provided amusement.

Such was the fate of Samuel Long, a pioneer daguerreotypist from Portsmouth, New Hampshire, who traveled into the nearby countryside to convince the curious that this new discovery could give them permanent pictures of their homes and farms. In one of these communities, in May 1840, Long gave a demonstration of the process, but during the long exposure time then needed, he failed to notice a grazing cow standing in his landscape view, its head moving from side to side. When Long proudly displayed the completed plate to the onlookers, their amazement sprang not from the accuracy of the landscape, but from the headless cow it contained! The report on Long's demonstration in the local paper did not fail to emphasize for its readers the incredible appearance of a headless cow.[1]

Only ten months later, however, it appeared that an accident such as Long's was becoming a problem of the past, for on January 4, 1841, it was announced that Daguerre himself had solved the daguerreotype's inability to record an object in motion. Daguerre's new invention was reported by François Arago to the Academy of Sciences, although no examples of this amazing improvement were exhibited nor was this new method described in any detail. Its very announcement, however, threw the infant daguerreotype business into turmoil. Potential operators hesitated before buying daguerreotype equipment that soon might be outdated, customers postponed portrait sittings, and collectors stopped acquiring existing daguerreotypes.

This situation was described in the January 30, 1841, issue of *The Athenaeum* of London, which also expressed its annoyance that no explanation of the process had followed the initial announcement. Once again, the world had to wait until late summer before Arago revealed the details of Daguerre's improvement. This "truly incredible" discovery, Arago said, resulted from using electricity to sensitize the plate.[2] A single spark made the plate so susceptible to receiving light that it was difficult to control the exposure time without slightly fogging the image. This was why, Arago said, Daguerre did not exhibit any specimens of this process. He wanted to disclose his new discovery at this time, Arago added, both to claim credit for its invention as well as to encourage others to join in perfecting it. Despite the official imprint Arago's presentation to the Academy gave to this new method, as well as Daguerre's enticing descriptions of the improvement's ability to "fix the image of objects in motion," no examples appear to have been made. The system faded from public awareness, as well as from the photographic literature.

Three years later, in 1844, Daguerre announced, again with Arago's endorsement, another new way to record moving objects.[3] He proposed a type of coating for the plates that was so sensitive he claimed it even allowed the camera to make sharp images of birds in flight. This process, too, appears to have been ignored by the now-enlarged daguerreian community. Even though Daguerre published a pamphlet describing in detail how the coating worked, no further evidence exists of its use.

What both these episodes reveal is how desirous the daguerreotypists were to improve the process so it could record events as they happened. Despite attempts like Daguerre's to capture actual movement, however, during its entire period of use, the daguerreotype never achieved this goal, nor did other subsequent photographic processes for most of the nineteenth century. It would be a long time before the grazing cow recovered its head from the blurred image on the plate made by the hapless Samuel Long.

That the daguerreian process could not depict moving objects was an enormous disappointment to those who had first hailed its discovery. Not completely informed of its limitations, they had imagined it capable of achievements that its technological state did not permit, one of which was capturing historical events as they happened. This misunderstanding is why Daguerre's later announcements that he had found ways for the daguerreotype to make instantaneous pictures were initially so eagerly received. The enthusiasm was not simply because of a wish to see, for example, birds in flight, but because of what such a possibility foretold. One newspaper

FIGURE 34
Kruger's Photographic Stand
Published in *Humphrey's Journal*, January 15, 1869, p. 262
Courtesy of George Eastman House

FIGURE 35
ETIENNE JULES MAREY
Measuring the Speed of a Swordburst by Means of Photography
Heliogravure published in *La Nature,* October 11, 1890,
p. 289
Courtesy of The Research Library,
Getty Research Institute

welcomed the news of Daguerre's improvements by saying that now there would be "no end to all that may be saved to futurity from oblivion."[4] Another journalist envisioned history being "written by pictures, even while its deeds" are taking place, recorded by a single electrical spark. Historians and reporters would now, he added, have the potential of seeing "vast assemblages of men, in the moment of animation and impulse . . . caught for eternity with the gesture of the moment in their limbs and its expression on the lips of each."[5]

Without the realistic availability of such an improvement, the only way daguerreotypists could produce visual images of historic events was to attempt to have the audience remain motionless. One such effort was planned as early as April 1840 to document the inaugural ceremony of railroad service in Courtrai, Belgium. The camera was described as being placed at a high spot where it could encompass the royal pavilion, the railroad cars, and most of the participants. At the sound of a cannon shot, the daguerreotypist was to remove the cover from the camera's lens, and the public was to assume "a general immobility" lasting for several minutes so that a "good representation of all personages" present could be obtained. Afterward, officials would enclose the plate in lead and place it in the cornerstone of the station. With what success this event was carried off we do not know, but the careful planning and the effort willingly expended to obtain a visual record of an ongoing event is impressive.[6]

For the time being, the daguerreotypist had to rely upon the willingness of the subjects to remain motionless. Eventually such ingenious devices as flexible posing stands were designed to permit a greater variety of positions, either in a relaxed pose or, more daringly, in the midst of action (Figure 34). Not until nearly fifty years after Daguerre's unsuccessful attempts, however, did experiments in photographing moving objects by Eadweard Muybridge (1830–1904) and Etienne Jules Marey (1830–1904) usher in the instantaneous recording of events (Figure 35).

Well into this century, photographers of historic events continued to rely on the participants remaining motionless during the exposure. For a daguerreotypist, successfully instilling a sense of time into the faithfully recorded image depended primarily on the maker's sensitive choice of the moment to depict—just before, during, or after an event—that would make the viewer believe in its reality.

PLATES

———◆———

Chapter Five

PLATE 63

UNKNOWN FRENCH PHOTOGRAPHER
Troops in Town Square
About 1855
Quarter plate
84.XT.402.5

PLATE 64

UNKNOWN FRENCH PHOTOGRAPHER
Crowd along the Street
About 1855
Quarter plate
84.XT.402.6

THIS DAGUERREOTYPIST HAS BEEN LURED from the confines of the studio to make two views of what appears to be an eagerly awaited event. From different points of view on high balconies or in dormer windows, the daring photographer aimed the camera down at the throng crowding the open spaces and crooked streets of what was probably a small provincial town located somewhere along a route between Paris and the Atlantic coast. What the crowds no doubt hoped to witness was a splendid procession of a member of the imperial family or a visiting dignitary passing through on the way to the nation's capital.

The mass of white bonnets that appears in the camera's downward-looking eye, filling the center of the lower plate with white dots, reveals that the farming population from the surrounding countryside has flocked into town in its native dress. In the other scene, the top-hatted men and their more fashionably dressed women have crowded into the windows and balconies above the square, with the less fortunate crammed into the upper dormer windows. The largest balcony (seen to the left of the top daguerreotype) appears to mark a municipal building where local officials are standing and sitting while waiting for the ceremony to begin. Immediately beneath this spot, astride their horses, wait cavalry troops looking in the direction of the expected visitors. What excitement they themselves must have created in this provincial town, for some wear the flowing robes and burnooses that mark them as part of the recently created corps of Chasseurs d'Afrique.[7] They add an exotic element to the scene, and their luster signifies France's recent victories in Algeria. As a section of the Imperial troops stationed in Paris, it was their duty to act as an honor guard accompanying visiting dignitaries.

Although we are deaf to the sounds of the crowd, it is easy to imagine from these views the excited hum of suppressed voices that must have characterized this moment before the event began. We shall never know exactly what this large crowd expected, but the daguerreotype has been able to preserve for us—for history—the intense excitement of a specific moment in time.

PLATE 65

FRANÇOIS A. CERTES
French (1805–1887)
Parade at the Place de la Concorde, Paris
About 1848
Whole plate
84.XT.265.7

FROM HIS POSITION ON THE ROOF of the National Assembly building, the daguerreotypist François Certes fixed his camera with a reversing prism so that the familiar monuments of Paris would be depicted in their correct relationship to one another while his lens took in this sweeping scene for a protracted length of time. From the young men sitting on the balustrade in the foreground, including one fully stretched out on one of the masonry blocks at the lower right, to the windmills on the distant butte of Montmartre, the lens has captured with extreme sharpness and clarity everything that has come into its view with one extraordinary exception: the distinctive blur of motion made by the cavalry troops as they move across the bridge and begin to fan out into the square.

The imposing architectural background that defines this great expanse is transformed into a varied, three-dimensional pattern of light and dark. Every detail of the architect's design is conveyed to us even more beautifully than it had been in earlier drawings and engravings of this model urban space. Over the vast plain of the square, scattered figures and carriages can be detected; and with the aid of a magnifying glass, we can even make out their stances and gestures. On either side of the great Luxor obelisk, erected where the equestrian statue of Louis xv originally stood, two bronze fountains are actively in play, their rising and cascading waters realistically reflected onto the daguerreotype surface.

Since its construction in the eighteenth century, this vast space had been the gathering place for innumerable public occasions, from royal celebrations of marriages and births to the end of the monarchy itself. It was here that the guillotine was erected, carrying out the sentences imposed by the revolutionary government as the newly created citizens crowded around. But since then, such memories had been erased by triumphal spectacles staged under Napoléon and subsequent rulers. The square, no longer an arena of death, has been restored to its original function as one of the most impressive theatrical stages within the urban fabric of Paris.

During the first months of the 1848 Revolution, the provisional government staged many festivals to symbolize the various public virtues that the new government of the people represented, such as the Feast of Fraternity on April 20 or the Feast of Concord on May 21. It is probable that Certes positioned himself so high up to take this daguerreotype because of one such celebration, not simply because he wished to record this stunning urban view. For when we look to the right of the square, across the moat in front of the Tuileries gardens, we discover a great number of festively dressed people seated on chairs along the terrace, where they wait for the event to take place. Because Certes has made such a long exposure, we also become witnesses to the event. Charging across the bridge comes the cavalry, about to fill the square where the riders will display their equestrian skill. On the silver plate, their swift movements are reduced to a blur, almost as if a brush loaded with oil paint had been swept across this area of the bridge. From the figures clearly delineated at the side of this mass, we know what we are seeing is the daguerreotype's record of swiftly moving objects—a blur that caricaturists will, from this time on, use as a symbol of motion.

Unlike the scenes in the provincial town in the two previous images (Plates 63 and 64), we are able to see the moment before the event took place as well as the beginning of the event. We might say, therefore, that within this single daguerreotype there exist two simultaneous moments of time. Here, once again, the daguerreotypist is able to use time as a communicative tool, something that previous artists could only represent sequentially or symbolically. By merging both moments within a single scene, the daguerreotypist has introduced a new reality into the work of art, a reality that would only be recognized and developed many years later.

ART CENTER COLLEGE OF DESIGN LIBRARY

PLATE 65

PLATE 66

UNKNOWN FRENCH PHOTOGRAPHER
Religious Ceremony on Martinique
Summer 1848
Half plate
84.XT.1581.12

BY THE MIRACLE OF THE DAGUERREOTYPE, we are privileged to be part of this joyous crowd celebrating a significant moment in the history of social justice.[8] We are allowed to share in a religious ceremony that the slaves of Martinique believed to be the only way they would become free people. Being reborn through baptism was more meaningful to them than any official decree of emancipation.

Although abolishing slavery in all its possessions was one of the first ideals declared by the French provisional government after the February 1848 revolution, no specific method of implementing it was provided by the new legislature. When news of this laudable goal reached Martinique in late March, the local government and plantation owners had little inclination to grant such freedom without further guidance. During the next two months, the slaves became increasingly mutinous as rumors spread of their promised emancipation. Aside from planting some "trees of liberty,"[9] little change in their lives resulted from this declaration. In Saint Pierre, a local riot occurred on April 21, but it was not until a month later that a major, widespread uprising of the slaves broke out on Martinique, resulting in substantial damage and bloodshed.[10] The following day, the local authorities took it upon themselves to declare the abolition of slavery, not knowing that in Paris, nearly a month earlier, the minister of the Marine and Colonies had signed an official decree granting emancipation to the slaves on Martinique and other French possessions.[11]

Over the summer of 1848, however, the relationship between the slave laborers—now to be treated as paid workers—and the plantation owners continued to be uneasy. The slaves remained distrustful over repeated declarations of freedom without specific action, and they had little faith in local elections. During this period they turned to the church for affirmation of their new lives by seeking to be rebaptized. "Liberty was proclaimed before the altar," is how one historian of the time described the actions of the slaves, and he quoted one missionary as saying "the slaves entered into liberty as if it were the second baptism."[12]

Our daguerreotypist was present for what was probably the most elaborate of these ceremonies, staged on the great parade grounds of Fort-de-France.[13] As can be seen from the accompanying map (Figure 35), this area was laid out with rows of tamarind trees and enclosed by the walls of the army barracks. Our photographer has climbed up onto the adjacent rampart to view the ceremony from above and to take advantage of the plentiful light coming from the southeast. From this point, the light gathers below the trees and skims across the parade ground, picking out the rows of trees. Beyond the trees, it reveals the regular pattern of the doors and windows stretching across the barracks.

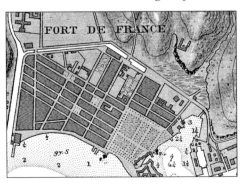

FIGURE 36
Fort-de-France, Martinique (detail)
Map published by Monnier, 1831

Although the daguerreotype was not able to reproduce the scene without blurring the moving figures in the center, the onlookers and priests already assembled by the temporary altar are clearly registered. (With a magnifying glass, even the arrangement of religious articles can be discerned within the shadowy recess of the altar.) The light enlivens the splendid attire of the black bourgeois, the braided uniforms and ornamented helmets of the troops, and the religious vestments with brocaded adornments, as well as the large plumes of the richly decorated portable canopy brought to the area to establish it as a sacred site. The density of all these individual items is brilliantly contained within a stage-like setting by the dominant curved lamp holder on the left and the truncated tree on the right.[14]

Our daguerreotypist has made us part of what was described at the time as "one of those rare, sublime, and joyous hours in which justice triumphs here on earth."[15]

PLATE 66

PLATE 67

Ezra Greenleaf Weld
American (1801–1874)
Fugitive Slave Law Convention, Cazenovia, New York
August 22, 1850
Reversed sixth plate (enlarged)
84.XT.1582.5

MANY OF THE PEOPLE shown in this view were targets of a law then being debated in Congress to encourage the capture and forceful return of runaway slaves to their owners. The law also would make criminals of anyone who aided in their escape. If enacted, the law would directly challenge the abolitionists' belief that, since all slavery was a sin, they were carrying out the work of the Lord by freeing slaves.[16]

To protest the Fugitive Slave Law, the prominent abolitionist leader Gerrit Smith (center) sent out a call for supporters to convene in August of 1850 in Cazenovia, New York. More than two thousand people overflowed the village, including nearly fifty runaway slaves, among whom were the legendary Edmonson sisters (dressed in plaid), whose hymns enlivened the two-day-long convention. Also attending were members of the abolitionist movement, including the famous orator and escaped slave, Frederick Douglass (seated below Smith).

The first day of the convention was held as planned in the antislavery Free Congregational Church, even though it could not possibly accommodate the crowd. After a day-long debate, the meeting adopted a document that, for the first time, endorsed violence as a means of ending slavery. Published as a letter from escaped slaves to those still in bondage, this document shifted the abolitionists' previous pacifist approach to one that reluctantly accepted the need for stronger measures. The newly defiant attitude produced a national outcry in both North and South. Aside from a few abolitionist papers, the national press objected to what seemed to be a call for slaves to revolt. One Southern journal described what took place at Cazenovia as "black deeds" coming from the witch's cauldron in *Macbeth*.

The nationwide reaction surpassed the feelings Smith and others had hoped the Cazenovia meeting would arouse. Ironically, this was achieved despite the failure of a theatrical highlight planned to attract attention to the event. William Chaplin, an active abolitionist in New York State, was to have made a dramatic appearance at the convention with some fugitive slaves he had spirited out of the South; but while aiding their escape, he was caught and jailed in Washington, D.C. There he remained, and the conventioneers were determined to take some action on his behalf.

On August 22, the second and last day of the convention, an apple orchard was made available where the entire group could assemble, and where this daguerreian scene was taken. Continuing their militant stance of the previous day, the convention members resolved that Chaplin must be released or civil revolution absolutely would follow. How this might be effected was left vague, but like the previous day's action, it represented a new direction in the antislavery movement.

The conventioneers further decreed that a daguerreotype be made of the signing of the declaration and sent to the imprisoned Chaplin as visual evidence of their support. Taken by the local daguerreotypist, Ezra Greenleaf Weld,[17] the image shows in the center, quill in hand, Theodosia Gilbert, Chaplin's fiancée, who had reported to the convention on her visit to him in jail. In this way Chaplin could share in the convention's success and see the crowd, several of whose luminaries, such as Frederick Douglass and the Edmonson sisters, he had helped to escape.

Today, of course, this piece goes far beyond any personal significance it had for Chaplin. It allows us to be present at an event at which antislavery supporters took a strong moral stand about the individuality and dignity of all men. The circles of time extend from this record of appreciation for the action of a single man, Chaplin, to encompass the emotions and conviction of all who came to Cazenovia in the summer of 1850. Happily, this outdoor site enabled the daguerreotypist to preserve for us the type of crowds that assembled to make their voices heard, to share in their emotions, and thus to acquire an insight into the long and intense battle of ideas and words that were waged before the impetuosity of a military commander turned the debate into war.

PLATE 67

PLATE 68

ALBERT SANDS SOUTHWORTH and JOSIAH JOHNSON HAWES
American (1811–1894; 1808–1901)
Early Operation Using Ether for Anesthesia
1847
Whole plate (reversed)
84.XT.958

IN THIS SCENE,[18] Albert Southworth and Josiah Hawes[19] have come close to realizing the ideal that early writers had hoped the daguerreotype would achieve—the visual depiction of history as it happened. Although the participants were required to maintain a few seconds of immobility, this daguerreotype records an actual operation that took place at a specific location— the teaching amphitheater of Boston's Massachusetts General Hospital.[20]

Not a single aspect of this scene is the result of the artists' imagination. The distant cases of surgical instruments, the bowls and vessels off to the side, the unused operating chair on the right, the frock coats of the physicians, and the socks worn by the patient are all details of the operation in process. In fact, since nothing could be omitted by the camera in favor of a more artistic presentation, this image has preserved for us the precise details of what a surgical operation looked like in the late spring of 1847—a time when an awareness of germs and the need for sanitary conditions were unknown.

To encompass this scene, Southworth and Hawes had to locate their camera at the highest point of the amphitheater, the lens aimed over the heads of the students sitting in the steeply ascending benches, to concentrate upon the operating area. An astonishing fact about this photographic feat is that it was carried out using only the light available from the skylight and lantern introduced into the dome by its original designer, Charles Bulfinch, to help illuminate the surgical operations carried out before the medical students.

This was not the first time Southworth and Hawes had been called upon to make a daguerreotype in this setting. Their earliest commission, in late 1846 or early 1847, was to make a visual document in honor of an historic event: the first public demonstration, on October 16, 1846, of the use of ether for surgery. The doctors who were part of that demonstration had not foreseen how historic that event would become, since previous attempts to find a successful anesthesia had failed.[21] Their success, however, transformed what had been an experiment into a significant moment in the history of medicine, marking the end of the horrors of surgery that previously had led to such screams and groans that surgeons hastily finished their work on writhing patients held down by attendants. No delicate surgery could be performed when opiates, straight jackets, strong liquor, and mesmerism were the only available means of relieving the excruciating pain. Ether opened a completely new era for surgery and its patients.

As news of the success of this demonstration spread almost immediately throughout the world, what had been considered an experiment took on the aura of a major step forward in relieving human suffering. Consequently, it was decided some months later that this historic demonstration and its participants should be memorialized by a visual depiction of the event. Surprisingly, the doctors involved did not follow the traditional practice of relying upon the artistic imagination of a painter to re-create the scene. Instead they turned to the new art of the daguerreotype to seek a record of the original experiment by restaging the event at the actual location where the demonstration had occurred—the amphitheater of the Massachusetts General Hospital—thereby forever associating the event and the site. Southworth and Hawes were the local Boston daguerreotypists commissioned to execute what was, at that time, an exceedingly daunting task (Figure 37).[22] Working for the first time within the cramped space below the dome of the amphitheater and using its far-from-adequate natural light, Southworth and Hawes carried out their assignment to make a daguerreotype of the reenactment with great success.

Probably due to this achievement they were again asked to bring their equipment to the same spot to carry out a new commission. This time, however, their task involved recording an actual operation, not simply a theatrical grouping.

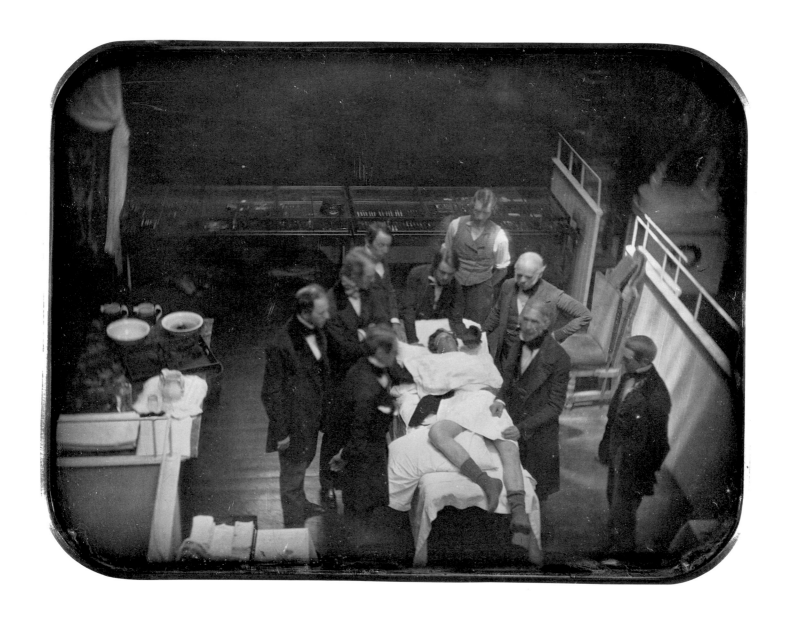

PLATE 68

FIGURE 37
ALBERT SANDS SOUTHWORTH and JOSIAH JOHNSON HAWES
American (1811–1894; 1808–1901)
*Reenactment of the First Public Demonstration of the Surgical Use
of Ether*
Late 1846
Whole-plate daguerreotype
Massachusetts General Hospital

The result was an historic achievement, a silver plate taken outside the photographers' studio depicting an event in progress (Plate 68). The figures are temporarily motionless, staring at the anesthetized body of the patient, next to whose head the anesthetist holds a sponge, ready to reapply ether if the need should arise. At the right, Dr. John Collins Warren has placed his hands on the area of the patient's leg to be operated upon while looking up toward the audience to explain what will occur during the operation. Behind him, with bent elbow, is Dr. Solomon Davis Townsend, who will actually perform the operation.

The historical moment captured here not only depicts an actual surgical operation taking place, but it also records another very specific moment. The daguerreotype marks a final appearance of Dr. Warren lecturing in the amphitheater at the end of his distinguished career as professor of anatomy and cofounder of the hospital. An avid fan of the daguerreotype, it is not surprising that Dr. Warren would have sought to have a record made of this moment in his career. He also would have advised Southworth and Hawes on how he wanted the photograph composed. Within the new possibilities and limita-

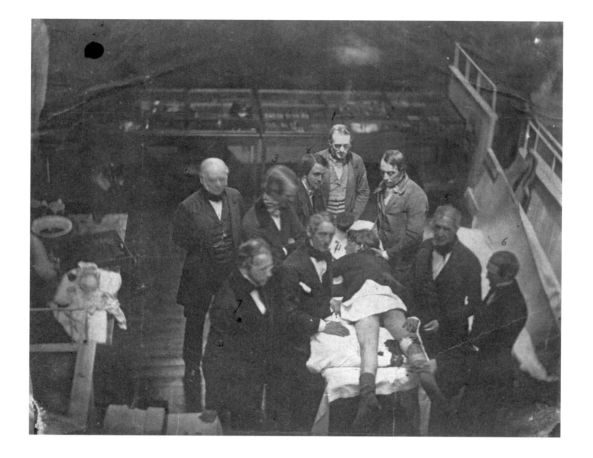

FIGURE 38
ALBERT SANDS SOUTHWORTH and JOSIAH JOHNSON HAWES
American (1811–1894; 1808–1901)
Post-Operation View of Early Use of Ether in Surgery
Late spring 1847
Paper copy of a lost daguerreotype (reversed)
Boston Medical Library in the F. A. Countway Library
of Medicine, Boston

tions of the daguerreotype, Dr. Warren would have wished them to emulate, as far as possible, Rembrandt's famous painting, *The Anatomy Lesson of Dr. Tulp*, which shows the principal surgeon of seventeenth-century Amsterdam using a corpse for an anatomy lesson. Dr. Warren had long equated his own career with this painting. He had a full-size (63 by 84 inches) oil copy made and displayed it in the front hall of his Park Street home for visitors and students to contemplate.

In addition to this daguerreotype honoring Dr. Warren, Southworth and Hawes gave us another view of this same operation (Figure 38), but taken slightly later. Now the operation has been completed, and the patient has been turned onto his stomach, showing the bandaged leg; there is evidence of blood on the sheets and in the water bowl where the surgeon has rinsed his hands. These two sequential scenes move us into the era of time-lapse photography; Southworth and Hawes carried the daguerreian art to a point where its role as a recorder of human events had not previously reached, perhaps surpassing what Daguerre had foreseen for his incredible discovery.[23]

Chapter Six

A Nation in Transition

W HEN, IN 1791, the French city planner Pierre-Charles L'Enfant first visited the virgin land on which he was to lay out a plan for the capital city of the world's newest republic, he described the highest section of the terrain as "a pedestal waiting for a monument." This 1846 daguerreian view of the United States Capitol shows the result of L'Enfant's acute observation (Plate 69). Upon the hill, he not only placed the building from which the representatives of the people would govern, but he established it as the exact center of his design for the entire capital city, designating its site as "zero degrees longitude." By this act, L'Enfant endowed the Capitol building, both physically and symbolically, as the keystone of the revolutionary form of government that was defined by both the Declaration of Independence and the Constitution.[1]

The maker of this daguerreotype, John Plumbe, Jr.,[2] has been able to show the imposing placement of the building because of the exceptional point of view into which he has maneuvered the camera. Although the Capitol was completed in 1829, the streets immediately around it were still mostly without buildings in 1846, as is the street shown in the foreground paralleling the fence that encloses the Capitol grounds. Designated on L'Enfant's plan as "Avenue A," the street has been graded and

flanked by trees, but its building lots remain empty, crossed here only by the long shadows of trees and of a structure under construction on the north side of its adjacent street, "Avenue B." It was from the top of this structure, or from a neighboring one, that Plumbe chose to point his camera toward the Capitol. The raw, wooden plank crossing diagonally before the lens in the left foreground sets the limits beyond which the daguerreotypist could not venture, leaving only a small rooftop enclosure where the camera could be set up. In addition to ensuring that his scene would have a superior point of view, Plumbe also chose the time of day that would give him the greatest opportunity for success. He uncapped his lens at an early morning hour at winter's beginning, when the sun would be at its brightest and the air at its clearest.

Armed with an extremely sharp lens and a perfectly polished plate, Plumbe used the light and the point of view to exercise his command of the art of the daguerreotype. Without his eye for detail and his sensitivity to the object portrayed, a less superior daguerreotypist would not have achieved the same result, even from the same point of view and in the same light.

Plumbe aimed the camera directly at the small square windows of the upper story of the building.

By using this viewpoint, he was able to capitalize on the strongly directional light illuminating equally both the upper and lower levels of the building. The light easily penetrates into the side and central porticos, even revealing the sculpture niches behind the columns and allowing the tall columns to play rhythmically across the side and central porches. The light is also so strong that the pilasters of the side wings and the other architectural elements composing their walls stand out, as if the architect's original drawing for the facade were set before us. Similarly, the stonework of the ground floor is as precisely delineated as if a draftsman's pen had inked in its shadows. In contrast to these suggestions of an underlying linear design, the central stairway is seen as a solid monumental structure, fulfilling its purpose in assuring the dominance of the building.

Above the square windows of the upper story, the side domes and their lanterns are clearly bathed in light. The perpendicular walls of the central dome's octagonal base are defined so strongly that we are made particularly sensitive to the swelling of the bell-shaped dome that rises over the interior rotunda. The delicate details of the balustrade crown the dome's upward movement, leaving a spacious amount of sky above and around the dome so its domination of the landscape is resonantly established.

In this daguerreotype, Plumbe not only illuminates the totality of the Capitol's building and setting, but goes beyond to reveal, as a small white object at the far left, a depiction of the President's House, now known as the White House, as seen in the detail of Plate 69 (page 186) In this single scene, therefore, Plumbe has illustrated the underlying organization and symbolic content of the plan devised by the capital city's brilliant designer. Although set out on maps (Figure 39) showing the Capitol as the center of the city and the President's House separated from it at the other end of the principal street, the emblematic relationship expressed in L'Enfant's concept for the city had never before been documented

in such a telling manner. The distant, but direct, relationship between the two divisions of governmental power were depicted here for the first time as an actuality, due to a daguerreotypist who understood the potential of his art.

The building Plumbe brilliantly photographed fulfilled the architectural ideals boldly put forth by the forefathers of the Republic at a time when the government was in its infancy. Matching their political aspirations for the nation, they set forth in the Constitution a provision for the creation of a totally new capital city six square miles in size—an area larger than Boston and, most critically, an urban center as large as Philadelphia, the city then most in contention to become the seat of the new national government. In addition to the scale of the new city, the desire was also expressed that its buildings, as George Washington said, "should look beyond the present day . . . in size, form and elegance." [3] In 1846, Plumbe visually expressed these initial bold ideas by making a series of views—this daguerreotype of the Capitol is one—of all the public buildings so far constructed.

In the early winter of 1846, *The National Intelligencer*, a local newspaper, announced that "elegant views" of the Capitol and other public buildings were now on view at the Plumbe National Daguerrean Gallery. [4] The next day, the *United States Journal*, another local newspaper, also mentioned the architectural daguerreotypes and noted that it was Plumbe's intention "to dispose of copies of these beautiful pictures either in sets or singly, thus affording to all an opportunity of securing perfect representations of the government buildings." [5]

Plumbe's decision to exhibit his daguerreotypes recording the capital city's public monuments along with his portraits of its major statesmen reflects the pride with which he viewed these buildings. Ironically, however, the architectural works do not represent so much a moment of achievement as they do one of transition. They stand for a time in

PLATE 69
JOHN PLUMBE, JR.
American (1809–1857)
The United States Capitol
About 1846
Half plate (enlarged)
96.XT.62

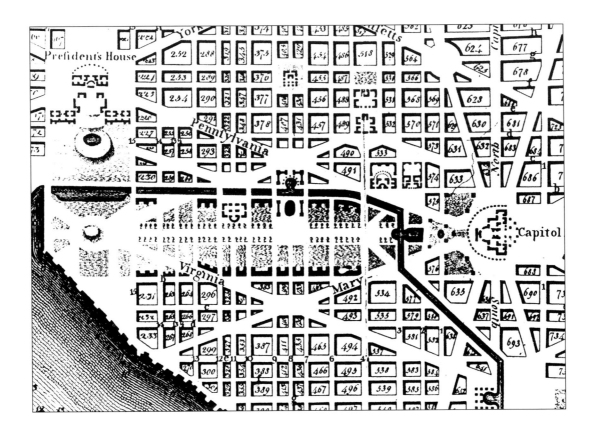

FIGURE 39
Official Plan of the City of Washington by Pierre L'Enfant
Detail of the Central Area
Engraving by Thackara & Vallance
Published October 1792
Library of Congress, Geography & Maps Division

the development of the country that precedes a period of enormous change, a period that is mirrored in the architectural expansion about to occur in the Capitol building itself. During the next decade, the building that Plumbe recorded in 1846 not only would have wings added on both sides, doubling its length, but its dome would be replaced by a loftier one that would forever tower over the city (Figure 40). As if conscious that, when the expansion was completed, the vast physical difference between the earlier and later versions of this seat of governmental power would appear too imperial, writers, critics, and statesmen went out of their way to refer to the new Capitol as the "people's palace."

FIGURE 40
THOMAS U. WALTER
American (1804–1887)
Design for Extension and New Dome of the U.S. Capitol
1855
Watercolor on paper
The Athenaeum of Philadelphia

Nevertheless, the difference between these two architectural expressions does reflect an equivalent change in the nation itself—not simply because it doubled in size, but because of the differences such an expansion meant to the life of every citizen. This momentous change occurred between the time President James Knox Polk gave his inaugural address on the steps of the East Front of the Capitol in March 1845 and his final address to Congress in 1848. During that time, he had presided over the enormous land expansion that added the territories of Oregon, Texas, and California; he had concluded a war with Mexico; and he was able to gild his final words with the announcement of the discovery of gold in California. His term marked an exceptional moment in America's history, a time of transition, when an ever larger, more diverse group of people would come to live within the principles laid down by the Founding Fathers and benefit from the form of government represented by Plumbe's daguerreian view of the Capitol.

This would be a time of opportunity for the individual as well as one that would mark the beginning of larger enterprises calling for collective efforts. It was also an epoch when the daguerreian artist was always at hand, recording these activities to a degree unequaled in any other country. From John Plumbe, Jr., who in 1846 decided that the public buildings of the nation's capital city deserved to be documented, to the photographers who, in the early 1850s, depicted the miners' camps and engineering projects in the West, American daguerreotypists embraced Louis Jacques Mandé Daguerre's revolutionary invention, which allowed detailed representations of the world to be carried away on a silver canvas, and brought it into its fullest expression. The images that follow are glimpses into the lives of the American people at mid-century.

P L A T E S

Chapter Six

UNKNOWN AMERICAN PHOTOGRAPHER
Grist Mill
About 1845
Sixth plate (enlarged)
84.XT.1581.8

BY STANDING ON A RISE nearly as high as the hill across the river behind this grist mill, the daguerreotypist—probably an itinerant one—was able to include in this scene a host of details defining one of the principal centers of an American village in the early 1850s. The grist mill was usually a family-owned enterprise that served an entire community by turning into flour the grain grown by the farmers from the surrounding countryside. As at this mill, the same water power that ground the grain frequently ran saws for cutting logs into lumber. Unsawn logs are visible to the left of the mill, with sawing machinery at the right rear; finished lumber can be seen drying in the upper window.[6]

The daguerreotypist set the camera at an angle to the mill, both to allow the three-dimensional form of the wooden structure to be clearly defined and to gain a sweeping view of the crowd of people and animals gathered in the foreground. As a result, the photographer expanded a simple record of the building into an insightful glimpse of rural life.

Although the river on which the mill was built, as well as nearby buildings, are visible, we do not see enough of the countryside around the mill to gain a hint as to its exact geographical location. Its basic design, however, was common throughout the eastern section of the nation. Such mills were constructed with large central openings to allow goods to be hoisted to each of the upper levels by means of a pulley attached at the peak of the roofline. Windows on either side of the openings, as well as on the sides of the building, brought light into the mill's work areas. The design of the mills derived directly from the function they were built to serve.

In this case, however, the quality of the building's architecture distinguishes it from many of its counterparts in other small towns. For this mill, the owner appears to have hired a builder/architect to create its design, rather than following the then-common practice of using a local carpenter. The classical detailing of the molding along the roofline, the heavy returns at the front corners, and the fact that the siding, as well as the trim, are painted, tell us that the proprietor wanted this building to make an impressive appearance. By cladding it in the currently fashionable Greek Revival style, the owner showed not simply an awareness of the latest favored architectural expression but a desire to make the mill a showcase.

Commissioning this daguerreotype was another act of displaying the owner's pride in the mill. To assure its being recognized as a hub of commercial activity, a crowd of people larger than might normally be present during the mill's daily operation appears to have been assembled. In addition to the men who would have been working at the mill, a large segment of the local population has arrived to "get into the picture," thereby providing us with a panoply of rustic details. Coming in from both sides are teams of oxen pulling wagons, their bulk dominating the area on the left. A pair of horses and a wagon fill the center stage; a rooting sow with her nursing piglets occupies the front center; a plowshare seen in profile is placed in the right foreground.

Because of a slip of paper pinned to the inner pad of the daguerreotype's case, we can link this scene with a specific person, a certain Willard Calkins, who, the inscription tells us, learned his trade at this mill.[7] His training and experience were valued commodities that would be welcomed by any new settlement where he might move. It was a time when, as President Polk had pointed out in his 1845 inaugural address, individuals in the nation "were entirely free to improve their own condition . . . by all their mental and physical powers."[8]

PLATE 70

PLATE 71

CHARLES H. FONTAYNE and WILLIAM SOUTHGATE PORTER
American (1814–1858; 1822–1889)
A Family Seated in Its Garden
1848–52
Three-quarter plate
84.XT.269.7

IN THIS DAZZLING PLATE, taken in the full summer sun, the daguerreotypists have made a casual view of members of one of the social classes emerging in America at the middle of the century. Far from being a formal family portrait, at first view it suggests that it was taken as a trial before the daguerreotypists formally posed the group. It probably represents, however, what could be called a rustic or natural portrait, one taken outside of the formality and controlled lighting of the daguerreian salon.

The casualness of the grouping is initiated first by the slanted angle of the bench on which the family is seated and by the awkward positions they necessarily assume upon it, from the little girl hidden under her bonnet and bunched into the corner to the awkward stance of the governess at the far right, one arm set akimbo on her apron and the other propped on the bench to shade her face. Overall, their positions appear to result more from avoiding the sunlight blinding their eyes than from any desire for an artistic composition. Why this family group has been posed in such a haphazard way is probably because the patriarch wanted a scene that would show off all his belongings: family, country estate, governess, and servant. Dressed as he is in his elegant top hat and formal clothes, he appears to have just arrived from his office in the city. An indication of his importance and wealth also is suggested by his ability to persuade the prestigious Cincinnati firm of Fontayne and Porter to leave its studio to travel into the country for this commission.

Cincinnati residents, as well as visitors from afar, prized the nearby countryside as a location for summer villas such as the one seen here. The city was surrounded by splendid vineyard-covered hillsides that afforded extensive views both up and down the Ohio River valley. Across the river, Covington, Kentucky, was a particularly favored area for such retreats because of its woods and the views it gave not only along the river but across it, to the busy steamship wharves of the growing town of Cincinnati.

Within the flickering foliage of light and dark, the photographers emphasized the casual atmosphere by enclosing the family on a light-colored bench that served as an informal posing stand. The daguerreotypists were positioned far enough away to embrace the entire scene, and that distance divided the plate's surface into bands of light and dark that, through the subtlety of their arrangement, make this daguerreotype an impressive work of art.

The upper third of the plate is transformed into a decorative filigree of branches and leaves against the sky, creating spots of light activating the surface. Across the center of the plate, a less sharply illuminated strip reveals the fanciful architecture of the house and isolates a solitary figure wearing a white shirt and dark vest, a tall African American holding a shovel. He was not caught accidentally by the camera, as was the figure on the front porch, but is posing for the camera as motionless as are the family members. His inclusion within the picture probably reflects his key role in overseeing the country estate, particularly during the time the family lived in the city. In these years, in this part of the nation, he most likely was a free man, not a slave; one whose ability had gained him his livelihood and independence.

This scene of daguerreian beauty contains in it a reflection on the silver canvas of the wealth of one family, representing a social class, and the many individuals who made their lifestyle possible.

PLATE 71

PLATE 72

UNKNOWN AMERICAN PHOTOGRAPHER
Three-Story House with Classical Porch
About 1851
Half plate
84.XT.269.18

As INDIVIDUALS PROSPERED in the 1840s, pride in personal accomplishment called for more than portraits of flourishing businessmen and their families. A more specific, detailed record of material success was desired, an attitude Daguerre had already foreseen when first announcing the possible use of the daguerreotype in his 1838 subscription brochure. The daguerreotype, he said, would be used to document every man's castle and country estate. Although at the time he was thinking of the leisure classes taking advantage of this possibility, life in the United States had broadened that opportunity to include other classes to pursue that instinct.

This house is certainly the primary reason the clients commissioned the daguerreotype, not only to show their pride in owning it but also to display its extensive remodeling. The three family members shown on the front porch are given far less prominence than the architectural details. These small figures are seated before the front door, completely dwarfed by the oversized columns of the massive porch, newly added to the original house. The capitals and heavy entablature were based on models from the Temple of Winds in Athens. Their elaborate design would have made them very expensive to duplicate, thus giving an insight into the lavishness of the remodeling. The scale of the porch also testifies to its being a recent addition to what originally must have been a tall and narrow three-story wooden house, most of whose wall area was given over to ample windows. Previously there probably was a much simpler porch in front of the down-to-the-ground windows of the entrance floor. Beneath its new classical cloak is hidden the form of a rural house whose stylistic origins are likely to be in the flat eastern farmland of Maryland or Delaware, where the suffocating summer heat dictated a house be high and open enough to catch any possible breath of air.[9]

The house appears to serve a double purpose: the small office-like wing with its own portico could be a private entryway for a doctor, a lawyer, or a private business. Given the probable location of the house in the mid-Atlantic and the extensive arbors seen to the right, it is possible that this is the home of a nurseryman on the outskirts of a town that already has extended paved streets, curbs, and sidewalks into its immediate surroundings. The owners have recognized the limits of their property by erecting a stone-capped brick wall, supporting a very up-to-date cast-iron fence of a kind that had become available only in recent years.[10] Locating this house even more specifically within a developed area of the eastern seaboard is the presence, under magnification, of a telegraph wire passing before the house, suspended from a pole mostly hidden from view by the leafy tree in the right foreground. The creation of Daguerre's fellow inventor, Samuel F. B. Morse, has here joined the daguerreotype.

Finally, we must not ignore the cart, the two-wheel dray so prominently set in the foreground. To include it and all the other details of the house and its grounds, the daguerreotypist had to climb up to a level from which the camera could encompass this entire scene. Together, all the objects gathered in this daguerreotype appear to tell us that we are the witnesses of a proud moment in the life of this proprietor. His business has enabled him to prosper and to hire others to work for him. The dray and its driver are as important in this scene as his newly refashioned house.

PLATE 72

PLATE 73

ROBERT H. VANCE
American (1825–1876)
Distant View of La Rancheria, California
1853–55
Half plate
84.XT.245

PLATE 74

ROBERT H. VANCE
American (1825–1876)
Street Scene in La Rancheria, California
1853–55
Half plate
84.XT.244

WHEN AN ASTONISHING DISPLAY of three hundred daguerreotype views of California by Robert H. Vance was exhibited in New York City in 1851, he was immediately established as one of the nation's most skillful daguerreotypists. A photographic critic viewing the exhibition praised the beauty and detail of his work, saying, "On looking upon these pictures, one can almost imagine himself among the hills and mines of California, grasping at the glittering gold that lies before him." [11] These two images by Vance take us, too, into the California landscape the early prospectors encountered, although not into a scene as picturesque as that conveyed by the Eastern reviewer. [12]

Only a few miles from the fabled Sutter's Mill, where gold was discovered in 1849, this miners' camp sprawled along La Rancheria Creek. [13] These two daguerreian views made by Vance, one from across the creek and the other close to the principal buildings, give a comprehensive picture of what such gold rush settlements looked like. These two factual records act to rectify the more common gold-mining daguerreotypes taken in the field that show a posed group of prospectors, at least one of whom holds a hat filled with rocks painted yellow.

Both of the Vance views display the desolate mountainous area of California to which men had come hoping to strike the one vein in the hillside, or the one spot on the river bed, that would make them rich. Scenes such as these give us an idea of the surroundings in which they carried out their quest. The view from across the creek, in particular, exposes the shabbiness of the buildings and records the bleakness of the landscape, where the few trees not cut down for lumber struggle to survive in the gulch's thin mountain soil.

In contrast to this dreary natural setting, the street scene of La Rancheria appears more civilized, showing close-up that a few buildings are made of clapboards and even painted. An almost festive air is given to the scene by the recently painted and artistically conceived hotel signs that were displayed on tall poles, rather than protruding from the sides of the building, like the more customary "GOOD STABELING" sign on the left.

Perhaps the spruced-up air of the camp reflects its importance in the region. A few years earlier, a gathering of nearby miners was held in La Rancheria to decide how the quartz mining rights would be assigned on four creeks in the surrounding area. This daguerreotype speaks, therefore, not just of the physical living conditions of these prospectors, but of their early attempts to establish a kind of communal order. Such efforts were rare within what was basically a lawless civil society. More common was the event that occurred in 1855, about the time these views were made, when the town was invaded by a gang of Mexican robbers who made off with the contents of a safe and murdered six inhabitants. Captured a few months later, the bandits were quickly hung, as frontier justice demanded.

These views of La Rancheria provide insight into the courage and strength it took for men to survive in this vigilante society. At the fringe of the country's expansion, the ideals for a man's existence as a citizen of a democracy had yet to be enforced. But even within this bleak outpost the art of the daguerreotypist was ably practiced by Robert Vance, whose sensitive eye coupled the geometrical forms of the simple buildings with the rhythmical line of human figures into a balanced composition of light and dark that many artists might envy.

PLATES 73 and 74

PLATE 75

Unknown American Photographer
Flume on the North Fork of the American River
About 1852
Half plate
84.XT.1581.7

After the first flood of prospectors came to California from all over the world to seek gold by pick and shovel, the early 1850s witnessed the formation of stock companies that replaced those primitive efforts. Although the gold rush remained an opportunity for independent, determined individualists, increasingly it was the entrepreneurs who took over. They could raise the large capital investment needed to hire the topographical surveyors and civil engineers whose experience on canal and railroad construction would turn the search for gold from a casual, lucky find into a profitable industry. Now mining operations relied on technological skills and learning to find and produce the elusive metal.

By the mid-1850s, few men were left who went out on their own to find a creek or a vein to explore. Their experience foretold the changes that the combination of wealth and power through stock enterprises would soon bring to the entire nation. The methods followed by the original forty-niners, of panning the streams at the base of the mountains in the hope that a nugget of gold might have tumbled down the creek, soon gave way to more sophisticated systems. These large engineering projects required building wooden trestles to bring down water and gravel from streams higher in the mountains through flumes or aqueducts. The gravel was swept by an increased current of water through wooden flumes that ran for miles across the land to the processing site. There the gravel was spread out onto platforms where employees, often Chinese, could more easily pan and rake for the sought-after metal.[14]

This daguerreotype, which records one of the ambitious achievements engineered on behalf of these new corporate powers, shows an aqueduct in the Sierra Nevada on the North Fork of the American River.[15] The daguerreotypist, probably hired by the corporation to provide a record for the shareholders of the flume's construction, appears to have had a daunting climb up the rocky terrain to find a point where the lens would encompass as much of the length of the structure as possible, while also giving an indication of its height. From this position, the camera includes at least 175 feet of the thirty-foot-high trestle, judging from the scale provided by the man with his dog at the ground level and the three men standing on the upper stages of the structure.

This daguerreotype achieves its task of reporting on specific construction details of the trestle as well as providing pride to its owners in accomplishing such an impressive feat of engineering. Also, by virtue of the chosen viewpoint, the daguerreotypist has been able to use the slashing diagonal of the trestle in a dramatic way that turns a straightforward document into a work of art.

PLATE 75

PLATE 76

UNKNOWN AMERICAN PHOTOGRAPHER
Canal Lock under Construction
About 1849
Whole plate
84.XT.1581.4

A COMMON SCENE across the landscape of the northeastern part of the nation in its early years was the construction of canals. By 1780, George Washington had already proposed building canals alongside the unnavigable portions of the Potomac River to turn it into a viable commercial link from the western regions of the country through the Appalachian Mountains to the eastern seaboard.

The most impressive engineering achievement of the new nation was the completion in 1825, in only eight years, of the Erie Canal, the vast 363-mile link between Lake Erie and the Hudson River that required eighty-three locks and massive stone aqueducts, some as high as five stories.[16] New York State bragged of its mammoth achievement by staging a great celebration called the Wedding of the Waters. To symbolize the union of the two parts of the state, a barrel of Lake Erie water, brought by barge through the new canal, was poured into the harbor of New York City.

This feat was considered a symbol of "Triumphant Republicanism," an accomplishment superior, it was claimed, to anything that could be realized under monarchies. Although some suggested its success was due to the favorable landscape laid out by the hand of God, the dominant reaction was a surge of nationalism. One resident of Albany, boasting of its new importance as a bustling port for the increased steamship traffic along the Hudson, said that the building of the canal gave him the same sense of pride that a Roman citizen must have felt during that city's golden era. In the canal's wall near Albany, a plaque was placed that sums up these sentiments: "Built by the enlightened wisdom of the citizens of this republican state."

News of this vast construction and its immediate commercial success in transporting agricultural products from the West to the industrial states of the East sparked numerous plans to connect all the major waterways throughout the eastern section of the country. By 1843, a network of over four thousand miles of canals was in operation, but few proved financially feasible; and by 1850, the commercial benefits of the newly introduced steam railroad began to outpace those of canal shipping.

One by-product of the early canal building was the experience gained from organizing and directing construction projects of such an enormous scale. These vast enterprises demanded the supervision of large crews of physical laborers, most of whom at that time were Irish or Welsh immigrants, as well as the creation of teams of engineers and draftsmen with adequate technical knowledge not only to plan vast projects but also to invent the machines needed for their successful execution.

The scale of these operations inevitably led to a central supervising bureau, one unable to assign individual inspectors to each site to oversee all aspects of the construction but still requiring to be informed about the progress of the work. Sending a daguerreotype like this one back to the central office was a perfect substitute for an on-site report—it was an indisputable record of the construction's progress. Such a use of daguerreotypes was apparently a recent innovation, one not restricted to the United States. At about the same time this record was made, a photographic journal reported that the emperor of Russia, Nicholas I, was receiving daily daguerreian views that detailed the erection of the suspension bridge over the Dnieper River at Kiev.[17]

The scene shown in this daguerreotype represents the progress on the building of a lock along a now-unidentified canal. The daguerreotypist provided an extensive view of the progress of the work by setting up a tripod on a construction rig similar to those seen in the distance. In the foreground, behind the lock's nearly completed gates, which will control the flow of water into the basin, we see stonemasons finishing the tightly joined side walls and carpenters laying the heavy lumber planks of the floor, both vital procedures for making the basin watertight. Along the left side, earth is being graded to prepare the towpath along which horses and donkeys will soon pull laden barges. The two sloping stone walls on either side mark the point where the canal descends from one level to another to match the land's natural drop.

PLATE 76

PLATE 77
UNKNOWN AMERICAN PHOTOGRAPHER
Canal Leading to Lock
About 1849
Half plate (reduced)
84.XT.1581.5

Another daguerreotype gives a vivid demonstration of the role a lock plays (Plate 77). For this smaller view, the camera was set on top of the almost-completed gates of a lock looking back at the straight ditch beginning to fill with water as it approached this point. Not until the rest of the lock is completed will the earthen barrier between it and the canal be removed. Barges then will be able to continue across flat countryside until once more they must be lowered or raised by another lock as the level of the terrain changes. As massive as such projects might have been, the canals were far superior for carrying goods and passengers than the only other existing routes for traveling, which were overland turnpikes or unreliable natural and hazardous river passageways.

This scene records a moment in time when America had quickly and successfully acquired all the talents, both native and immigrant, to move beyond anyone's expectation to reach its next great stage—the settlement of the other two-thirds of the continent. This great expansion also would force a reshaping of the concepts and ideals Washington and Jefferson had set forth for the Republic. In this sense, the daguerreotype before us is symbolic of the forces that moved the country from an agrarian to an industrial culture.

Epilogue

The Emergence of an American Identity

THROUGHOUT THESE YEARS of enormous geographical expansion and population increase, the original small republic, still intact at the beginning of Polk's term as president and represented by Plumbe's daguerreotype of the U.S. Capitol, was raised to a new level of nationhood. The architectural monument containing the people's governing body was expanded to echo this growth, the entrepreneurial spirit of the individual was encouraged, and some began to find success in becoming part of great enterprises. But the nature of the American spirit described in 1835 by the French visitor, Alexis de Tocqueville, did not significantly change during the following two decades. As he had described, human freedom and political equality continued to be the basis of the American system.

All of the daguerreotypes we have seen in this chapter tell us about different facets of life in the America of the 1840s and 1850s. From these individual scenes we have gained an insight into the kind of people that were forming the society of the larger nation. Not presented in these views, however, is the evil of slavery that was just beginning to make its political impact clear, although the Compromise Act of 1850 had temporarily defused it. The period from 1846 until almost fifteen years later was one of relative peace, the Mexican War (1846–1848) having had little effect upon the country as a whole.

The spirit of the country and the "Genius of America" were concepts that had become increasingly difficult to put either into words or visual form. The key phrase of the time—Manifest Destiny—was more a political slogan with divine overtones than a national motto like *E Pluribus Unum*. Such a national maxim would face its own fight for survival in the future Civil War, but in the 1840s and 1850s its acceptance was not threatened. What was changing, however, was how the people related the accomplishments of their own nation to those of the distant past. The link to the ancient Greek or Roman republics was a bond no longer felt by the growing nation, and even the classical style in art was beginning to lose its earlier dominance. A new sense of nationalism had begun. People took pride in owning objects that were made in America. When, in the 1850s, the new Congressional Library was built within the U.S. Capitol building, its architect, Thomas U. Walter, proudly announced that all the parts of its cast-iron construction and furnishings were of American manufacture.

Nowhere was this changed attitude more dramatically demonstrated than in the case of the colossal statue of George Washington, which, from the

FIGURE 41
HORATIO GREENOUGH
American (1805–1852)
George Washington
1832–40
Marble
National Museum of American Art, Smithsonian
Institution; transfer from the U. S. Capitol

building's inception, had been intended to occupy the central Rotunda of the Capitol.[18] Not until 1832, however, was money for its execution finally appropriated by Congress. It was commissioned from the young American sculptor, Horatio Greenough of Boston, a member of the group of American artists resident in Italy.

Originally conceived by Congress as a standing figure with a head based on Washington's death mask, Greenough argued against making the monument a mere likeness of the man, but instead wanted it to be a sculpture embodying Washington's spirit. Greenough took as his ideal the statue of Zeus by Phidias, which ancient writers had acclaimed as embodying the spirit of Greek civilization. Greenough and his

supporters intended that the colossal sculpture of Washington in the Capitol should achieve the same purpose for the people of the United States.

Greenough worked on developing the eleven-foot-high marble sculpture for the next eight years. On its installation in the Rotunda in December 1840, the mammoth, seminude statue of Washington, seated on what resembled a throne holding the sword of Liberty and raising his finger to heaven, aroused a national response, but it was an almost totally negative one (Figure 41). Despite favorable newspaper accounts, the public was strongly unsympathetic, and Congress was unanimous in disliking it. No matter what changes were introduced into its lighting or placement in the Rotunda, Congress demanded it be removed. So in the fall of 1843, this "ponderous mass of immobility," as one congressman described it, was hauled down the great east stairway to a distant position on the Capitol grounds, where it contemplated the East Front, but was not welcome inside the halls of Congress.

Plainly the ideals of the country, and even of its founders, could no longer be represented by the kind of imperial statuary Greenough had envisioned. In fact, classical sculptural allegories and architectural symbols were not adequate to represent the growing and changing nation.

America did not see itself represented by ideals of the past. It was now a vigorous, young America, aware of the opportunities presented to it and willing to take on the challenges needed to achieve them. It had become a nation of individual entrepreneurs and collective industries making their own way, no longer following a hero of the past. If we look for a voice from that time that understood the country, it is Walt Whitman's, which celebrated the freedom and dignity of individuals, in all their idiosyncrasies, to fulfill their own potential. Just as Whitman reflected the spirit of these times, so, too, American daguerreotypists gave us the images of this period and its people directly. Theirs was a tri-

PLATE 78
Jeremiah Gurney
American (1812–1895)
Portrait of an American Youth
1852–56
Quarter plate with applied color
84.XT.1564.27

umph of realism over the kind of idealized classicism represented by the statue of George Washington.

Indeed, a more fitting symbol of the American Republic at this time could be the daguerreotype by Jeremiah Gurney of the youth with hands held in a boxer's pose (Plate 78). The "Spirit of America" is how John Wood, one of America's insightful interpreters of daguerreotypes, has aptly entitled him.[19] Not only does he appear to represent physically, in his youthful, unblemished body, the state of the American nation, but this meaning is projected so strongly because Gurney speaks the language of the daguerreotype so eloquently.

The bare chest of this young American is itself a clear statement of the strength of the daguerreo-

type's portrayal of the human body. On the silver surface, the flesh is molded so softly through the almost imperceptible shading of light and dark that the background becomes an atmospheric space in which the figure stands. All the muscles of the upper body are suggested in the way the daguerreotypist has captured, in the minuscule grains of the plate, the light playing across the youth's skin. The daguerreotype's ability to render precise detail is responsible for defining his face in startling clarity, echoing his stance and making his gaze a resolute challenge to the viewer.

The aptness of this daguerreian image to this particular moment of transition in our nation's history also encompasses the aim of this book to demonstrate the new depth of meaning the daguerreotype has brought to our entire visual experience. This example stands as a model of the new language that the artist Louis Jacques Mandé Daguerre introduced into our culture, the result of his sensitivity to the difference between reality and appearance and to his determination to make a tangible record of that on a silver canvas.

Notes

Prologue
The Magician of Light

1. Any account of the life and work of Daguerre is dependent, first of all, upon the book originally published in 1956 by Helmut and Alison Gernsheim, *L. J. M. Daguerre: The History of the Diorama and the Daguerreotype*, 2d rev. ed. (New York: Dover Publications, 1968). Amazingly, for over forty years this presentation has remained the only publication in any language to give a comprehensive treatment of Daguerre's work. It is limited in its contribution, however, because their account of Daguerre's life is drawn solely from earlier secondary publications which in themselves are based on traditional tales handed down by Daguerre's contemporaries and their immediate descendants. The most reliable of these earlier accounts is that of Paul Carpentier, *Notice sur Daguerre* (Paris: Bonaventure et Ducessois, 1855) whose accuracy earned the congratulations of Daguerre's widow. The most cautious review of facts about Daguerre's early life is contained in Georges Potonniée, *Histoire de la découverte de la photographie* (1925; reprint of 1936 English translation, New York: Arno Press, 1973).

An excellent brief summary of Daguerre's life and work is given in Beaumont Newhall's introduction to the republication of Daguerre's original 1839 manuals in both English and French in L. J. M. Daguerre, *An historical and descriptive account of the various processes of the daguerreotype and the Diorama* (New York: Winter House, 1971), 1–25.

Michel Frizot, in *1839; La Photographie révélée* (Paris: Centre national de la photographie, 1989), 27, deplored the lack of attention scholars paid to Daguerre, and gave as an indication of this situation the fact that the Gernsheims' book had yet to be translated into French.

2. The most informative history of Daguerre's early work at the panorama, the theater, and the Diorama is Germain Bapst, *Essai sur l'histoire des panoramas et des dioramas* (Paris: Imprimerie nationale, 1891), reprinted in Robert Sobieszek, ed., *The Prehistory of Photography: Five Texts* (New York: Arno Press, 1979).

3. For dimensions of the panorama, see Barry V. Daniels, "Notes on the Panorama in Paris," *Theatre Survey* 19 (November 1978): 171.

4. Bapst, in Sobieszek, *Prehistory*, 17.

5. The description of a visit to view the panorama of the city of Rome appeared in *Journal des Débats* (May 13, 1804) first quoted in Daniels, "Notes on the Panorama," 174–176. A more detailed account of Daguerre's work as a painter and designer of illusionistic spectacles is found in Georges Potonniée, *Daguerre: Peintre et décorateur* (Paris: Paul Montel, 1935), also reprinted in Sobieszek, *Prehistory*. This book is the source of most of the Gernsheims' account of this period in Daguerre's life, including the critical reviews they quote about the reception of Daguerre's work in the theater and Diorama.

Illustrations of Daguerre's designs for the theater and Diorama are best seen in the article by Janet E. Buerger

and David Kwasigroh, "Daguerre: The Artist," *Image* 2 (June 1985): 2–20.

6. A collection of the critical acclaim given Daguerre's works in journals of the period can be found in Potonniée, *Daguerre: Peintre et décorateur*, in Sobieszek, *Prehistory*, 19–22.

7. A vast literature exists on these aesthetic controversies in nineteenth-century France. The most recent treatment of these issues can be found in Charles Rosen and Henri Zerner, *Romanticism and Realism: The Mythology of Nineteenth Century Art* (New York: Viking Press, 1984).

8. A complete description of the work by Ciceri and Daguerre on *Aladdin or the Marvelous Lamp* is given in Barry V. Daniels, "Cicéri and Daguerre: Set Designers for the Paris Opera, 1820–1822," *Theatre Survey* 22 (May 1981): 69–90.

9. Review of July 12, 1822, in *Le Miroir* quoted by Potonniée, in *Histoire*, 53–54.

10. Ibid. 56.

11. The simplest and most forthright description of the new Diorama presentation is set forth in an original broadside distributed at the time. This rare piece of ephemera is in the J. Paul Getty Museum, accession number 84.XV.1007. We appreciate Michael Hargraves's bringing this broadside to our attention.

12. Gernsheim, *Daguerre*, 34, quoting a description not published until 1841.

13. Ibid. 36, quoting a description from *L'Artiste* [ser. 1], vol. 10, no. 11, 1835.

14. The connection between the Diorama and photography is discussed in Heinz Buddemeier, *Panorama, Diorama, Photographie* (Munich: W. Fink, 1970), which includes reprints (sometimes incomplete) of early sources.

The most important and original discussion of the relationship between these two inventions by Daguerre and their impact on painting after 1839 is in Janet Buerger, "The Genius of Photography," in *The Daguerreotype: A Sesquicentennial Celebration*, ed. John Wood (Iowa City: University of Iowa Press, 1989), 43–59.

Fortified Vision

15. Beginning in August 1841, with the publication of *Historique de la découverte improprement nommée daguerréotype* by Isidore Niépce (Paris: Astier, 1841; reprinted in Sobieszek, *Prehistory*), many books claimed the older Niépce to be the inventor of photography, but none were based on conclusive documentary evidence. More damning for their cause was the absence of any examples of Niépce's work.

An example of a still-life photograph on glass was once believed to be a work of Niépce (discussed by Gernsheim, *Daguerre*, 68–69), but recently it has been shown to be a work from about 1850 by a relative,

Abel Niépce de Saint-Victor. See Bernard Lefebvre, *À Niépce de Saint-Victor et la Table Servie*, privately printed in Rouen in 1984.

In 1952, the Gernsheims, following up on information about Niépce's London visit in 1827–1828, tracked down and recovered an original work Niépce had left in England (Figure 7). Their brilliant discovery, naturally, shaped their attitude about the Daguerre-Niépce priority issue in favor of the latter.

In addition to having, for the first time, an example of Niépce's work, new key documentary evidence had surfaced in 1949 with the publication of *Dokumenty po istorii izobreteniia fotografii*, edited by Torichan P. Kravets, (Moscow: Izd-vo Akademii nauk, 1949; reprinted New York: Arno Press, 1979). It contains a massive amount of original Daguerre-Niépce correspondence (also translated into Russian) conserved by Niépce's family and later housed in the Russian Academy of Sciences. The Gernsheims paid scant attention to these documents, although they are key to understanding how these two men came to work together and what their goal was. In our account of their relationship, a necessarily brief one given the intention of our book, we have depended essentially upon these documents, as well as upon the few others in diverse repositories, all of which have been catalogued by Pierre G. Harmant in *Joseph Nicéphore Niépce: Correspondances, 1825–1829* (Rouen: Pavillon de la photographie, 1974). Unfortunately no similar trove of documentary records from Daguerre is known.

An elaborate volume on Niépce by Paul Jay, *Niépce: Genèse d'une invention*, was published in 1988 by the Musée Nicéphore Niépce at Chalon-Sur-Saône, France, but contains little information not previously published.

16. Gernsheim, *Daguerre*, 56–57.

17. Referred to in a letter to Daguerre from Niépce, October 23, 1829. Kravets, no. 91.

18. An inscription on a letter of September 1829 states that the plate was sent to Daguerre by Niépce on October 2, 1829. Kravets, no. 87.

19. Both Lemaître and Daguerre responded to Niépce within ten days. Kravets, nos. 89, 90.

20. One difference is that the plate in Austin is of pewter, while Niépce mentions that the plate sent to Paris was silver-plated (Kravets, no. 88). In February 1828, after returning from England, Niépce switched from pewter to silver plates, which he first received from Paris in June 1828 (Kravets, nos. 78, 79). The plate sent to Daguerre was therefore made sometime between June 1828 and September 1829.

21. All are views of the courtyard of his home taken from an upstairs window, where, it is reasonable to assume given the length of time needed to expose the plates, that he probably had constructed some permanent emplacement for the camera obscura. As a scientist he would have wished to control his experiments in this way so as to make accurate comparisons of his results.

22. Letter of October 12, 1829. Kravets, no. 89.

23. Letter of October 12, 1829. Kravets, no. 90.

24. Scientific experiments have been carried out on the single existing Niépce plate, in the collection of the University of Texas at Austin, by Jean-Louis Mariginier, research scientist for the National Center for Scientific Research, Paris. His work has defined and clarified for the first time some of the chemical mysteries surrounding these early experiments. Most of his research has appeared in *Le Photographie* (December 1989–January 1990; July 1990–January 1991; September-November 1992), but one paper given in May 1995 at the annual meeting of the Society for Imaging Science and Technology has been published in English in *The New England Journal of Photographic History* 144–145 (1995): 37–46. Although the author states that his physical research has been correlated with the written evidence of Niépce and Daguerre, no rigorous relationship has been published so far, which still leaves room for doubt in some of his conclusions. Nevertheless, the primary result of his examination of the Austin plate establishes without question that the length of exposure time necessary to achieve the image was in the range of four to five days.

25. Letter of October 23, 1829. Kravets no. 91.

26. Both Beaumont Newhall in *Latent Image: The Discovery of Photography* (Garden City: Doubleday, 1967), 40, and Gernsheim in *Daguerre*, 69, believed Niépce and Daguerre never saw one another after signing the agreement, but the correspondence demonstrates that this is not true. Daguerre visited Niépce in June 1830 for fifteen days, in May and June 1832, and in November 1832. See essay by Paul Jay on Niépce in *1839: La Photographie révélée*, 21.

27. Kravets, no. 140 (May 1835).

28. Kravets, nos. 134–139.

29. Kravets, no. 141.

30. The Gernsheims describe this article as an example of Daguerre's boasting (*Daguerre*, 73), but nothing substantiates such a reading. It is in their presentation of this period in the development of the daguerreotype that their bias toward Niépce seems to have guided their reading of the documents.

31. This little known description is the most detailed evidence proving that by early winter 1836 Daguerre already had been able to produce a view that could be examined by others and that was clear enough to show minute details. See Eugène-Emmanuel Viollet-le-Duc, *Lettres de Italie: 1836–1837 adressée à sa famille* (Paris: L. Laget, 1971), 165.

32. Kravets, no. 148, gives the contract.

33. This remains the earliest extant example of a daguerreotype, unfortunately now totally effaced.

34. Kravets, no. 151.

35. The lack of protection a patent would provide was put succinctly by the Minister of Interior in his address when introducing the bill to recompense Daguerre and Niépce on June 15, 1839: "No patent that can be taken out will protect their invention. As soon as a knowledge of it be acquired, every body may apply it to their own purpose. . . . The process will, therefore, become the property of every body or for ever remain a secret." From page 2 of the address, reproduced in Daguerre, *Historical*.

36. Kravets, no. 151.

37. Kravets, no. 152. An original and interesting interpretation of Arago's reason for supporting Daguerre's invention is given in Anne McCauley, "François Arago and the Politics of the French Invention of Photography," published in *Multiple Views: Logan Grant Essays on Photography, 1983–89*, ed. Daniel P. Younger (Albuquerque: University of New Mexico Press, 1991), 43–69.

The Dream Has Come to Pass

38. For Arago's text, see Gernsheim, *Daguerre*, 82–84.

39. Mentioned by a correspondent when viewing Daguerre's plates, *The Athenaeum: Journal of Literature, Science, and the Fine Arts* [London](March 9, 1839): 187.

40. An excellent summary of the press during the early period, including brief quotes from many of the articles, is given in Keith I. P. Adamson, "1839—The Year of Daguerre," *History of Photography* 13 (July / September 1989): 191–202. Quotations or references in our text, however, are from the original sources unless otherwise noted.

Two articles by Martin Gasser deal in part with this period. They are keenly analytical and bring in additional critical reactions that are mostly beyond our immediate concern: "Between 'From Today Painting is Dead' and 'How the Sun Became a Painter,'" *Image* 33 (Winter 1990–1991): 9–29; and "Histories of Photography 1839–1939," *History of Photography* 16 (Spring 1992): 50–61.

41. Jules Janin, *L'Artiste*, ser. 2, vol. 2, no. 11 [January 28, 1839]: 146.

42. This comparison was made by a correspondent interviewing Daguerre on January 16, 1839, as reported in *The Athenaeum* [London] (January 26, 1839). It was also used as a term of comparison by Samuel Morse after visiting Daguerre's studio on March 7, 1839. Morse's March 9 letter about the visit was published in the *New York Observer* on April 20, 1839.

43. The term "pencil of nature" was first used to describe daguerreotypes in an article in *The Literary Gazette* [London] (February 2, 1839): 74. This is where Larry J. Schaff, in *Out of the Shadows: Herschel, Talbot, & the Invention of Photography* (New Haven: Yale University Press, 1992), 138, suggests Talbot first saw it and used it for the title of his own 1844 publication. The relationship between the rays of the sun and the pencil of nature was a frequent metaphor in early descriptions.

44. Comment by Alexander von Humboldt, who with Arago and Biot was one of the three scientists who reported to the Academy on Daguerre's achievement.

He described the daguerreotype as having "satin-like shadows as in the finest black chalk drawing." See Newhall's introduction in Daguerre, *Historical*, 16.

45. The first news about Daguerre's discovery appeared in *The Literary Gazette* [London] issues of January 12 and 19, 1839.

46. The exhibition was described by Talbot in a letter of January 30 to the editor of *The Literary Gazette* [London] entitled "Photogenic Drawing." Printed in the issue of February 2, 1839, 73–74. It was also reported in *The Athenaeum* [London] (February 2, 1839): 96, where the writer did not hesitate to say that the two processes were "almost identical"—even though no daguerreotype had yet to be seen in England.

47. Letter of February 9, 1839, quoted by Schaff, *Out of the Shadows*, 174, note 5.

48. Talbot's letter claiming to have invented the process much earlier was submitted to the Academy of Sciences on February 4, 1839, as reported in *The Athenaeum* [London], (February 9, 1839): 114, which also described Arago's reaction.

49. Samuel I. Prime, *The Life of Samuel F. B. Morse* (New York: Appleton, 1875), 400–402. Morse's letter was published in *The New York Observer* (April 20, 1839).

50. In an account in the *New York Mirror* (May 25, 1839): 380, Arago is quoted as having said that he was acquainted personally with Daguerre's process and that in ten minutes he had obtained a perfect view of the "Boulevard de [sic] Temple." Presumably this refers to a work by Arago that was later said to have been consumed in the flames of the Diorama. Gay-Lussac, *Report to the Chamber of Peers* (July 30, 1839), 36. Published in Daguerre, *Historical*.

51. Schaff, *Out of the Shadows*, 67, calls Talbot's refusal of the invitation by Daguerre inexplicable. At this time none of the principals in England had yet seen a daguerreotype but had formed their idea of the process from news reports and by seeing the works by Niépce that had remained in England. On March 8, 1839, Talbot had accompanied Charles Wheatstone to the home of Francis Bauer, both to show him his own work (Kravets, no. 154) and to pick up the Niépce pieces that were to be exhibited at the Royal Society on March 9. Presumably Talbot's concept of what Daguerre's work looked like was based on his viewing of Niépce's work of twelve years earlier.

In a letter of April 24, 1839 (Kravets, no. 159), Bauer wrote Isidore Niépce about the distinguished artists, scientists, and nobles who had attended the exhibition of March 9, 1839, and that they all agreed that the daguerreotype was only a ridiculous usurpation of Niépce's work and that "England would never grant that name [daguerreotype] to the art."

52. For the letter to Talbot, see Schaff, *Out of the Shadows*, 75. For comments about "childish amusements," see Gernsheim, *Daguerre*, 88, taken from *Comptes rendu des séances de l'Académie des Sciences* (May 27, 1839): 838. In all likelihood, Herschel and his companions expected

Daguerre's work to resemble what they knew of Niépce's earlier work.

53. For example, see *The Athenaeum* [London] (June 8, 1839): 435, "Now we have long since stated, and after an attentive examination of both, that all comparison between photogenic drawings and the works of M. Daguerre, is quite ridiculous, and a candid acknowledgment of this we thought due to the Frenchman's great and undoubted merits."

54. Letter written on May 20, 1839, quoted in Graham Smith, "James D. Forbes and the Early History of Photography," in *Shadow and Substance: Essays on the History of Photography in Honor of Heinz K. Henisch* (Bloomfield Hills, Michigan: Amorphous Institute Press, 1990): 11.

The Secret Is Disclosed

55. Arago's address was not officially recorded, with the consequence that several different versions exist. We have used the texts given in Gernsheim, *Daguerre*, 98–100, as well as that in Beaumont Newhall, *Daguerreotype in America*, 3d. rev. ed. (New York: Dover Publications, 1976), 19.

56. The first and most comprehensive technical explanation of the formation of the daguerreian image is found in M. Susan Barger and William B. White, *The Daguerreotype: Nineteenth-Century Technology and Modern Science* (Washington, D.C.: Smithsonian Institution Press, 1991).

57. Alfred Donné, *Journal des Débats* (August 20, 1839). Reprinted in William F. Stapp, *Robert Cornelius: Portraits from the Dawn of Photography* (Washington, D.C.: Smithsonian Institution Press, 1983), 130–134.

58. Gernsheim, *Daguerre*, 106–107. The contract between Daguerre, Niépce, and Giroux for making the equipment was signed on June 22, 1839; it is reproduced in Gernsheim, *Daguerre*, 189–191. A complete bibliography compiled by Newhall of Daguerre's instruction manuals is included in Gernsheim, *Daguerre*, 198–205.

59. We are indebted to Matthew R. Isenberg for patiently taking us through the steps of making a daguerreotype using original equipment from his collection.

60. For a detailed description of the technical process and equipment used throughout the daguerreian era, see Floyd Rinhart and Marion Rinhart, *The American Daguerreotype* (Athens: University of Georgia Press, 1981), 156–190.

61. Jules Janin, *L'Artiste* ser. 2, vol. 3, no. 17 (August 25, 1839): 277.

62. Jules Janin, *L'Artiste* ser. 2, vol. 4, no.1 (September 1839): 1–3.

63. Gernsheim, *Daguerre*, 104.

Chapter 1
The World Poses for the Sun

1. For the moon hoax, see Herma Silverstein and Caroline Arnold, *Hoaxes That Made Headlines* (New York: Julian Messner, 1986), 76–79; and Carl Sifakis, *Hoaxes and Scams: A Compendium of Deceptions, Ruses and Swindles* (New York: Facts on File, 1993), 184–185.

2. Rinhart, *American Daguerreotype*, 19.

3. The poem, signed NUGATOR, appeared in *Southern Literary Messenger* 6, no. 3 (March 1840), reference courtesy of Gary W. Ewer.

4. The eyewitness account is by Ludwig Pfau, who was present during Arago's speech and later wrote in detail about this time in Paris in *Kunst und Gewerbe* (Stuttgart: Ebner & Seubert, 1877), 115–117; quoted extensively in Gernsheim, *Daguerre*, 100–101.

5. A Danish scientist, in Paris to learn the daguerreian process, stated that opticians would renew the plates for a fee: Ida Haugsted, "Un Danois fait ses premières daguerréotypes á Paris," *Paris et le daguerrèotype* (Paris: Paris-Museés, 1989), 40.

6. "La Description du Daguérotype [sic]," *L'Artiste* ser. 2, vol. 3, no. 17 [August 25, 1839]: 282.

7. Advertisement in *La Presse* (January 6, 1840), cited in Elizabeth Anne McCauley, *Industrial Madness: Commercial Photography in Paris, 1848–1871* (New Haven: Yale University Press, 1994), 78, 96–97.

8. For the king's request, see *Paris et le daguerréotype*, 41. A valuable statistical survey of workers in photographic studios was made in 1847–1848 for the Parisian Chamber of Commerce. Reprinted in Jean-Claude Lemagny and André Rouille, eds., *History of Photography*, trans. Janet Lloyd (Cambridge: Cambridge University Press, 1987), 82–86.

9. For a thorough account and dictionary of photographers working in the Near East, see Nissan N. Perez, *Focus East* (New York: Abrams, 1988).

10. For a general discussion, see Gernsheim, *Daguerre*, 109–110, but the individual developments are too complex to be easily summarized. For Fizeau's method, see Noël-Marie Paymal Lerebours, *Traité de photographie: derniers perfectionnements apportés au daguerréotype*, 4th ed., (Paris: N. P. Lerebours, 1843), where he not only described Fizeau's method but expressed his wish that it had been available earlier to be used in his publications. He did include three plates made by the Fizeau method in later issues of the *Excursions daguerriennes* (Noël-Marie Paymal Lerebours, *Excursions daguerriennes: Vues et monuments les plus remarquables du globe* (Paris: N. P. Lerebours, 1840–1844).

Examples of the different processes used to duplicate the daguerreotype are illustrated in *Paris et le daguerréotype*, 259–263.

Poitevin received a prize in 1847 from the Société d'Encouragement for his work on engraving daguerreian images. See Frédéric Proust, "Le 3e homme de l'histoire de la photographie: Alphonse Poitevin (1819–1882)," *Prestige de la photographie* 2 (September 1977): 10.

11. Gernsheim, *Daguerre*, 110.

12. Beaumont Newhall, "The Value of Photography to the Artist, 1839," *Image* 11 (1962): 27.

13. See Robert Sobieszek, *Masterpieces of Photography from the George Eastman House Collection* (New York: Abbeville Press, 1985), 18, for a comparison of the difference between the appearance of the same site as seen in a lithograph made from a daguerreotype and an artist's interpretation of the site using artistic liberty.

14. Mentioned in the advertisement for the *Excursions daguerriennes* that appeared in Marc Antoine Gaudin and Noël-Marie Paymal Lerebours, *Derniers perfectionnements apportés au daguerréotype* (Paris: N. P. Lerebours, 1841).

15. The most comprehensive description of Lerebours's *Excursions daguerriennes* is found in Janet E. Buerger, *French Daguerreotypes* (Chicago: University of Chicago Press, 1989), 28–40; a complete listing of the views appearing in the publication is found on pages 246–250.

16. This plate appeared in the third fascicle of plates issued in 1840. In later editions, Lerebours often switched the order of the plates.

Our appreciation of the quality of light and dark as conveyed by the aquatint translation of the daguerreotype by Lerebours must take into account that, for an additional fee, all of the views were made available in hand-colored editions.

Plate 1

17. The Pantheon in Paris was designed by Jacques Germain Soufflot (1709–1780). It was begun in 1757 and completed about 1780. Originally intended as a religious edifice, it was secularized during the French Revolution and became a monument and mausoleum for illustrious Frenchmen. Voltaire was the first to be so honored.

18. Poitevin made another view of the building from the same point of view, but at a slightly earlier time of day, thereby not revealing as clearly the relief panels in the rear of the porch. It is now in the collection of the Canadian Centre for Architecture in Montreal.

Plate 2

19. Ozymandias was an alternate name for Ramses II (1292–1225 B.C.), said to be the pharaoh referred to in Genesis and Exodus and one of Egypt's greatest builders. The impressive statue of Ramses II was contained in the first court of his vast mortuary temple known as the Ramasseum. Comprehensive plans and views of the site are given in *Monuments of Egypt: The Napoleonic Edition* (Princeton: Princeton Architectural Press, 1987), which is

a reprint of the archeological plates from the official publication of Napoleon's campaign, *La Description de l'Egypte* (Paris: Imprimerie imperiale, 1809–1823).

20. Described in 60–57 B.C. by the Greek historian Diodorus, in *Diodorus of Sicily*, trans. C. H. Oldfather (London: Heinemann, 1933; New York: Putnam, 1933), vol. 1, 169.

21. Itier's work was rediscovered only twenty years ago. See Gilbert Gimon, "Jules Itier," *Prestige de la Photographie* 9 (April 1980): 6–31, and by the same author, "Jules Itier, Daguerreotypist," *History of Photography* 5 (July 1981): 225–244. Itier's work with the daguerreotype in China in 1843–1846 was noted in *La Lumière* 3 (October 22, 1853) at the time his *Journal d'un voyage en Chine* (Paris: Dauvin et Fontaine, 1848–1853) was published.

22. Vivant Denon, *Voyage dans la Basse et la Haute Egypte pendant les campagnes du Général Bonaparte* (Paris: Didot, 1802).

23. The visible vaulted brick chambers were cursorily noted by Napoleon's expedition, partially explored by Lepsius in the late 1840s and by Mariette in 1850–1863, but not fully excavated until 1906–1909. An elaborate restoration is still in progress.

Plate 3

24. In addition to being one of the New World's earliest daguerreotypists, Dr. Bemis was a maker of watches and surveying instruments, but he was particularly noted for his major improvements to false teeth. His work in these fields is listed in Charles E. Smart, *The Makers of Surveying Instruments in America Since 1700* (Troy, New York: Regal Art Press, 1962), which was brought to our attention by Sherry Welding-White of the New Hampshire Historical Society. For Bemis's photographic work, see the brief biography by Janet Buerger, "American Landscape Photography from the Nineteenth-Century Collections," *Image* 25 (June 1982): 4–7. A fuller discussion of his work appears in Richard Rudisill, *Mirror Image, The Influence of the Daguerreotype on American Society*, (Albuquerque: University of New Mexico Press, 1971), 69–70.

25. Today Bemis's entire daguerreian outfit, including the original bill of sale ($51 for the equipment), is in the collection of the International Museum of Photography and Film at George Eastman House, having been purchased in 1937 from a legatee of Bemis's estate. Newhall, *Daguerreotype in America*, 30–31, describes Bemis's equipment.

26. We are grateful to James L. Garvin, architectural historian at the New Hampshire Division of Historical Resources, for assisting us with information about the turnpike and inns.

27. One view in the International Museum of Photography collection (80.788.3) shows a corner of this barn, the fields further down the turnpike, and a mile-post marker with the numeral "6" (reversed), therefore placing it close to the inn where Bemis stayed.

In this area today, a barn still exisits of the same type seen in this daguerreotype; it could well be from the same period. Barn types generally changed little within an area as the local builders repeated the designs they originally learned. For this type of barn see Allen G. Nobel, *Wood, Brick and Stone*, vol. 2 "Barns and Farm Structures," (Amherst: University of Massachusetts Press, 1984), 17–18.

28. Only twelve Bemis daguerreotypes were known until 1980, when additional examples were discovered in the stone house Dr. Bemis had built for himself in 1855–1859 in Hart's Location, across the road from the inn where he had originally stayed. Bemis's house was run as an inn in the 1920s by Florence Morey, the daughter-in-law of the property manager to whom Bemis had left his entire estate, including the house and its contents, upon his death in 1881. In November 1980, the last legatee put the furnishings and unexpected treasure trove of daguerreotypes up for auction by Arthur Smith in Middlebury, Vermont. A report on the auction by William B. Becker appears in *Maine Antique Digest* (January 1981): 15A. For another Bemis plate in the J. Paul Getty Museum collection, see plate 61.

For a detailed, documented history of Bemis's enormous land holdings in Crawford Notch, see Marion L. Barney, *Hart's Location in Crawford Notch* (Portsmouth, New Hampshire: Peter E. Randall, 1997), 50–95.

Plate 4

29. This plate is one of a pair with plate 59, both of which are identical in size and are marked on their backs with an early inscription "Martinique."

30. Decrees put into effect describing the paving and care of the streets in Martinique identify this street as the type specifically used in Saint Pierre. Henry Delinde, *Guide des sources de l'architecture d'après les registres du conseil privé* (Fort-de-France: Archives departmentale de la Martinique, 1991).

An unusual aspect of this street is the stone gutters, whose presence is explained by a description of the city that mentions the street as being frequently hosed down. See Jules Charles-Roux, *Colonies et pays de protectorats* (Paris: Commission Exposition Universelle de 1900, 1900), 63.

31. Eugène Revert, *La Martinique: Étude géographique et humaine* (Paris: Nouvelles editions latines, 1949), 302.

Plate 5

32. Review by Francis Wey of Eugéne Piot, *L'Italie Monumentale*, in *La Lumière* 1 (August 17, 1851): 111.

33. See Frederick Hartt, *Florentine Art under Fire* (Princeton: Princeton University Press, 1949), 80, 86, 135.

Plate 6

34. A detailed account of Mayall's entire life is given in Léonie L. Reynolds and Arthur T. Gill, "The Mayall Story," *History of Photography* 9 (April-June 1985): 89–107. Helmut Gernsheim, *The Origins of Photography*, rev. 3d ed. (New York: Thames & Hudson, 1982), 141–142, covers his daguerreian career. A rare description of his life in Philadelphia in 1846, including an 1846 portrait of him, is found in Pamela C. Powell, *Reflected Light* (Westchester, Pennsylvania: Chester County Historical Society, 1988), 17–18.

35. Gernsheim, *Origins of Photography*, 141–142, refers to several contemporary articles including, *The Photographic Art-Journal* (October 1849): 294, which describes a Mayall daguerreotype as "the largest picture which the pure pencil of the sunbeam has ever produced." *Humphrey's Journal* 4 (April 1, 1853): 365 states "Mr. Mayall's pictures are the largest taken in the city of London."

36. See *The Athenaeum* (October 4, 1851): 1051, and particularly the laudatory description reprinted from *The Morning Chronicle* [London] in *The Photographic Art-Journal* 2 (November 1851): 315–316.

37. John Tallis, *Tallis's History and Description of the Crystal Palace and the Exhibition of the World's Industry in 1851* (London: J. Tallis, 1852), vol. 1, 197.

38. Quoted in John McKean, *Crystal Palace: Joseph Paxton and Charles Fox* (London: Phaidon, 1994), 33.

39. *The Photographic Art-Journal* 2 (November 1851): 315 states "Mr. Mayall appears to have tried all points and corners of the place, until there is hardly a possible variety of view which he has not seized."

40. See *The Athenaeum* (October 4, 1851): 1051.

Chapter 2
Stealing from the Mirror

1. Kravets, nos. 142–143, 145, 150–151.

2. The only known copy of the March 1838 prospectus is in the collection of the International Museum of Photography and Film at George Eastman House, reproduced and translated by Beaumont Newhall, *Image* (March 1959): 32–36.

3. The writer for *La Presse* was Jules Pelletan (January 24, 1839): 1–2.

4. Janin's article, entitled "Le Daguereotype"[sic], was published in *L'Artiste*, ser. 2, vol. 2, no. 11, [January 28, 1839]: 145–148.

5. Gernsheim, *Daguerre*, 95.

6. No early portraits by Daguerre exist. Apparently he did not produce any until about 1843, after the obstacles in making a portrait had been removed by others. See Buerger, *French Daguerreotypes*, 8.

7. First published in *The Literary Gazette* (October 26, 1839): 685. Quoted in Rudisill, *Mirror Image*, 61.

8. Newhall, *Daguerreotype in America*, 25.

9. For the contribution of Philadelphians to shortening exposure time, see Stapp, *Robert Cornelius*, 36–38.

10. William Welling, *Photography in America: The Formative Years: 1839–1900*, (New York: Thomas Y. Crowell, 1978), 38–39.

11. See Barger and White, *Daguerreotype*, 38, for a description of the gilding process.

12. The daguerreotype's use was restricted only in England, where Daguerre had patented his process.

13. Marc Antoine Gaudin and Noël-Paymal Lerebours, *Derniers perfectionnements apportés au daguerréotype*, 3d ed. (Paris: N. P. Lerebours, 1842), 57.

14. Such comments are found in the Langenheim Brothers' account books cited by Julius F. Sachse, "The Dawn of Photography: Early Daguerreotype Days [X]," *American Journal of Photography* 18 (March 1897): 106.

15. E. De Valicourt, *Nouveau manuel de photographie sur papièr, sur métal et sur verre* (Paris: Librairie encyclopedique de Roret, 1851), 213.

16. For a comprehensive survey, see Floyd Rinhart and Marion Rinhart, *American Miniature Case Art* (South Brunswick and New York: A. S. Barnes, 1969; London, Thomas Yoseloff, 1969).

For thermoplastic cases, which came into use in about 1853, see Clifford Krainik, *Union Cases: A Collector's Guide to the Art of America's First Plastics* (Grantsburg: Centennial Photo Service, 1988).

17. From an advertisement about 1842 on the reverse of a daguerreotype portrait by Byron Dorgeval in the collection of Robert Shimshak. It is reproduced and translated in Robert Flynn Johnson, *The Power of Light: Daguerreotypes from the Robert Harshorn Shimshak Collection* (San Francisco: Fine Arts Museums of San Francisco, 1986), 9.

18. Such manuals were issued during most of the nineteenth century, beginning as early as 1842. The most comprehensive instructions were given by Marcus Aurelius Root, *The Camera and the Pencil* (1864; reprinted Pawlet, Vermont: Helios, 1971).

19. The poem was published in *The Museum of Foreign Literature, Science and Art* 14 (August 1841): 501. Reference courtesy of Gary W. Ewer.

20. Plate 7 is inscribed on the green silk pad of the case "Edward Carrington, Jr. 1842;" Plate 8 is inscribed on its pad "UNCLE ED/EDWARD/CARRINGTON."

21. Originally a jeweler, Gurney learned daguerreotyping in March 1840 and opened one of the earliest galleries in New York that same year. He consistently was awarded prizes for his widely exhibited work, culminating in winning, in 1853, the prestigious Anthony Prize, an ornately chased silver pitcher, awarded to the best entrant by a distinguished panel including the two pioneers in the field, Samuel Morse and John Draper.

22. Using a vase within the portrait inscribed with the name and location of the daguerreotypist was a rare but not exceptional practice in the 1840s. Three examples of it exist in the Smithsonian Institution's collection, one by Phineas Pardee of New Haven; two by E. W. Vose of Philadelphia.

23. For a brief biographical summary of Ford see Rinhart, *American Daguerreotype*, 391.

24. We wish to thank Peter E. Palmquist for his knowledgeable information about Ford and early California daguerreotypists, which led to our being able to assign a date for the images and provided an insight into the character of these portraits.

Plate 13

25. See Julius F. Sachse, "Philadelphia's Share in the Development of Photography," *Journal of the Franklin Institute* 135 (April 1893): 271–287. Also see Kenneth Finkel, *Nineteenth-Century Photography in Philadelphia: 250 Historic Prints from the Library Company of Philadelphia* (New York: Dover Publications, 1980).

26. The Langenheims advertised their agency and its five agents beyond Philadelphia in *The New York Herald* (August 27, 1843); reference courtesy of Gary W. Ewer.

27. Early business documents about the concern are given in a series of articles by Julius F. Sachse entitled "The Dawn of Photography. Early Daguerreotype Days," published in *American Journal of Photography* 16 (June 1895): 259–266 and 17 (July 1895): 306–310. Their advertisements from the 1840s are reproduced in number 18 (March 1897): 104–105. For a more recent account of the studio see George S. Layne, "The Langenheims of Philadelphia," *History of Photography* 11 (January-March 1987): 39–52. A factual summary biography appears in Rinhart, *American Daguerreotype*, 399.

28. The official report on the Great Exhibition of 1851 appeared in eight luxurious volumes. Four contain the reports of the juries for each class, the third of which contains the section on photography which was included in Class 10, which combined "Philosophical, Musical, Horological and Surgical Instruments." Other references to the photographs on display also occur in other volumes. Our quotation comes from volume three, page 522.

Plate 14

29. For sources on Mayall's career, see chapter 1, note 34.

30. See *Humphrey's Journal* 4 (1853): 365.

31. Reproduced in Reynolds and Gill, "Mayall Story," 91.

Plate 15

32. We have profited enormously from discussing this piece with Kenneth Finkel, whose book *Nineteenth-Century Photography in Philadelphia* reproduces on plate 35 a Root daguerreotype with an ornamental mat identical to the one seen here.

Root started daguerreotyping in Philadelphia in 1844, and in 1846 he purchased the studio of Mayall upon his return to England. The most recent biography of Root is by Clyde H. Dilley, "Marcus Aurelius Root: Heliographer," *The Daguerreian Annual 1991*: 42–47.

33. Marcus Aurelius Root, *The Camera and the Pencil*, (1864; reprint Pawlet, Vermont: Helios, 1971).

34. Cited by Dilley, "Marcus Aurelius Root," 44, note 7, quoting Root's article, "Qualification of a First-Class Daguerreotypist," *The Photographic Art-Journal* 6 (August 1853): 113.

Plate 16

35. The most complete and recent work on the Flandrin brothers is the catalogue of the exhibition held in 1984 and 1985 in Paris and Lyon, *Hippolyte, Auguste et Paul Flandrin; Une fraternité picturale au XIX siècle* (Paris: Ministre de la culture, 1984). A family memoir using letters and journals was privately published in Paris in 1984, entitled *Les frères Flandrin: Trois jeunes peintres au XIX siècle*.

Plate 17

36. We are grateful to Philippe Garner, senior director, Sotheby's London, for providing us with unpublished documentation recording Constable's description of his invention in a letter of April 11, 1854. Garner has amassed a substantial collection of copies of unpublished manuscript material related to Constable that he is hoping to include in a later publication. In the meantime, a short biography by Garner has appeared in *History of Photography* 15 (Autumn 1991): 236–240, as well as in the entry for Constable in the British *Dictionary of National Biography*.

37. Constable also invented a "sand clock," described as a "very convenient addition to the paraphernalia of the Daguerreian." *The Daguerreian Journal* 1 (January 1, 1851): 111.

38. Unfortunately, none of Constable's daguerreian portraits of this type has been published. One of Henry Grece at the Smithsonian Institution, dated winter of 1841–1842, is particularly expressive.

Plate 18

39. No general biography of Hughes exists, only abbreviated dictionary entries, from which we learn that he began working in 1847 as an assistant to Mayall and opened his own studio in Glasgow in 1849. He stayed there until 1855, when he returned to London and bought Mayall's studio.

40. At the time this daguerreotype was made, John Werge was working as a colorist in Hughes's studio.

41. The date of the daguerreotype has to fall between the time the uniform was adopted in 1852 and Hughes's departure from Glasgow in June 1855. We are grateful to W. Y. Carman, of Sutton, Surrey, England, for identifying the uniform and the time it came into use. We wish to thank Peter Harrington, curator, Anne S. K. Brown Military Collection, Brown University, for contacting Carman on our behalf.

Plate 19

42. The most exhaustive treatment of Poe's images is found in the exemplary book by Michael J. Deas, *The Portraits and Daguerreotypes of Edgar Allan Poe* (Charlottesville: University Press of Virginia, 1989).

Plate 20

43. We wish to thank Dale Gluckman, curator of costumes and textiles at the Los Angeles County Museum of Art, for discussing with us the headdress, which she described as being very hard to identify since headdresses changed from village to village as well as through time, and as to whether or not the wearer was married. She agreed with us that the subject was a well-to-do burgher's wife, or chatelain, but stated she was not part of a religious order.

Plate 21

44. Previous references to the daguerreotypes of Eynard have incorrectly given his last name as Eynard-Lullin ever since the photographs in his family archive first came onto the market. Lullin is the family name of his wife. It never was used by him nor was he referred to as Eynard-Lullin during his long career. We are grateful to Daniel Girardin, curator, Musée de l'Elysée Lausanne, for verifying this.

45. Lerebours, *Traité*, describes his daguerreotypes as "amongst the most beautiful we have ever seen." Similar admiration for Eynard's work was expressed by J. Thierry, *Daguerréotypie* (1847; reprint, New York: Arno Press, 1979), 86.

46. Eynard's authorship also has been referred to as a joint endeavor with a Jean Rion on the basis of an inscription on one daguerreotype that says that Eynard's servant, Rion, assisted him in his daguerreotyping. In our opinion, this identification has elevated Rion beyond his actual participation as an assistant. To apply the same standard in the case of Talbot, for example, would require always citing Nicholaas Henneman, the servant who assisted him, as coauthor. Although Rion no doubt removed the lens cap for the self-portraits, Eynard was the photographer.

47. Eynard's objections to Vernet's portrait are detailed in an 1831 letter quoted in Reneé Loche, "Un cabinet de peintures à Genéve au XIXe siècle," *Genava* 27 (1979): 217.

48. The view shows the Temple of Saturn at the left and the Temple of Vespasian at the right taken from the Arch of Severus, an unusual point of view, superior, in terms of its sensitivity to the expressive quality of the lofty columns, to other early views that generally encompass more of the Forum. For an example see Buerger, *French Daguerreotypes*, fig. 56.

49. Cited in Christopher M. Woodhouse, *Capodistria: The Founder of Greek Independence* (London: Oxford University Press, 1973), who gives a full account of Eynard's primary role in this struggle.

50. For a recent account of Eynard's life, see Catherine Santschi, *J.-G. Eynard au temps du daguerréotype; Genève 1840–1860* (Neuchatel, Ides et Calandes, 1996).

Plate 22

51. The principal source of information about this firm is Charles L. Moore, *Two Partners in Boston: the Careers and Daguerreian Artistry of Albert Southworth and Josiah Hawes* (Ph.D. dissertation, University of Michigan, 1975). An exhibition catalogue based on the information in this dissertation is by Robert A. Sobieszek and Odette M. Appel, *The Spirit of Fact: The Daguerreotypes of Southworth and Hawes, 1843–1862* (Boston: Godine, 1976). Other works by this firm can be seen in plates 51 and 68.

Plate 23

52. Easterly is one of the few American daguerreotypists to have been the subject of a scholarly monograph: Dolores A. Kilgo, *Likeness and Landscape: Thomas M. Easterly and the Art of the Daguerreotype* (Saint Louis: Missouri Historical Society Press, 1994). It is an exemplary model.

Plate 24

53. Although prominent at the time in Philadelphia and frequent winners of awards at the Franklin Institute annual exhibition, the scarcity of their work today has kept them from being well known. See Welling, *Photography in America*, 98–100, as well as Rinhart, *American Daguerreotype*, 105–106, 393, 400.

54. For information concerning the jewelry and the probable material and color of the gown we are grateful to Joan Severa of Madison, Wisconsin, and to John Adams-Graf, curator, the Neville Public Museum, Green Bay, Wisconsin, who first identified the "pelerine" and cited as his source the *Ladies' Memorial* (Boston 1850), 47.

55. We have been unable to discover this impressive urn in any other daguerreotypes by these makers, a conclusion concurred with by Kenneth Finkle, who generously shared his opinion with us. Alice Frelinghuysen, curator, the Metropolitan Museum of Art, has suggested that it may be a unique piece made by a European firm for display at an exhibition earlier in the century. Philadelphia had several importers of fine china, porcelain, and Parian ware beginning in the 1830s.

Plate 25

56. A documented account of one of America's most important daguerreotypists is still lacking. In the *Daguerreian Annual 1994*, 49–56, Clifford Krainik made an update of the information given by Robert Taft in his pioneering article on Plumbe that appeared in *American Photography* 30 (January 1936): 1–12. Krainik straightened out some of the conflicting information, but the most complete biography of the artist continues to be the publication by George Gilbert, *Photography: the Early Years; A Historical Guide for Collectors* (New York: Harper and Row, 1980), 7–20.

Plumbe is discussed in various sections of Rinhart, *American Daguerreotype*, and a factual biographical entry is provided on page 406. The same authors published an informative biography in *New Daguerreian Journal* 3 (September 1974): 4–9. An account of Plumbe giving new information is found in Alan Fern and Milton Kaplan, "John Plumbe, Jr. and the First Architectural Photographs of the Nation's Capitol," *The Quarterly Journal of the Library of Congress* 31 (January 1974): 3–17. It is essentially concerned with his scenes of Washington, D.C., but most importantly includes a checklist of known daguerreian images by Plumbe.

57. A circular published on September 1, 1841, under the title of "United States Photographic Institute" describes in detail the benefits of Plumbe's system, including the cost of operation and the potential profit for the maker. The adjacent leaf of the circular, bearing the additional citation of Granite House, Exeter, New Hampshire, goes into greater detail about Plumbe's new camera and the promise of this new profession for "supplying the means of genteel support." It is suggested that Plumbe's camera "is so portable as to be carried in a lady's work bag." The statement signed by Plumbe is accompanied by some twenty endorsements of his work. Despite these self-serving notices, the circular is an impressive new document for the early history of the American daguerreotype and we are indebted to the generosity of Dennis Waters of Exeter, New Hampshire, in sharing it with us.

58. Plumbe laid particular stress on his system's ability to be used "in an ordinary room, *without opening a window.*" *Boston Advertiser* (March 17, 1841), cited by Rinhart, *American Daguerreotype*, 66–67. Plumbe again emphasized the advantage of this aspect of his system as saying it allowed a likeness to be taken "in an ordinary room, *without* requiring any peculiar adjustment of the light." This advertisement appeared in *The Exeter News-Letter* (August 3, 1841): 4 and was brought to our attention by Dennis Waters. This notice appears to discount any idea that a skylight was required, as is suggested in Rinhart, *American Daguerreotype*, 64.

Plate 26

59. For information concerning the subject's clothing— the fact that the boy's clothes are brand new with "room to grow" and that he was not simply dressing in imitation of a sailor—we are indebted to Susan J. Jerome, Mystic [Connecticut] Seaport Museum. We are also grateful to Thomas Moore, curator of photography, The Mariners' Museum, Newport News, Virginia, who added to our information about this young sailor by informing us that it was not until the "1880s that naval uniforms became strictly regulated."

Plate 27

60. Although Claudet is one of the most important fig- ures in the history of photography from the standpoint of both artist and scientist, no monograph has been pub- lished on his work. The late Arthur T. Gill completed con- siderable research on Claudet and published the most detailed biography in "Antoine Claudet, Photographer," *Modern Camera Magazine* (November 1961): 459–462ff. Research about Claudet's lifetime of work is hampered by the destruction of much of his work and papers in December 1867, a month after his death.

We have been fortunate to have had access to two theses written about Claudet, both of which include substantial amounts of unpublished material and were written with the cooperation of the Claudet family. The earlier one is by Linda Vance Sevey, *The Question of Style in Daguerreotype and Calotype Portraits by Antoine Claudet* (Master's thesis, Rochester Institute of Technology, 1977). The second is by Joan G. Coke, *Antoine François Jean Claudet: Artist, Photographer, and Scientist* (Master's thesis, University of New Mexico, 1985). We are grateful to both for being willing to share their valuable research with us.

61. A revealing illustration and a concise description of the use of the focimeter is given in Julius F. Sachse, "The Dawn of Photography: Early Daguerreotype Days [VI]," *American Journal of Photography* 13 (December 1892): 550. A more technical explanation is given in an unsigned article in *Image* 1, no. 2 (February 1952): 1–2.

62. The stereograph was introduced to the public at the Crystal Palace Exhibition in 1851 and was particularly admired by Queen Victoria.

63. Starting in 1851, most of Claudet's portraits were stereographs. Sevey, *Question of Style*, 42–43.

64. The existence and explanation of the four stereo daguerreotypes made for this experiment was first dis- closed in Sevey, *Question of Style*, 43. Another piece from this series with "4" given as the large numeral was auc- tioned at Sotheby Parke Bernet, New York, sale num- ber 3867, May 4, 1976. A further description with an illustration of the setup of the two cameras is given in Urs Tillmanns, *Geschichte der Photographie* (Frauenfeld: Huber, 1981), 187.

Plates 28 and 29

65. For a detailed account of the competition between Claudet and Beard during the early years of their studios see Gernsheim, *Origins*, 121–149. A thoughtful reappraisal of Beard's role is given by Roy Flukinger in "Beard and Claudet; a Further Inquiry," in *The Daguereotype: A Sesqui- centennial Celebration*, 91–96.

Plate 33

66. Despite the distinctive nature of this young girl's costume, we have been unable to associate it with any specific region. The barn in back left is a Western type, probably three-aisled with a peaked central nave. We are grateful to Alberta Parker Horn of Berkeley, California, for her information about the barn, and to John Adams- Graf, for his observations about the costume.

Plate 34

67. Little is known about Warren Thompson. The best account and illustrations of other self-portraits can be found in Buerger, *French Daguerreotypes*, 108–114, 229–231.

68. For details of his coloring process see Rinhart, *Ameri- can Daguerreotype*, 210.

69. The lengthy review of Thompson's entries at the 1849 exposition did not appear until 1851, since *La Lumière* only began publication that year. Laborde's review appeared on page 10.

70. Both of these feats were praised in *La Lumière* (1851): 11 and (1851): 161.

71. Cited by Buerger, *French Daguerreotypes*, 110 and 186, note 38.

Plate 38

72. Beneath the mat, an additional but not complete part of the hand holding the book is visible, as is slightly more of the lower arm. The bottom part of the plate has been roughly cut off by approximately one-half inch, but this change does not affect the image's basic character.

Chapter 3
The Artificial Retina

1. For Biot's comments, see the quotation in Gernsheim, *Daguerre*, 84, from *Comptes rendus* (January 7, 1839). An excellent chapter on the daguerreotype as a scientific tool is found in Barger and White, *Daguerreotype*, 72–97.

2. *Niles' National Register* 14 (March 18, 1843); reference courtesy of Gary W. Ewer.

3. See Rinhart, *American Daguerreotype*, 102–104, for daguerreotypes of the moon. See Sally Pierce, *Whipple and Black: Commercial Photographers in Boston* (Boston: Boston Athenaeum, 1987) for an excellent overview of Whipple's work. Barger and White, *Daguerreotype*, 82–94, deals extensively with astronomical applications of the daguerreotype.

4. The inadequacy of drawings made from a microscope is described in Dionysis Lardner, *The Museum of Science and Art*, vol. 6 (London 1855), 99. For Donné, also see Buerger, *French Daguerreotypes*, 85.

5. Jay Ruby, *Secure the Shadow: Death and Photography in America* (Cambridge: MIT Press, 1995), is the most reliable study of postmortem paintings and daguerreotypes.

6. James Stuart and Nicholas Revett, *The Antiquities of Athens* (London 1762).

7. *Boston Evening Daily Transcript* (December 6, 1854): 2; reference courtesy of Gary W. Ewer.

8. Edgar Allan Poe, "The Daguerreotype," *Alexander's Weekly Messenger* (January 15, 1840); reprinted in Alan Trachtenberg, ed., *Classic Essays on Photography* (New Haven: Leete's Island Books, 1980), 37–38.

Plate 41

9. On the advantages of photography for the geologist see Jules Girard, *La photographie appliqué aux études géographiques* (Paris 1871), 82–83.

10. For information on early geologists see Archibald Geikie, *The Founders of Geology*, 2d ed., (1905; reprint, New York: Dover Publications, 1962). Also see "Earth Sciences," *New Encyclopaedia Britannica* (Chicago 1995) 17:619–620.

11. The description and appreciation of the work of the Bisson frères in Switzerland appeared in an article signed A. T. L., "La photographie appliquée á la géologie," *La Lumière* 5 (September 15, 1855): 146.

Plate 42

12. We are able to locate this scene so specifically because the inscription (in French) on the back of the daguerreotype reads: "Sachi [Arabic for water-wheel] established on the right bank of the Nile across from the ruins of the Temple of Ombos 1845."

13. Excerpts from the journal of Maxime Du Camp's voyage in Egypt are published in the exhibition catalogue *En Egypte au temps de Flaubert; les premiers photographes; 1839–1860*, 2d ed. (Paris: Kodak-Pathé, 1980), 27.

14. For a general overview of French daguerreotypists and anthropology, see Buerger, *French Daguerreotypes*, 90–91, and Frizot, *Nouvelle historie de la photographie* (Paris: A. Biro, 1994), 47. The book *Anthropology and Photography: 1860–1920*, edited by Elizabeth Edwards (New Haven: Yale University Press, 1992) deals only with photography in Great Britain.

15. The article by Serres appeared in *La Lumière* 2 (August 7, 1852): 130.

Plate 43

16. Johann Caspar Lavater, *Essai sur la Physiognomie* (The Hague: n.p. 1781–1803).

17. The principal book dealing with the subject is *Seeing the Insane* (New York: Wiley, 1982) by Sander L. Gilman, who personally was of great assistance to us in discussing this work.

18. Another way of raising funds for an asylum was tried in the United States through the sale of the book *The Mind Unveiled* (Philadelphia: Hunt, 1858) by Isaac Newton Kerlin, the director of the Philadelphia Asylum. It included tipped-in photographs of the inmates. See Gilman, *Seeing the Insane*, 172.

Plate 44

19. We want to thank David Cherinin, D.M.D., who assisted us in identifying the dental problems of the subject, and Professor William Sharp who, on the basis of his expertise in directing theatrical productions, judged the subject was not attempting to express any emotion. Previous description of this piece identified it as a man yawning.

Plate 45

20. Schoolcraft's descriptions are found in his *Historical and Statistical Information Respecting the History, Condition and Prospects of the Indian Tribes of the United States: Collected and Prepared under the Direction of the Bureau of Indian Affairs, per Act of Congress of March 3d, 1847*. Schoolcraft's original reading of the pictographs is discussed on pages 109–111 of Part 1, published in 1851. His revised conclusion is found on pages 119–120 of Part 4, published in 1854.

21. We have dated the daguerreotype to July 7, 1853, to accord with the date inscribed by Seth Eastman on a beautiful, delicate pencil drawing of Dighton Rock from his sketch book in the collection of the Peabody Museum,

Harvard University. We are grateful to Jane Emack-Cambra, of the Old Colony Historical Society, Taunton, Massachusetts, for uncovering King's vital statistics.

22. Concerning Eastman's daguerreotypes of Indians see Harold Francis Pfister, *Facing the Light: Historic American Portrait Daguerreotypes* (Washington, D.C.: Smithsonian Institution Press, 1978), 198. Its source is the book written by Eastman's wife about their life while Eastman was stationed at Fort Snelling (1841–1848). Mary Eastman, *Dahcotah, or, Life and Legends of the Sioux Around Fort Snelling* (1849; reprint, New York: Arno Press, 1975).

23. Another, slightly out of focus, image shows Eastman in a top hat, reclining barefoot on the rock. Collection, Massachusetts Historical Society, Boston.

Plate 46

24. The comment by Oliver Wendell Holmes was originally published in "The Stereoscope and the Stereograph," *Atlantic Monthly*, June 1859. Reprinted in Vicki Goldberg, ed., *Photography in Print* (Albuquerque: University of New Mexico Press, 1988), 110.

Plate 47

25. The label on the reverse does not bear a reproduction of the medal Durheim won at the Paris Exposition of 1855, therefore this daguerreotype presumably predates 1855. While giving the same address in Bern, his labels appear in both French and German. Accordingly, his name is given as Charles or Carl. See the exhibition catalogue *Swiss Photographers from 1840 until Today* (Zurich: A. Niggli, 1977), fig. 24.

Plate 48

26. Janin, *L'Artiste*, ser. 2, vol. 2, no. 11 [January 28, 1839]: 147.

27. This 1841 daguerreotype may be the first to have been made of a recently painted work. Ingres is regarded as one of the first painters to have his own work photographed, but up to now the evidence has only come from literary sources. Aaron Scharf, *Art and Photography* (London: Penguin Books, 1986), 49, quotes a letter by Ingres of December 10, 1842, about not varnishing a painting until after a daguerreotype was made of it.

28. The complex history of this painting is detailed by Hélène Toussaint, *Les portraits d'Ingres: Peintures des musées nationaux* (Paris: Ministere de la culture, 1985), 79–96.

29. For information on Brevière see Jules Adeline, *L. H. Brevière* (Rouen 1876), 95–97. Examples of his experimental etched daguerreotypes can be found in Stefan Richter, *The Art of the Daguerreotype* (London: Viking, 1989), 120–121.

30. For the 1843 letter from Ingres regarding the daguerreotypes of Cherubini see Boven d'Agen, ed., *Ingres d'après une Correspondance Inédite* (Paris 1909), 362.

Plate 49

31. All information about the painting, the legend of Florinda, and critical reactions comes from the exhibition catalogue *Franz Xaver Winterhalter et les cours d'Europe de 1830 à 1870* (Paris: Musée du Petit Palais, 1988), 45–46, 195–196, and cat. no. 38.

32. The painting shown in the Salon of 1853 is now in the collection of The Metropolitan Museum of Art, New York, bequest of William H. Webb, 1899. We are grateful to Rebecca A. Rabinow, Department of European Paintings, for her help.

33. The very large engraving (28 by 38 inches) was commissioned and published by the art gallery Goupil et Cie. of Paris in April 1858, as recorded on the final print, a copy of which is in the collection of the Philadelphia Museum of Art. We are grateful to John Ittmann, curator of prints at the museum, for his help in obtaining this information. The engraver was Philipp-Herman Eichens (1813–1886), who began to make reproductions of paintings for Goupil in 1849.

Such black-and-white prints were not only advertisements for paintings on sale, but were widely popular themselves as pictures to be hung in Victorian parlors. Long out of favor, these prints today are difficult to locate, as is information concerning them. Particularly valuable in this regard is the catalogue by Brenda D. Rix for the Art Gallery of Ontario's 1983 exhibition entitled *Pictures for the Parlour* (Toronto: Art Gallery of Ontario, 1983).

34. Despite its huge size, a daguerreotype could have been made from the painting because the ample, skylit galleries of Goupil et Cie. would easily have provided enough light to make the photograph.

35. The margins surrounding the print can be seen beneath the metallic mat that frames the daguerreotype. They are without the information concerning owner, title, date, artist, or name of engraver, which would be added before final printing. An identical, but smaller (sixth-plate) daguerreotype of the proof descended in the family of the Meade Brothers Studio (active New York 1850–about 1863) and is now in the collection of the National Portrait Gallery, Washington, D.C.

Plate 50

36. Information concerning Claudet is from Gernsheim, *Daguerre*, 150; Lerebour's sets of nude studies are discussed in Welling, *Photography in America*, 187.

37. This lithograph was reproduced in McCauley, *Industrial Madness*, 168, and we are indebted to her for guiding us to its source.

38. Delacroix's enthusiasm for the daguerreotype has been discussed in many articles and books, but the most concise treatment can be found in Van Deren Coke, *The Painter and the Photograph; from Delacroix to Warhol*, rev. ed. (Albuquerque: University of New Mexico Press, 1972), 7–10.

39. Quoted in Coke, *Painter and Photograph*, 12.

Plate 51

40. The principal catalogue of the works of Powers is by Richard Wunder, *Hiram Powers, Vermont Sculptor, 1805–1873* (Newark: University of Delaware, 1991). Although the author documents the different versions of this piece, he does not detail the specific differences between them and, disappointingly, does not include daguerreotypes on his list of graphic reproductions of the sculpture.

Although six marble versions of *The Greek Slave*, each slightly different from the other with respect to drapery and chains, were made in Powers's studio in Italy, only four came to the United States. The versions now at the Corcoran Gallery of Art and the Newark [New Jersey] Museum of Art are the ones that possibly could be the subject of this daguerreotype. Another, now at the Brooklyn Museum of Art, shows differences from the daguerreotype and was not completed until after 1866, too late for a daguerreotype to be a likely means of copying. The version at the Yale University Art Gallery has an elaborate pedestal, unlike that shown here. Because only the back of the sculpture is seen in this daguerreotype, in order to identify which of the two possible versions is represented, we examined and photographed each from the viewpoint of the daguerreotype. The manner in which the folds of cloth hang, and the way the fringe is arranged around the base, allowed us to determine that the Newark version is the one shown here. The Newark version was exhibited in Boston in 1848 and 1849. For their generous assistance we wish to thank Joseph Jacobs, curator of painting and sculpture, The Newark Museum; Julia Solz, of the Corcoran Gallery of Art; and Judith Lanius.

41. Contemporary reactions by viewers of the sculpture are found in Wunder and particularly in Donald M. Reynolds, *Hiram Powers and His Ideal Sculpture* (New York: Garland, 1977).

42. The letters between Powers and his tour manager, Miner K. Kellogg, are preserved in the Hiram Powers papers at the Archives of American Art. A description of the preferred installation and a sketch of the design of the gas lamp to be used for illumination are found in a letter of August 29, 1847, from Kellogg to Powers. Microfilm 1131.

43. Apparently a concern on the part of Powers whether his tour manager, Kellogg, had profited unduly some six years earlier from selling the rights to photograph *The Greek Slave* led to an exchange of letters between Whipple and Powers. In that context, Whipple told, in a letter of April 1854, about the restrictions put on him at the time, but added that "Southworth had first copied the slave" and exhibited an example which had made Kellogg "furious." See Archives of American Art, microfilm roll 1137, letters April 1, 1854, January 1, 1855, February 13, 1855. We are grateful to Joan Murray for having directed our attention to this exchange.

44. This previously unnoticed article praising the three-view plate by Southworth and Hawes appeared in *The Boston Evening Transcript* (July 21, 1848): 2.

45. The description by Southworth and Hawes of the magnification of the daguerreotype and the illusion it created in their studio appeared in an advertisement written by them for *The Boston Directory* (Boston 1851), 32.

46. After 1850, many daguerreotypes and, in particular, paper stereographs were issued of various versions of *The Greek Slave*. Most, however, are based on terra-cotta models fashioned after the marbles. One such set shows an arm bracelet on the sculpture. This marks it as a photograph of a later copy in which the casting joint was disguised by the bracelet. We wish to thank Julian Wolff for sharing with us his daguerreotypes representing several versions of *The Greek Slave*.

Chapter 4
An Intruder in the Realm

1. For the history and popularity of lithographs, see Beatrice Farwell, *French Popular Lithographic Imagery: 1815–1870*, vol. 1 (Chicago: University of Chicago Press, 1981).

2. Conte's invention is described and illustrated in *Monuments of Egypt: The Napoleonic Edition* (Princeton: Princeton Architectural Press, 1987), 26–29. For statistics see pages 27–28.

3. Report on the diagraphe and the discusssion of the 1831 meeting of the Société libre des Beaux Arts is reproduced in Heinz Buddemeier, *Panorama, Diorama, Photographie* (Munich: W. Fink, 1970), 194–196. A long discourse on the difference between the products of the machine, the diagraphe, and true artistic genius appears in *L'Artiste* of 1833, reprinted in Buddemeier, 196–199. On the diagraphe and Versailles see Buddemeier, 331–332, which reproduces a letter from *Le Journal des Artistes* of 1836.

4. Following the *The Spectator*'s report of February 2, 1839, on the daguerreotype, the invention of Collas is discussed, page 115. The report in *The Literary Gazette* [London] (August 24, 1839): 538–539 appeared after Arago's disclosure of Daguerre's secret.

Interestingly, the first edition of Daguerre's manual that Susse frères published in 1839 included, in the back, an extensive price list of their inventory of reduced copies of sculpture.

A discussion on reproducing sculpture by photographic and mechanical means occurs in Robert Sobieszek "Sculpture as the Sum of its Profiles," *The Art Bulletin* 62 (December 1980): 617–630. Collas is discussed particularly on pages 624 and 627.

5. *L'Artiste*, ser. 2, vol. 2, no. 11 [January 28, 1839]: 148.

6. Charles Seignobos, *La Révolution de 1848—Le Second Empire* (Paris 1920–1922), 19–20.

7. For reaction to the report about the daguerreotype from his father see Viollet-le-Duc, *Lettres,* 166–167. He also disparages the work of Gavard.

8. Delaroche apparently was consulted immediately by Arago, as his opinion is quoted in the January 7, 1839, report appearing in *The Literary Gazette* [London] (January 19, 1839): 43. In these remarks Delaroche spoke primarily about the painterly effects of light and shade on objects of different textures and how even the time of day they were taken could be determined from their appearance. Arago apparently ignored this early attitude of Delaroche in favor of one less threatening to the painter. The widely quoted phrase "From today, painting is dead" was not attributed to Delaroche until 1874, when Gaston Tissandier cited it. Gernsheim, *Daguerre*, 95, states that they could find no earlier use of it.

9. François Arago, *Report to the Chamber of Deputies* (July 3, 1839), 23.

10. Daguerre's broadside, reproduced in *Image* 8 (March 1959): 36.

11. For Biot's comments, see Barger and White, *Daguerreotype*, 26, quoting from Robert Lassam, *Fox Talbot, Photographer* (Tisbury, Wiltshire: Compton Press, 1979), 26.

12. From a speech by Morse at the National Academy of Design on April 24, 1840, published in Root, 392.

13. The lithographic series *Voyages pittoresques et romantiques en l'ancienne France* appeared in numerous parts and was edited by Taylor, Nodier, and Cailleux.

14. Now at the Walker Art Gallery, Liverpool. A Diorama of this subject opened October 20, 1823, in Paris. Gernsheim, *Daguerre*, 180.

15. Letter concerning drawing received by Niépce from Daguerre, April 3, 1827. Kravets, no. 48.

16. Arago, *Report*, 17.

17. This concept is discussed in the seventeenth century by Roger de Piles. See Thomas Puttfarken, *Roger de Piles' Theory of Art* (New Haven: Yale University Press, 1985) for a new appraisal of de Piles's theories and their relevance for the appreciation of "painterly" representation. Titian's anecdote appears on page 87. For the continued application of Titian's principle see the exhibition catalogue by E. de Johng, *Still Life in the Age of Rembrandt* (Auckland: Auckland City Art Gallery, 1982), 111, where its use by Diderot is discussed.

Evidence that the "bunch of grapes" continued to be understood as a painterly expression well into the nineteenth century is given in the article by Peter Hecht, "Candlelight and Dirty Fingers," *Simiolus* 11 (1980): 31–34. A Parisian publication of 1826, *Dictionnaire du dessin*, includes an entry discussing the principle.

18. This unusual work has been ignored up to now by most photographic historians. Howard R. McManus of Roanoke, Virginia, described this daguerreotype in his article "Daguerreotype Treasures at the Smithsonian Institution," *The Daguerreian Annual 1996*, 256–257.

19. Affixed to the front of the framed work is the following inscription: "Painting by *Daguerre* the Inventor of the Art Presented / by Madame Daguerre to *Meade Brothers* at Bry sur Marne / France 1853."

20. Adrien Mentienne, *La Découverte de la photographie* (1892; reprint, New York: Arno Press, 1979), 111–112, refers to Daguerre's execution of monochrome paintings at the end of his life.

The dark portions on center of left side of figure 31 are the result of the brown velvet accidentally adhering to the substance which formed the image.

21. Edward Weston, "Photographic Art," *Encyclopedia Britannica*, 14 ed. (1941), vol. 17, 769–799. We thank Weston Naef for calling our attention to this comment.

Plate 52

22. For an attempt to reconstruct the extensive art gallery gathered by Eynard and his brother and father, see Renée Loche, "Une Cabinet de peintures à Genève au xix siècle," *Genava* 27 (1979).

Plate 53

23. Our ability to describe the location of these two figures within the courtyard of the hospital is due to our familiarity with this spectacular monument.

Plate 54

24. Inscribed on the backing is the note "Lisette Gilliard / cuisiniere / Susette / fermiere."

Plate 55

25. Again we are indebted to Dale Gluckman, curator of costumes and textiles, the Los Angeles County Museum of Art, who brought to our attention the correct identification of this object. At the time this daguerreotype was made, soap was produced in large wheels like cheese and cut into wedges for use. The laundress is seen here in the midst of rubbing soap into the more soiled parts of the garments.

Plate 56

26. This work has tentatively been attributed to Bruno Braquehais by Serge Nazarieff in *Early Erotic Photography* (Cologne: Taschen, 1993), 180–181. He admits, however, to having no specific evidence to confirm his judgment (p. 151). Our reason for rejecting this attribution is apparent from our discussion of the qualities of this work.

Plate 58

27. See Mary D. Sheriff, *Fragonard: Art and Eroticism* (Chicago: University of Chicago Press, 1990).

28. Beatrice Farwell, *French Popular Lithographic Imagery: 1815–1870, vol. 11, Pinups and Erotica*, (Chicago: University of Chicago Press, 1995). The author was generous in sharing the pre-publication manuscript of the volume and discussing many of the issues surrounding this representation. See also the critical exhibition catalogue edited by Beatrice Farwell, *The Cult of Images* (Santa Barbara: UCSB Art Museum, 1977).

29. An example is the 1833 lithograph by Pierre Numa, entitled *Le Toucher* in the collection of the Bibliothèque Nationale and illustrated as image 2G3 of the microfiche of volume 11 in Farwell, *French Popular Lithographic Imagery*.

30. A detailed discussion of the Parisian trade in pornographic photography is found in McAuley, *Industrial Madness*, chapter 4.

31. McAuley, *Industrial Madness*, 157, discusses obscene photographs made to order.

32. *The Sleepers*, or *Le Sommeil*, is in the collection of the Musée de Petit Palais, Paris. See the exhibition catalogue *Courbet Reconsidered*, ed. Sarah Faunce and Linda Nochlin, (Brooklyn: Brooklyn Museum, 1988), particularly the essay by Michael Fried, "Courbet's 'Femininity.'"

Plate 59

33. The inscription on the back, in period script, reads *"Veduta dell. lung arno — di Pisa / — mai 1844 / prise de l'hotel delle tre dunzelle."* The mixture of Italian and French words is typical of a traveler trying to pick up the local language but combining it when needed with a native tongue, in this case French, as indicated by the use of the phrase *prise de l'hotel* and the word *mai*.

34. In addition to revealing the writer's nationality as French, the inscription on the rear also gives us the date (May 1844) and the location (Hotel of the Three Damsels), from which the image was made.

Plate 60

35. Daguerreotype views of Spain are exceedingly rare, but this example is one in a series of six such views in the J. Paul Getty Museum collection. One view, taken in the Court of the Lions at the Alhambra, shows, posed by the fountain, a male figure who resembles Gautier in a later portrait (1849) taken by Gustave Le Gray. Gautier's trip in Spain lasted from May to September 1840 and included a visit to the Escorial as well as to the Alhambra.

The other earliest views of Spain—three are included in the first fascicles issued by Lerebours in 1840—do not correspond to the Getty views of the same subject. The Escorial was never included in the *Excursions daguerriennes*.

36. The basic work is George Kubler, *Building the Escorial* (Princeton: Princeton University Press, 1982). See particularly chapter 1, "The Changing Fame of the Escorial." Gautier is cited on page 10.

37. Théophile Gautier, *Wanderings in Spain* (London: Ingram, Cooke, 1853), 103–112. Gautier's writings first appeared serially from 1840 to 1843 in various French publications and were collected in book form in 1843 with the title *Tra los Montes*; reprinted in 1845 as *Voyage en Espagne*.

Also see Ann Wilshire, "Gautier, Piot and the Susse Frères Camera," *History of Photography* 9 (October–December 1985): 275–278.

Plate 61

38. We are grateful to James L. Garvin, architectural historian, the New Hampshire Division of Historical Resources, for assisting us with information about the turnpike and inn.

39. An example of its popularity as a tourist site can be seen in the description given in *The Fashionable Tour: A Guide to Travelers Visiting the Middle and Northern States*, 4th ed., (Saratoga Springs 1830). On page 339 the author remarks on the increase in the number of visitors to the White Mountains and suggests it is due to the interest excited by the avalanche.

Plate 62

40. Most of the accounts referred to come from extracts given in the basic book by Charles Mason Dow, *Anthology and Bibliography of Niagara Falls* (Albany: State of New York, 1921). For the French accounts see pages 22–25, 47–48.

41. These visitors to the falls approached from the bottom, along the Canadian shore.

42. Emmeline Stuart-Wortley, *Travels in the United States . . . during 1849 and 1850* (London: R. Bentley, 1851). Extract in Dow, *Anthology and Bibliography*, 246–247.

43. *Peck's Tourist's Companion to Niagara Falls* (Buffalo: Peck, 1845), 70.

44. Patrick V. Mc Greevy, *Imagining Niagara* (Amherst: University of Massachusetts Press, 1994), 2.

45. Anthony Trollope, *North America* (London: Chapman & Hall, 1862). Extract in Dow, *Anthology and Bibliography*, 300.

46. Anthony Bannon, *The Taking of Niagara: A History of the Falls in Photography* (Buffalo: Media Study / Buffalo, 1982), 14. Newhall, *Daguerreotype in America*, 68–69, speaks of the umbrellas.

47. We thank William H. Titus, registrar, the Heckscher Museum of Art, for his assistance in providing us with information about the painting.

48. Frederick Marryat, *Diary in America* (London: Longman, 1839). Extract in Dow, *Anthology and Bibliography*, 223–224.

Chapter 5
Capturing the Moment

1. "The Daguerreotype," *Portsmouth [New Hampshire] Journal* (May 12, 1840). We are indebted to Dennis Waters for providing us with this reference.

2. Arago's description of Daguerre's process was reported in *The Athenaeum* [London] (July 14, 1841): 539–540. See also Gernsheim, *Daguerre*, 120–121.

3. See Gernsheim, *Daguerre*, 123–124. The title page of Daguerre's brochure is reproduced opposite page 97.

4. *The Art Union* [London] (September 1841): 156.

5. *The Athenaeum* [London] (July 17, 1841): 540.

6. *Journal of the Franklin Institute of the State of Pa. And Mechanics Register* (April 1840), reproduced in *New Daguerreian Journal* 1 (April 1972).

Plates 63 and 64

7. We again appreciate Peter Harrington's assistance in identifying military uniforms, although the view is not detailed enough to say more than they are in Arabian dress. For information on the formation of the Algerian battalions see Maxime Weygand, *Histoire de l'Armée Française* (Paris: Flammarion, 1961), 271–273. For illustrations and discussion see the invaluable microtext by Beatrice Farwell, *French Popular Lithographic Imagery: 1815–1870* (Chicago: University of Chicago Press, 1983), vol. 3, 20.

Plate 66

8. This plate is one of a pair (see plate 4) that are identical in size and contain the early inscription "Martinique" on the back.

9. For the use of the "tree of liberty" during the Revolution of 1848 see Charles Seignobos, *La Révolution de 1848—Le Second Empire* (Paris 1920–1922), 25; and vol. 6 in *Histoire de France contemporaine depuis la Révolution jusqu'à la Paix de 1919*, Ernest Lavisse, ed. (Paris: Hachette, 1920–1922).

10. The *Boston Evening Transcript* of June 20 and 29, 1848, reported on the massacre at Martinique as beginning on May 22. For an account of the disturbances in Martinique see Seignobos, *La Révolution* 333, as well as the more recent account in Lyne Rose Beuze, *De la Chaine à la Liberté: l'Esclavage et la Martinique pendant deux siècles* (Fort-de-France: Bureau de Patrimonie, 1988), 85–88. Another account of the insurrection is in Marie-Hélène Leotin, *La Revolution Anti-esclavagiste de Mai 1848 en Martinique* (Fort-de-France: Apal Production, 1991).

11. Interestingly, the signer of the declaration was François Arago, the scientist most responsible for the introduction of the daguerreotype. He had assumed this ministerial post in the provisional government in 1848.

12. Augustin Cochin, *The Results of Emancipation*, trans. Mary L. Booth, 2d ed. (Boston: Walker, Wise, 1863), 275.

13. The identification of the view shown here was based on the description of Fort-de-France in Jules Charles-Roux, *Colonies et pays*, 53, and the 1831 map of the entire island by Monnier, corrected in 1868 and again by the U.S. Navy in 1887. The representation of the parade grounds remains the same through all emendations. We are grateful to Arlene Olivero of the Map Collection of Harvard University for her assistance.

14. The giant truncated tree, one of two famous trees described in early travel accounts as standing in this section of the parade ground, probably was damaged in the earthquake and hurricane of 1839 (see Charles-Roux, *Colonies et pays,* 53). (The world's first photographic exhibition was held in Paris on June 24, 1839, by Hippolyte Bayard for the benefit of the victims of this disaster.) This type of tree is concentrated in the New World tropics and is highly susceptible to wind damage. *Hura crepitans* is its botanical name, but it is known as the sand-box tree because its large fruits were exported to Europe, where they were hollowed, filled with sand, and used to blot ink on written documents.

15. Cochin, *Results of Emancipation*, 275.

Plate 67

16. All of the information concerning this scene and the events surrounding it have been taken from the exemplary article by Hugh C. Humphreys of Madison County, whose research disclosed the date and circumstances of the event as well as the maker of the daguerreotype— "'Agitate! Agitate! Agitate!' The Great Fugitive Slave Law Convention and its Rare Daguerreotype," *Madison County* [New York] *Heritage* 19 (1994): 3–64.

17. In his article, Judge Hugh Humphreys published a half-plate daguerreotype belonging to the Madison County [New York] Historical Society which, as it is reversed from the smaller Getty daguerreotype, was presumed to be the original. Since Judge Humphrey's article, however, a daguerreotype has been identified in a Pennsylvanian private collection that is apparently identical in size and image to the Madison County daguerreotype. Its existence raises questions about their relationship, and under what circumstances and when copies were made of an original. In Humphrey's article, he quotes the 1885 *Cazenovia Republican* as referring to "some fine old daguerreotypes of the scene" in existence at the time.

There is no doubt, however, that the Getty plate is a copy of another daguerreotype. It is smaller, and the reasons for believing it to be reversed are plausible and convincing. However, in this smaller copy the maker has concentrated only on the center of the scene, cropping out, as it were, the lower and upper portions that were out of focus. The smaller Getty version may well be one made at the time to be sent to other abolitionist figures (even perhaps to Chaplin himself) who were unable to attend what was, up to then, the strongest declaration of their opposition to slavery.

Plate 68

18. This is probably the most reproduced photograph of a medical subject. It became an icon when Beaumont Newhall published it in his first edition of *The American Daguerreotype* (New York: Duell, Sloan & Pearce, 1961), pl. 56.

What Newhall reproduced, however, was not an original daguerreotype but a paper print made in 1946 by the Boston print dealer Richard Holman from an old glass-plate negative he had recently found in material coming from the former Southworth and Hawes studio. Newhall correctly identified it as a copy from a "lost daguerreotype," but, following Holman, mistakenly stated it was a "reenactment" of the original October 16, 1846, operation that was, as we describe and illustrate in figure 36, a very different scene. In the years since Newhall's publication of the "lost original," the scene has been persistently misidentified and variously interpreted and dated. Our date is based on the surgical records available in the archives of the Massachusetts General Hospital.

During this period, the first publication of the original daguerreotype—nearly sixty years earlier—went unnoticed. In the book M. A. De Wolfe Howe, *Boston: The Place and the People* (New York: Macmillan, 1903), 326, it was correctly identified as an early operation using ether. At that time, the original daguerreotype was in the possession of Josiah B. Millet, of Cambridge, Massachusetts; in 1947, it emerged briefly on display at the New York Medical Society, where it was noted as being in the possession of Mrs. William H. Osborne. Its whereabouts were not recorded again until it was offered for sale in the early 1970s; it became part of the collection of the J. Paul Getty Museum in 1984.

19. Southworth and Hawes announced in *The Massachusetts Register: A State Record for the Year 1852* (Boston 1852), 328, that "We have made several pictures of the Surgeons of the Massachusetts [General] Hospital with the patient under the influence of ether, all accurate likenesses."

20. Now known as the "Ether Dome," this amphitheater, designed by Charles Bulfinch in 1816, was restored in 1996 to resemble its appearance in 1846 based on the daguerreotypes by Southworth and Hawes. An earlier restoration in 1896 followed the daguerreotype scenes, but without recognition that the daguerreotype image was reversed.

21. There is vivid controversy as to who first used ether for surgery. There are several contenders. Crawford Long of Georgia is credited with having preceded William T. G. Morton in such a practice, but made no public disclosure

of his findings, as Morton did. At the time, Boston recognized Morton as the principal individual responsible and rewarded him accordingly.

22. This is the first time this daguerreotype has been published. When the hospital placed its daguerreotypes on loan at Harvard's Fogg Art Museum, it was cataloged as being by "Mr. St. Clair," as it was inscribed on the back "Photographed by Mr. St. Clair 3/28/47." However, we have found documents in the hospital's archives that identify Mr. St. Clair as a photographer who was commissioned in 1947, at the time of the *centennial* of the operation, to copy the original daguerreotype, thus effectively removing him as the "daguerreotypist," as he previously had been identified.

Hospital records explain in detail the operation in which Dr. Warren removed a tumor from the neck of a young man who was anesthetized with ether from a glass flask (visible in the daguerreotype).

In addition to the reenactment daguerreotype, Massachusetts General Hospital owns one representing a woman patient and another one which is a similar view of the same operation as the Getty's daguerreotype. All three are on deposit at the Fogg Museum of Art.

23. The extended research which we undertook about this daguerreotype and its related images was made possible through the generous assistance of many people. As well as sharing his wide knowledge about the events surrounding this scene, Richard Wolfe, curator, rare books, Harvard's Countway Library of Medicine, allowed us to copy the paper print of the post-operation daguerreotype. We also wish to acknowledge Deborah Martin Kao, assistant curator, photographs, the Fogg Museum of Art, for her continued assistance and Michelle Marcella of the archives of the Massachusetts General Hospital, who made its records available to us and permitted us to publish its daguerreotype. Phyllis Ducette openly shared the research into these daguerreotypes she uncovered for her senior thesis at the University of Massachusetts, Boston. We wish to thank them all for their significant contributions.

A full monograph putting all these daguerreotypes into their proper setting, as well as making clear the genius of Southworth and Hawes in carrying out these assignments, is to be published separately.

Chapter 6
A Nation in Transition

1. See Bates Lowry, *Building a National Image: Architectural Drawings for the American Democracy, 1789–1912* (Washington, D.C.: National Building Museum, 1985; New York: Walker, 1985), 10–35, for descriptions and illustrations of L'Enfant's city plan and the extremely complicated building program for the Capitol from the first drawings for its design through its 1850s expansion.

2. For biographical information about Plumbe, see plate 25 and its note 56.

3. Letter of March 8, 1792, reproduced in "The Writings of George Washington Relating to the National Capital," *Records of the Columbia Historical Society* 17, 1914.

4. Although described in newspaper accounts of 1846, no actual examples of these key works were known until the early 1960s, when this daguerreotype of the Capitol was purchased in a shop in Massachusetts. It remained in a private collection until auctioned on October 5, 1995. A cache of other views by Plumbe of public buildings was found in a California flea market in 1971, six of which were purchased by the Library of Congress. Another view of the Capitol similar to this one but showing less of the surrounding area, was purchased by the Connecticut collector, Matthew R. Isenburg.

For a personal account of the flea market discovery and later identification of the daguerreotypes see Mike Kessler, "Once in a Lifetime: The True Story of the Plumbe Daguerreotypes," *The Photographist* no. 99 (Fall 1993): 10–22.

The Library of Congress daguerreotypes (which include a frontal view of the Capitol) are reproduced and discussed in Alan Fern and Milton Kaplan, "John Plumbe, Jr., and the First Architectural Photographs of the Nation's Capitol," *The Quarterly Journal of the Library of Congress* 31 (January 1974): 3–20. The Isenburg view of the Capitol is reproduced and discussed in Richard Field and Robin Jaffee Frank, *American Daguerreotypes from the Matthew R. Isenburg Collection* (New Haven: Yale University Art Gallery, 1989).

5. Announcements of Plumbe's views of public buildings were given in *The National Intelligencer* (January 28, 1846): 5; *The United States Journal* (January 29, 1846): 2; *Daily Times* [Washington] (February 20, 1846): 2.

The reference in *The United States Journal* (January 29, 1846): 2 to "sets" being offered by Plumbe has led to speculation that he intended to reproduce these views by the process he called "Plumbeotype," which scholars believe is no different from a lithograph. He began publishing "Plumbeotypes" in 1846 or 1847, but examples of them are extraordinarily rare, suggesting it was not a profitable venture. Of the thirty prints known to exist, only two deal with architectural subjects, one a view of the Washington Monument in Baltimore, the other a view of the Capitol directly from the east, seen at ground level, which corresponds to the Plumbe daguerreotype in the Library of Congress. It is a sketchy rendition without detail and could have been made without depending upon a daguerreotype as other similar views already existed in lithograph form. The most complete treatment of the Plumbeotype is found in Alan Fern "John Plumbe and the 'Plumbeotype,'" *Philadelphia Printmaking: American Prints before 1860* (West Chester, Pennsylvania: Tinicum Press, 1976), 149–164.

Plate 70

6. An overall history of the grist mill is given in John Storck and Walter Dorwin Teague, *Flour for Man's Bread* (Minneapolis: University of Minnesota Press, 1952).

7. Although there is no indication of the physical location of this mill either on the plate or on the label pinned to the interior of the case, the family name *Calkins* points to a New England location. According to the 1850 national census, that family name was found in Massachusetts, Connecticut, New Hampshire, Vermont, Rhode Island, and even New York; its presence in any of the southern states was limited to four individuals.

8. John J. Farrell, ed., *James K. Polk: 1795–1849* (Dobbs Ferry, New York: Oceana Publications, 1970), 26.

Plate 72

9. Discussions with many architectural historians led to no identification of this particular house, whose idiosyncratic style defies easy classification. All believed the location to be in the mid-Atlantic area; several believed it to be the site of the business of a nurseryman. For all their musings we are particularly indebted to Ford Peatross and Denys Peter Myers.

10. Both Margot Gayle, of the Friends of Cast Iron Architecture, and Barbara Rotundo, a historic-cemetery consultant, examined the cast iron fence but were not able to identify it specifically for date or location of manufacture.

Plates 73 and 74

11. *The Photographic Art-Journal* 2 (October 1851): 253.

12. The date of these two images has been determined by the location of Vance's studio given on the case. We appreciate Peter E. Palmquist's help in matters relating to Vance. See also his articles "Western Photographers, II: Robert Vance: Pioneer in Western Landscape Photography," *American West* 18 (September-October 1981): 22–27 and "Robert H. Vance: Pioneer Photographer," *The Argonaut* 8 (Spring 1997): 1–36.

13. The mining camp took its name from the creek, which was variously spelled as Rancheree, Ranchoree, or Rancherie. See Edwin G. Gudde, *California Gold Camps* (Berkeley: University of California Press, 1975).

Plate 75

14. We are grateful to Matthew R. Isenburg for showing us original stock certificates from gold mining companies, one of which is illustrated with a view of the entire mining operation, beginning with a depiction of a trestle high in the mountains, much like the one in this daguerreotype. It was issued by the Bear River & Auburn Water & Mining Company, which was capitalized in 1851 at $650,000.

15. A note in the daguerreotype case identified the scene as being on the North Fork of the American River.

Plate 76

16. Ronald E. Shaw, *Canals for a Nation* (Lexington: University of Kentucky Press, 1990), 200–203.

17. *The Photographic Art-Journal* 6 (October 1853): 222–223.

Epilogue—The Emergence of an American Identity

18. See Nathalia Wright, *Horatio Greenough: The First American Sculptor* (Philadelphia: University of Pennsylvania Press, 1963) and Sylvia E. Crane, *White Silence: Greenough, Powers and Crawford: American Sculptors in Nineteenth-Century Italy* (Coral Gables: University of Miami Press, 1972).

19. John Wood, ed., *America and the Daguerreotype* (Iowa City: University of Iowa Press, 1991), 181, 241.

Roster of Daguerreian Makers

in the Getty Museum Collection

Compiled by Michael Hargraves

The following is a list of daguerreotypists represented in the J. Paul Getty Museum as of the date of this publication. The number in brackets to the right indicates the number in the collection by examples by, or attributed to, the maker. Active dates are approximate.

Abadie, Martin (Russian, 1814–1855) [1]

Amadio, Joseph (British, active 1855) [2]

Anson, Rufus (American, active 1851–1867) [6]

Artaria, Ferdinando (Italian, 1781–1843) [1]

Atelier Héliographique (French, active late 1840s–1850s) [1]

Babbitt, Platt D. (American, d. 1879) [4]

Baker, Elisha W. (American, active 1843–1851) [1]

Beard, Richard A. (British, 1802–1885) [5]

Beard, Richard A. (British, 1802–1885) and **Foard, James F.** (British, active mid-1850s) [1]

Beckers, Alexander (American, b. Germany, active 1842–1869) [2]

Bell, William H. (American, b. England, 1830–1910) [2]

Bemis, Samuel A. (American, 1793–1881) [4]

Betts, Benjamin (American, active 1852–1857) and **Carlisle, Nelson** (American, active 1853–1857) [1]

Biewend, Dr. Hermann Carl Eduard (German, 1814–1888) [1]

Bisson, Louis Auguste (French, 1814–1876) [2]

Bogardus, Abraham (American, 1822–1908) [1]

Brady's Gallery (American, active 1852–1860) [2]

Brady, Mathew B. (American, 1823–1896) [1]

Braquehais, Bruno (French, 1823–1875) [7]

Broadbent, Samuel (American, 1810–1880) [1]

Bruder, I. (Swiss, active 1840s) [1]

Burbach, J. J. (German, active 1850s) [2]

Byerly, Jacob (American, about 1809–1881) [519]

Calderon, Marcos (Venezuelan?, active 1850s) [1]

Calvet, A. (French, active 1855–1871) [1]

Carleton, Samuel L. (American, 1822–1908) [1]

Cary, Preston M. (American, active 1845–1860) [1]

Certes, François Adolphe (French, 1805–1887) [2]

Chabrol, F. (French, active 1840–1855) [1]

Chase, Lorenzo G. (American, active 1844–1856) [1]

Churchill, Remmett E. (American, active 1840s–1860s) [1]

Clark, David (American, active 1853–1855) [1]

Claudet, Antoine François Jean (French, 1797–1867) [25]

Clausel, Alexandre-Jean-Pierre (French, 1802–1884) [1]

Collins, Thomas Painter (American, active 1846–1871) [3]

Constable, William (British, 1783–1861) [1]

Crespon, Antonie, Fils (French, active 1842–1895) [1]

Cutting, James Ambrose (American, 1814–1867) and **Turner, Austin Augustine** (American, about 1813–1866) [1]

Delamotte, Philip Henry (British, 1820–1889) [3]

De Lancy, W. J. A. (American, active 1840–1860) [1]

Delanoy, C. (French, active 1842) [1]

Devisuzanne, Félix (French, b. 1809, active 1845–1860) [3]

D'Olivier, Louis-Camille (French, 1827–after 1870) [2]

Dubois (French, active 1840–1855) [1]

Duboscq-Soleil, Louis Jules (French, 1817–1886) [6]

Durheim, Carl or Charles (Swiss, 1810–1890) [1]

Easterly, Thomas M. (American, 1809–1882) [1]

Elder, Anton (German, active 1845–1850) [1]

Ennis, T. J. (American, 1815–after 1856) [1]

Eynard, Jean-Gabriel (Swiss, 1775–1863) [92]

Fehrenbach, Emilian (British, active 1840–1855) [2]

Fish, Addison & Company (American, active 1850s) [1]

Fixon, E. (French, active 1840–1855) [1]

Fizeau, Armand-Hippolyte-Louis (French, 1819–1896) [2]

Fontayne, Charles H. (American, 1814–1901) and **Porter, William Southgate** (American, 1822–1889) [1]

Ford, James May (American, 1827–about 1877) [2]

Fraenkel, S., Jr. (German, active 1842–1852) [1]

Galle, A. (French, active 1850s) [1]

Gautier, Théophile (French, 1811–1872) [6]

Gay, Charles H. (American, active New London, Connecticut, 1847–1851) [1]

Germon, Washington L. (American, 1823–1877) [1]

Gros, Jean Baptiste Louis (French, 1793–1870) [1]

Gurney, Jeremiah (American, 1812–1895) [13]

Gurney, Jeremiah (American, 1812–1895) and **Gurney, Benjamin** (American, active 1840s–1874) [2]

Gurney Studio (American, active 1840s–1860s) [1]

Guy (British, active 1850s) [1]

Hale, Luther Holman (American, 1821–1885) [2]

Hamilton, George D. (American, active 1852–1865) [1]

Harrison, Gabriel (American, 1818–1902) and **Hill, George Waldo** (American, active 1852–1856) [1]

Heer, Samuel (Swiss, active 1839–1851) [3]

Heller, Johann Jacob (German, active 1840s) [1]

Herzog, L. von (German, active 1840–1855) [1]

Hesler, Alexander (American, b. Canada, 1823–1895) [1]

Hewitt, John M. (American, active 1844–1855) [1]

Higgins, Oscar T. (American, active 1854–1864) [1]

Hogg, Jabez H. (British, 1817–1899) [1]

Hughes, Cornelius Jabez (British, 1819–1884) [3]

Hutchings, George (American, active 1846–1847) [1]

Isenring, Johann Baptiste (Swiss, 1796–1860) [4]

Itier, Alphonse-Eugène-Jules (French, 1802–1877) [4]

Jacobs, Edward (American, b. England, 1813–1892) [1]

Jacquith, Nathaniel C. (American, active late 1840s–1850s) [1]

Johnson, George H. (American, b. 1823, active Sacramento and San Francisco, 1849–1852; New York City, 1879–1880) [1]

Keely, Robert Neff (American, active 1846–1856) [1]

Keenan, John A. (American, active 1848–1861) [1]

Kelsey, Calvin C. (American, active Chicago, 1849–1857, d. 1887) [1]

Kent, William Hardy (British, 1819–1907) [2]

Kerston, Marcellus (American, active 1853–1857) [3]

Kilburn, William Edward (British, active London, 1846–1862) [7]

King, Horatio B. (American, 1820–1889) [1]

Knickerbocker, Fredericks (American, active 1844–1845) [1]

Langenheim, Frederick (American, b. Germany, 1809–1879) and Langenheim, William (American, b. Germany, 1807–1874) [5]

Langenheim, William (American, b. Germany, 1807–1874) [1]

Lerebours, Nöel-Marie-Paymal (French, 1807–1873) [1]

Long, Enoch (American, 1823–1898) [1]

Long, Horatio H. (American, active 1844–1851, d. 1851) [1]

Lorenzen, Hermann (German, active 1850–1855) [1]

McClees, James Earle (American, 1821–1887) [1]

McClees, James Earle (American, 1821–1887) and Germon, Washington L. (American, 1823–1877) [3]

McElroy, John (American, active 1859) [1]

McIntyre, Sterling C. (American, active 1850–1851) [1]

Maguire, James (American, b. Ireland, 1816–1851) [1]

Margaritis, Philippos (Greek, 1810–1892) and Perraud, Philibert (French, b. 1815, active late 1840s) [11]

Matter (French?, active late 1840s?) [1]

Mayall, John Jabez Edwin (British, 1810–1901) [5]

Mayer, Léopold Ernest (French, 1817–about 1865), Mayer, Louis Frédéric (French, 1822–1913) and Pierson, Pierre Louis (French, 1822–1913); active as a group, 1855–1861 [1]

Meade, Charles Richard (American, 1827–1858) [1]

Meade, Charles Richard (American, 1827–1858) and Meade, Henry William Matthew (American, 1823–1865) [2]

Middlebrook, C. S. (American, active 1845–1854) [1]

Miller, James Sidney (American, active 1853–1860) [1]

Millet, Désiré François (French, active 1840–1868) [3]

Moulin, Jacques Antoine (French, 1802–after 1869) [2]

Moulthrop, Major (American, 1805–1890) [1]

Mucker (American, active 1840–1855) [1]

Nauman, W. (German, active 1840–1855) [1]

Négre, Charles (French, 1820–1880) [2]

Nichols, Sheldon K. (American, active 1849–1854) [1]

North, William C. (American, 1814–1890) [3]

Norwich (American, active 1855) [1]

Oehme, Carl Gustav (German, 1817–1881) [1]

Outley, John J. (American, active 1850s, d. 1892) and Wells, S. P. (American, active 1850s) [1]

Photographic Portrait Gallery (British, active 1850s) [1]

Plumbe, John, Jr. (American, b. Wales, 1809–1857) [12]

Plumier, Victor (French, active 1840s) [1]

Poitevin, Louis-Alphonse (French, 1819–1882) [7]

Price, R. T. (American, active 1850s) [1]

Ritton, Edward D. (American, 1823–1892) [1]

Root, Marcus Aurelius (American, 1808–1888) [3]

Root, Samuel (American, 1819–1889) [1]

Sabatier-Blot, Jean-Baptiste (French, 1801–1881) [2]

Saugrin, Louis François (French, active 1855) [1]

Schneidau, John Frederick Polycarpus von (American, b. Stockholm, 1812–1859) [2]

Schhtz, Thomas (German, active 1850s) [1]

Schweizer (Swiss, active about 1840–1855) [1]

Schwendlen, F. A. (German, active 1840–1855) [1]

Shew, Myron (American, 1824–1891) [1]

Shew, William J. (American, 1820–1903) [3]

Shlaer, Robert (American, b. 1943) [5]

Smith (American, active Boston, 1840–1842) [1]

Southworth, Albert Sands (American, 1811–1894) and Hawes, Josiah Johnson (American, 1808–1901) [10]

Stelzner, Carl Ferdinand (German, 1805–1894) [5]

Stone, Jesse (American, active 1851–1855) [1]

Tallett, G. R. (American, active 1850s) [1]

Tannenberg (German, active 1840–1850s) [1]

Thomas, Eugene (French, active 1856–1858) [1]

Thompson, Warren T. (American, active Philadelphia, 1840–1846; Paris, 1849–1860) [2]

Tompkins, Joseph H. (American, active 1855–1876) [1]

Tyler, Edward M. and Company (American, active 1854–1860) [1]

Upton, Benjamin Franklin (American, 1818–1899) [21]

Vance, Robert H. (American, 1825–1876) [9]

Walker, Samuel Leon (American, 1802–1874) [1]

Wehnert-Beckmann, Bertha (German, active 1850s) [1]

Weld, Ezra Greenleaf (American, 1801–1874) [1]

Werge, John (British, 1825–about 1902) [1]

Weston, James (Guillermo) P. (American, active South America, 1849; New York City, 1851–1852, 1855–1857) [5]

Whipple, John Adams (American, 1822–1891) [3]

White, Asa (American, active 1843–1851) [1]

Whitney, Edward Tompkins (American, 1820–1893) [1]

Williams, Thomas Richard (British, 1825–1871) [9]

Williamson, Charles Henry (American, b. Scotland, 1826–1874) [3]

Williamson, Charles Henry (American, b. Scotland, 1826–1874) and **Williamson, Edward M.** (American, active 1857–1859) [1]

Winter, Charles (French, active 1848–1880s) [1]

Woolen, J. (American, active 1852–about 1860) [1]

Young, H. C. (American, active 1850s) [1]

Unknown photographer (American) [731]

Unknown photographer (British) [62]

Unknown photographer (Chilean) [1]

Unknown photographer (Czechoslovakian) [1]

Unknown photographer (French) [89]

Unknown photographer (German) [6]

Unknown photographer (Italian) [5]

Unknown photographer (Swiss) [8]

Unknown photographer (place of origin unattributed) [37]

Selected Bibliography

Barger, M. Susan, and William B. White. *The Daguerreotype: Nineteenth-Century Technology and Modern Science.* Washington, D.C.: Smithsonian Institution Press, 1991.

Buerger, Janet E. *French Daguerreotypes.* Chicago: University of Chicago Press, 1989.

Borcoman, James. *Intimate Images: 129 Daguerreotypes: The Phyllis Lambert Gift.* Ottawa, National Gallery of Canada, 1988.

Daguerre, L. J. M. *An Historical and Descriptive Account of the Various Processes of the Daguerreotype and the Diorama by Daguerre.* 1839. Reprint, New York: Winter House, 1971.

The Daguerreian Annual: The Official Yearbook of the Daguerreian Society. Pittsburgh, The Daguerreian Society, 1990–.

Field, Richard, and Robin Jaffee Frank. *American Daguerreotypes from the Matthew R. Isenburg Collection.* New Haven: Yale University Art Gallery, 1989.

Foresta, Merry A., and John Wood. *Secrets of the Dark Chamber: The Art of the American Daguerreotype.* Washington, D.C.: Smithsonian Institution Press, 1995.

Gernsheim, Helmut. *The Origins of Photography.* 3d ed. New York: Thames & Hudson, 1982.

Gernsheim, Helmut, and Alison Gernsheim. *L. J. M. Daguerre: The History of the Diorama and the Daguerreotype.* 2d rev. ed. New York: Dover Publications, 1968.

Humphrey, Samuel D. *American Hand Book of the Daguerreotype.* 1858. Reprint, New York: Arno Press, 1973.

Kempe, Fritz. *Daguerreotypie in Deutschland.* Seebruck am Chiemsee: Heering, 1979.

Kilgo, Dolores A. *Likeness and Landscape: Thomas M. Easterly and the Art of the Daguerreotype.* Saint Louis: Missouri Historical Society Press, 1994.

Kravets, Torichan P., ed. *Dokumenty po istorii izobreteniia fotografii* [Documents on the history of the invention of photography]. 1949. Reprint, New York: Arno Press, 1979. [Letters in French, with Russian translation.]

Moore, Charles L. *"Two Partners in Boston: The Careers and Daguerreian Artistry of Albert Southworth and Josiah Hawes."* Ph.D. Diss. Ann Arbor: University Microfilms, 1975.

Newhall, Beaumont. *The Daguerreotype in America.* 3d rev. ed. New York: Dover Publications, 1976.

———. *The History of Photography from 1839 to the Present.* Rev. ed. New York: The Museum of Modern Art, 1982.

———. *Latent Image: The Discovery of Photography.* Garden City: Doubleday, 1967.

Paris et le daguerréotype. Essays by Shelley Rice, Françoise Reynaud, Jean-Louis Bigourdan, Ida Haugsted, Christian Tuxen Falbe, Grant B. Romer, M. Susan Barger, Anne Cartier-Bresson. Paris: Paris-Musées, 1989.

Pfister, Harold Francis. *Facing the Light: Historic American Portrait Daguerreotypes.* Washington, D.C.: Smithsonian Institution Press, 1978.

Pierce, Sally. *Whipple and Black: Commercial Photographers in Boston.* Boston: Boston Athenaeum, 1987.

Richter, Stefan. *The Art of the Daguerreotype.* London: Viking, 1989.

Rinhart, Floyd, and Marion Rinhart. *The American Daguerreotype.* Athens: University of Georgia Press, 1981.

———. *American Miniature Case Art.* South Brunswick and New York: A. S. Barnes, 1969.

Root, Marcus Aurelius. *The Camera and the Pencil.* 1864. Reprint, Pawlet, Vermont: Helios, 1971.

Rudisill, Richard. *Mirror Image: The Influence of the Daguerreotype on American Society.* Albuquerque: University of New Mexico Press, 1971.

Sobieszek, Robert, ed. *The Prehistory of Photography: Five Texts.* New York: Arno Press, 1979. Includes reprints of Germain Bapst, *Essai sur l'historie des panoramas et des dioramas* (1891); G. F. Grander, *Kurze beschreibung einer ganz neuen art einer camerae obscurae* (1769); Georges Potonniée, *Daguerre: peintre et décorateur* (1935); Henry Vivarez, *Le physionotrace* (1906); Isidore Niépce, *Historique de la découverte improprement nommée daguerrétype* (1841).

Sobieszek, Robert, and Odette Appell. *The Spirit of Fact: The Daguerreotypes of Southworth and Hawes, 1843–1862.* Boston: Godine, 1976.

Stapp, William F. *Robert Cornelius: Portraits from the Dawn of Photography.* Washington, D.C.: Smithsonian Institution Press, 1983.

Stenger, Erich. *The History of Photography.* 1989. Reprint, New York: Arno Press, 1979.

Taft, Robert. *Photography and the American Scene: A Social History, 1839–1889.* 1938. Reprint, New York: Dover Publications, 1964.

Thierry, J. *Daguerréotypie.* 1847. Reprint, New York: Arno Press, 1979.

Welling, William. *Photography in America: The Formative Years; 1839–1900.* New York: Thomas Y. Crowell, 1978.

Wood, John, ed. *America and the Daguerreotype.* Iowa City: University of Iowa Press, 1991. Essays by John F. Graf, Brooks Johnson, Dolores A. Kilgo, Peter E. Palmquist, David E. Stannard, John R. Stilgoe, Jeanne Verhulst, and John Wood.

———, ed. *The Daguerreotype: A Sesquicentennial Celebration.* Iowa City: University of Iowa Press, 1989. Essays by Ken Appollo, M. Susan Barger, Janet E. Buerger, Roy Flukinger, Matthew R. Isenburg, Ben Maddow, Grant B. Romer, Alan Trachtenberg, and John Wood.

———. *The Scenic Daguerreotype: Romanticism and Early Photography.* Iowa City: University of Iowa Press, 1995.

INDEX

Note: page numbers in italics refer to illustrations